To Become
an American

RHETORIC AND PUBLIC AFFAIRS SERIES

- *Eisenhower's War of Words: Rhetoric and Leadership*, Martin J. Medhurst, editor
- *The Nuclear Freeze Campaign: Rhetoric and Foreign Policy in the Telepolitical Age*, J. Michael Hogan
- *Mansfield and Vietnam: A Study in Rhetorical Adaptation*, Gregory A. Olson
- *Truman and the Hiroshima Cult*, Robert P. Newman
- *Post-Realism: The Rhetorical Turn in International Relations*, Francis A. Beer and Robert Hariman, editors
- *Rhetoric and Political Culture in Nineteenth-Century America*, Thomas W. Benson, editor
- *Frederick Douglass: Freedom's Voice, 1818–1845*, Gregory P. Lampe
- *Angelina Grimké: Rhetoric, Identity, and the Radical Imagination*, Stephen Howard Browne
- *Strategic Deception: Rhetoric, Science, and Politics in Missile Defense Advocacy*, Gordon R. Mitchell
- *Rostow, Kennedy, and the Rhetoric of Foreign Aid*, Kimber Charles Pearce
- *Visions of Poverty: Welfare Policy and Political Imagination*, Robert Asen
- *General Eisenhower: Ideology and Discourse*, Ira Chernus
- *The Reconstruction Desegregation Debate: The Politics of Equality and the Rhetoric of Place, 1870–1875*, Kirt H. Wilson
- *Shared Land/Conflicting Identity: Trajectories of Israeli and Palestinian Symbol Use*, Robert C. Rowland and David A. Frank
- *Darwinism, Design, and Public Education*, John Angus Campbell and Stephen C. Meyer, editors
- *Religious Expression and the American Constitution*, Franklyn S. Haiman
- *Christianity and the Mass Media in America: Toward a Democratic Accommodation*, Quentin J. Schultze
- *Bending Spines: The Propagandas of Nazi Germany and the German Democratic Republic*, Randall L. Bytwerk
- *Malcolm X: Inventing Radical Judgment*, Robert E. Terrill
- *Metaphorical World Politics*, Francis A. Beer and Christ'l De Landtsheer, editors
- *The Lyceum and Public Culture in the Nineteenth-Century United States*, Angela G. Ray
- *The Political Style of Conspiracy: Chase, Sumner, and Lincoln*, Michael William Pfau
- *The Character of Justice: Rhetoric, Law, and Politics in the Supreme Court Confirmation Process*, Trevor Parry-Giles
- *Rhetorical Vectors of Memory in National and International Holocaust Trials*, Marouf A. Hasian Jr.
- *Judging the Supreme Court: Constructions of Motives in Bush v. Gore*, Clarke Rountree
- *Everyday Subversion: From Joking to Revolting in the German Democratic Republic*, Kerry Kathleen Riley
- *In the Wake of Violence: Image and Social Reform*, Cheryl R. Jorgensen-Earp
- *Rhetoric and Democracy: Pedagogical and Political Practices*, Todd F. McDorman and David M. Timmerman, editors
- *Invoking the Invisible Hand: Social Security and the Privatization Debates*, Robert Asen
- *With Faith in the Works of Words: The Beginnings of Reconciliation in South Africa, 1985–1995*, Erik Doxtader
- *Public Address and Moral Judgment: Critical Studies in Ethical Tensions*, Shawn J. Parry-Giles and Trevor Parry-Giles, editors
- *Executing Democracy: Capital Punishment and the Making of America, 1683–1807*, Stephen John Hartnett
- *Enemyship: Democracy and Counter-Revolution in the Early Republic*, Jeremy Engels
- *Spirits of the Cold War: Contesting Worldviews in the Classical Age of American Security Strategy*, Ned O'Gorman
- *Making the Case: Advocacy and Judgment in Public Argument*, Kathryn M. Olson, Michael William Pfau, Benjamin Ponder, and Kirt H. Wilson, editors
- *Executing Democracy: Capital Punishment and the Making of America, 1835–1843*, Stephen John Hartnett
- *William James and the Art of Popular Statement*, Paul Stob
- *On the Frontier of Science: An American Rhetoric of Exploration and Exploitation*, Leah Ceccarelli
- *The Good Neighbor: Franklin D. Roosevelt and the Rhetoric of American Power*, Mary E. Stuckey
- *Creating Conservatism: Postwar Words That Made an American Movement*, Michael J. Lee
- *Intertextuality and the 24-Hour News Cycle: A Day in the Rhetorical Life of Colin Powell's U.N. Address*, John Oddo
- *Superchurch: The Rhetoric and Politics of American Fundamentalism*, Jonathan J. Edwards
- *Rethinking Rhetorical Theory, Criticism, and Pedagogy: The Living Art of Michael C. Leff*, Antonio de Velasco, John Angus Campbell, and David Henry, editors
- *Imagining China: Rhetorics of Nationalism in an Age of Globalization*, Stephen J. Hartnett, Lisa B. Keränen, and Donovan Conley, editors
- *Political Vocabularies: FDR, the Clergy Letters, and the Elements of Political Argument*, Mary E. Stuckey
- *To Become an American: Immigrants and Americanization Campaigns of the Early Twentieth Century*, Leslie A. Hahner

To Become an American

IMMIGRANTS AND AMERICANIZATION CAMPAIGNS OF THE EARLY TWENTIETH CENTURY

Leslie A. Hahner

MICHIGAN STATE UNIVERSITY PRESS • *East Lansing*

Copyright © 2017 by Leslie A. Hahner

∞ The paper used in this publication meets the minimum requirements of ANSI/NISO Z39.48-1992 (R 1997) (Permanence of Paper).

Michigan State University Press
East Lansing, Michigan 48823-5245

Printed and bound in the United States of America.

26 25 24 23 22 21 20 19 18 17   1 2 3 4 5 6 7 8 9 10

RHETORIC AND PUBLIC AFFAIRS
SERIES EDITOR
Martin J. Medhurst, *Baylor University*
EDITORIAL BOARD
Denise M. Bostdorff, *College of Wooster*
G. Thomas Goodnight, *University of Southern California*
Robert Hariman, *Northwestern University*
David Henry, *University of Nevada, Las Vegas*
Robert L. Ivie, *Indiana University*
Mark Lawrence McPhail, *Southern Methodist University*
John M. Murphy, *University of Illinois*
Shawn J. Parry-Giles, *University of Maryland*
Angela G. Ray, *Northwestern University*
Mary E. Stuckey, *Georgia State University*
Kirt H. Wilson, *Penn State University*
David Zarefsky, *Northwestern University*

LIBRARY OF CONGRESS CATALOGING-IN-PUBLICATION DATA
Names: Hahner, Leslie Ann, author.
Title: To become an American : immigrants and Americanization campaigns of the early twentieth century / Leslie A. Hahner.
Description: East Lansing : Michigan State University Press, [2017] | Series: Rhetoric and public affairs series | Includes bibliographical references and index.
Identifiers: LCCN 2016049792| ISBN 9781611862539 (pbk. : alk. paper) | ISBN 9781609175351 (pdf) | ISBN 9781628953046 (epub) | ISBN 9781628963045 (kindle)
Subjects: LCSH: Americanization—History—20th century. | Immigrants—United States—Social conditions—20th century. | United States—Emigration and immigration—History—20th century.
Classification: LCC JV6455 .H28 2017 | DDC 325.7309/041—dc23
LC record available at https://lccn.loc.gov/2016049792

Book design by Charlie Sharp, Sharp Des!gns, East Lansing, Michigan
Cover design by Erin Kirk New.
Cover image is from the National Photo Company Collection, Prints and Photographs Division, Library of Congress, LC-DIG-npcc-29272.

Michigan State University Press is a member of the Green Press Initiative and is committed to developing and encouraging ecologically responsible publishing practices. For more information about the Green Press Initiative and the use of recycled paper in book publishing, please visit www.greenpressinitiative.org.

Visit Michigan State University Press at www.msupress.org

*This book is dedicated to
Scott, Kennedy, and Annika.*

Contents

ACKNOWLEDGMENTS · ix

INTRODUCTION · xiii

CHAPTER ONE. Public Culture and the Americanization of Immigrants · · 1

CHAPTER TWO. The Visual Pedagogy of Americanization · · · · · · · · · · · · 29

CHAPTER THREE. The American Lifestyle through Housing Reform · · · · 65

CHAPTER FOUR. Displaying Americanization in Public Celebration · · · · · 91

CHAPTER FIVE. Recognizing Americans through Scouting · · · · · · · · · · · 123

CHAPTER SIX. The Paradox of Americanization · · · · · · · · · · · · · · · · · · · 153

CONCLUSION · 177

NOTES · 197

BIBLIOGRAPHY · 245

INDEX · 273

Acknowledgments

Completing this manuscript has been a long journey. It is a project that began partially during my days as a Hawkeye at the University of Iowa and has continued through two subsequent universities, Truman State and Baylor. At all of these sites, I have been encouraged, challenged, and supported by my mentors, colleagues, and family. It is with great pleasure that I finally have the opportunity to thank them here.

The possibility of this book was inaugurated by my advisors and teachers in both undergraduate and graduate school. These educators shaped how I think and how I write. At the University of Central Missouri, Barbara L. Baker and Kendall R. Phillips appreciated my intellectual curiosity. They noticed my rhetorical aptitudes even before I did. At Iowa, I was surrounded by a wealth of professors who invited me to embrace rigorous academic inquiry. David Depew, David Hingstman, John Durham Peters, Takis Poulakos, James Throgmorton, and many others proved exemplary in teaching me how to do the work of rhetorical criticism and academic analysis. The late Bruce Gronbeck was one of my very favorite teachers at Iowa, but our true scholarly relationship developed after graduation. Bruce read and responded to many of the chapters I wrote and took special pleasure in reassuring me that this book was worthwhile. His absence is felt deeply by so many. At Iowa, the most influential person in my life was Barbara Biesecker. Barb shaped me from an underprepared student into a confident rhetorical critic. She spent a considerable amount of time honing my scholastic aptitudes. When I look back on those years, I am amazed she invested so much in me and in all her students. I remain forever grateful for her mentorship during my time at Iowa and in the years that followed.

My cohort from Iowa also deserve recognition for their loyal support and, in keeping with the Iowa tradition, their insightful, relentless criticism. Michael Albrecht, Rachel Avon Whidden, Rafael Cervantes, Michael Lawrence, Joan Faber McAlister, Kim Hong Nguyen, Megan Foley, Chuck Goehring, Hemani Hughes, Meryl Irwin, Erin Rand, Rae Lynn Schwartz-DuPre, Adam Roth, Gerald Voorhees, Nathan Wilson, and others, listened to fledgling ideas about this project and still told me to continue. In more recent years, Michael Albrecht and Megan Foley were careful reviewers of chapters. My ideas here and in other pieces have been transformed by their advice.

My colleagues at Baylor have been extraordinary in terms of their support. David Schlueter has been an outstanding chair, finding monies when I needed research materials or travel while reminding me that me that my work was important. I cannot think of another chair who makes it a point to attend as many of his colleagues' conference presentations as possible. That kind of backing is incredibly generous. I am surrounded by some of the smartest rhetorical critics in the discipline, including Jeff Bass, Matt Gerber, and Sam Perry. I am thankful for their counsel and friendship. I have been bolstered over the years by members of my on-campus writing group. Kara Poe Alexander, Beth Barr, and Theresa Varney Kennedy have all read more pages than I care to count. Finally, I cannot overstate my indebtedness to Marty Medhurst. He was the first to suggest I submit this project to a university press and talked at length with me about how to fashion my early ideas into the project now in print. Marty works diligently to shape the field, to ensure that careful historical analysis can always find an outlet and ready audience. He is truly one of a kind.

Friends and colleagues across the country have proved invaluable readers, interlocutors, and allies. Abe Khan, Caitlin Bruce, Cara Finnegan, Amanda Davis Gatchet, Roger Davis Gatchet, Casey Ryan Kelley, Ron Greene, Tom Goodnight, and Zornitsa Keremidchieva have each become champions of this book during its various stages. Kristen Hoerl and Chris Lundberg were conscientious readers and respondents to different chapters. John M. Sloop was kind enough to publish the essay that launched this project and found marvelous reviewers for that process. Likewise, the anonymous reviewers for this manuscript supplied ample and astute guidance. I want to offer special thanks to Heather Ashley Hayes. She has become one of my most trusted confidants in the field. Her friendship and support of this book are rendered even more meaningful by the fact that she still makes it a point to visit Waco whenever she can, treats my children as her own, and advocates for her friends and colleagues all over the globe.

I have been lucky to receive financial and archival assistance for this project. Baylor University supported me through departmental funds and travel monies from the University Office of the Vice Provost for Research. Yevgeniya Gribov was the most skilled and competent archivist I have ever encountered. Her assistance at the Girl Scouts of the United States of America National Historic Preservation Center was unparalleled. Fellow Baylor bear Tab Lewis supplied outstanding archival support at the National Archives in Maryland.

I am also grateful to have an opportunity to revise ideas printed elsewhere. An earlier version of chapter 5 was originally published in "Practical Patriotism: Camp Fire Girls, Girl Scouts, and Americanization," *Communication and Critical/Cultural Studies* 5 (2008): 113–34. A few ideas from chapter 4 originally appeared in the following: "Generative Arguments: The Display of National Loyalty in Americanization Parades," in *The Functions of Argument and Social Context (Selected Papers from the 16th Biennial Conference on Argumentation)*, ed. Dennis Gouran (Washington, DC: National Communication Association, 2010), 145–50. As I revised these academic ideas, I have been bolstered by the staff at Michigan State. Julie Loehr, Annette Tanner, Lauren Spitzley, Kristine M. Blakeslee, Bonnie Cobb, and Anastasia Wraight have been outstanding in their work.

My family members have long been cheerleaders for everything I do—from failed attempts at team sports to finishing a PhD. I am grateful for them and their playful reminders that no matter how much education I attain, I ought not get "too big for my britches." Kenneth and Donna Hahner taught me the value of perseverance. They continually tell me how proud they are of me and ensured that the distances of life never enabled us to drift apart. My siblings, Chad and Sasha Hahner, Luke and Carrie Guittar, and Kalisa Hahner, have always been there for me. My nieces and nephews, Salena Havner, Austin Hahner, Taylor Hahner, Justin Beamer, and Peyton Guittar, provided wonderful sources of laughter and distraction. My in-laws, Jo Ann and Joe Varda, have welcomed me as one of their own, and I am truly grateful for the time they spend encouraging and caring for us. Greg, Amy, and Hazel Gall and Anthony Varda, my family by marriage, remind me to stay focused on what matters and that I joined an incredibly smart brood. Finally, I want to express my humble gratitude to my mother, Maureen Henthorn, and my stepfather, Roland Henthorn. From the day I was born, my mother told me to keep achieving. She let me devour books, even those that weren't exactly age-appropriate. Her efforts ensured that I loved to learn and knew that my ambitions could be materialized through diligence. She and Rolly have taken such good care of me and my family as I finished this project.

One of the best decisions I ever made was to marry Scott Varda. Scott is my best friend, my most challenging academic critic, and the greatest partner one could imagine. Scott has sacrificed so much to bolster my own work. He is a fierce advocate for good scholarship, and a rigorous reader who insists on precision in scholarly arguments. Without him, this project simply could not exist. He edited every single page (nearly a dozen times), took on an enormous amount of extra labor so that I could work, and demanded I seek excellence. He did all of this while being a loving partner, a gracious colleague, and a prolific coach and scholar. As our firstborn might say, he is "my very best." And while words fall short of expressing gratitude fully, I remain in awe of his intelligence and in debt to his selflessness. To my children, Kennedy Grace and Annika Elyse, you remind me every day to be grateful and humble. I am thankful to be yours.

Introduction

In 1916, President Woodrow Wilson declared Flag Day an official nationwide day of celebration. As United States involvement in the First World War loomed, the holiday became a spectacular affair showcasing American history, the dedication of the citizenry, and the nation's preparedness for international conflict. The event was concurrently deemed Preparedness Day, a moniker emphasizing home-front readiness. Over 150 cities took up Wilson's call, organizing parades, pageants, and other commemorations. The revelry followed the Lincoln Highway (a route that spanned from New York to San Francisco, somewhat following today's I-80). Towns on this course arranged festivities, including lectures on American history; parades with marchers carrying flags; red, white, and blue bunting adorning every conceivable public fixture; schoolchildren singing, "The Star-Spangled Banner"; and rifle and cannon salutes. In the New York City parade, 125,000 Flag Day marchers crossed under an enormous electric sign emblazoned with the words "Absolute and Unqualified Loyalty to Our Country."¹ These happenings were designed, as Wilson maintained, to combat the "influences which have seemed to threaten to divide us in interest and sympathy."² In keeping with Wilson's directive, Flag Day celebrations emphasized patriotism above all.

Public exhibitions of patriotism reached a new zenith during this period. Although citizens of the republic had long promoted fidelity, this zealous patriotism was propelled by the recognition that large numbers of recent immigrants hailed from war-torn nations. While immigrants have often been viewed with suspicion, at the beginning of the twentieth century, many Americans railed against large numbers of immigrants from Southern and Eastern Europe—newcomers who were seen as difficult, if not impossible, to assimilate given their unique circumstances and customs. The perceived need to make true Americans out of this new stock became an imperative as violence erupted abroad. The demand for loyalty rested on the presumption that a nation of many immigrants could not congeal public opinion on the war, develop capable troops, or sustain a national identity. Immigrants' material and emotional connections to the homeland became seen as obstacles to preparedness.

Within this milieu, experts positioned Americanization as an educational practice capable of transforming all immigrants into 100 percent Americans. The term "Americanization" typically denoted the process of becoming an American in word, deed, and heart. Throughout the nineteenth and early twentieth centuries, Americanization was undertaken by thousands of institutions, organizations, and individuals that varied wildly in their goals and approaches.³ At best, Americanization provided a path to inclusion in the nation; at worst, its programs demanded complete capitulation to jingoism. As the twentieth century progressed, Americanization became an organized campaign. Federal organizations, such as the Bureau of Education and the Committee on Public Information, as well as national programs, like those conducted by the National Americanization Committee and the Young Men's and Young Women's Christian Associations, joined forces to systematize and nationalize efforts. Local programs run by unions, employers, churches, and others also assisted these broader campaigns. With the advent of war, loyalty and patriotism became the watchwords of those missionaries warning that without direction, immigrants might remain faithful to their countries of origin and thereby undermine military and home-front readiness.

Americanization endeavors during this period often focused on creating an emotional connection to the United States. These pedagogues relied on teaching methods thought to evoke the sentiments of patriotism. Pointedly, Flag Day was merely one of myriad events designed to stir affection in immigrants. As President Wilson proclaimed, Flag Day reinstated those "happy traditions of united purpose and action of which we have been so proud," to better feel the "compulsion of this supreme allegiance."[4] Flag Day was not simply a patriotic holiday for the citizens of the nation, but an event orchestrated to fashion a nation of faithful residents. As part of this emotional emphasis, new forms of visual and performative educational materials began to surface in Americanization initiatives. Dramatic displays, nationalistic films, patriotic pageants, sympathetic home teachers, photographic textbooks, and other tools aimed to transform the hearts of immigrants. Particularly for progressives, the tactics of Americanization during this period used the sensational to create a love of country that might sever ties to the former homeland.

The visual and aesthetic pedagogies of Americanization have largely been a footnote to its history. A number of historians of this period have noted that Americanization authorities commonly relied on visual methods, including magic lantern shows, films, posters, demonstrations, and the like.[5] For example, in his classic treatise *The Movement to Americanize the Immigrant*, Edward Hartmann repeatedly mentions the visual tools employed by Americanization agents.[6] Yet, Hartmann's detailed history merely records that films, parades, and pamphlets were employed. He fails to engage period arguments about the promise of these media for changing the emotions of immigrants. In his discussion of Ford Motor Company's Americanization program, Stephen Meyer writes that graduation from the Ford English School was "the most spectacular aspect" of the program.[7] Indeed, a number of historians have recounted Ford's ritualistic pageant, a stage performance where workers walked from a boat scene, down a gangway, into a giant pot representing the school, emerging as flag-waving Americans.[8] Similar to Hartmann, Meyer and other scholars simply acknowledge that the pageant was a spectacle evidencing Ford's paternalism. In his history of the Christian film industry, Terry Lindvall remarks that the Young Men's Christian Association screened educational films in front of immigrant audiences to overcome English illiteracy and economically tutor them in the American way of life.[9] Thus, while authors have identified the visual or aesthetic pedagogies used for Americanization, there is little appreciation for the significance of these approaches, especially in relationship to the larger stakes of Americanization.

This volume examines methods of Americanization used in the early part of the twentieth century to better understand how these lessons changed the rhetorical structures of patriotism and nationalism. I focus on visual and aesthetic education, the use of visual media, performative rituals, and aesthetic methods to instruct students on becoming an American. Americanization educators insisted the use of new media, design principles, and pageantry could more effectively teach immigrants than rote methods of English and civics instruction. Pedagogical rationale for these novel methods maintained that dramatic displays overwhelmed the senses to fuel emotional nationalism, a consuming love of country. I illuminate an important shift in public culture by employing a rhetorical lens to analyze the visual and aesthetic practices of Americanization. Namely, these pedagogies not only tutored students in the practices of Americanism, but engendered a normative visual rubric that modified how Americans would come to understand, interpret, and judge their own patriotism and that of others.

To wit, one of the most interesting aspects of Americanization education during this period is the emphasis on publicly demonstrating the process and products of Americanization. Organizers often instructed pupils to display their allegiance, or invited students to exhibit their own successful assimilation. For instance, participation in 1916 Flag Day events publicized the patriotism of some immigrant organizations. Group members typically advertised their dedication via emblems of loyalty—marchers carried American flags, publicly crooned "The Star-Spangled Banner," and shouted "100% Americanism" as their slogan. These performances announced to onlookers that the patriotism of immigrants need not be questioned, despite outcry to the contrary. Likewise, the selection of these specific practices was obviously not arbitrary. Patriotic performances such as displaying the American flag, singing national anthems, and shouting jingoistic slogans were publicly identified as demonstrative of loyalty. In this way, Americanization was focused not merely on extracting the allegiances of newcomers to the United States, but on rendering *visible* the passion of patriotism.

In short, the early twentieth century witnessed the codification of patriotism into a set of normative expectations transforming what it meant to be an American. The discourses and practices of Americanization, particularly as manifest in visual and aesthetic education, fashioned the terms through which patriotism became recognizable. Displaying oneself as an American not only took on renewed importance, but the work of Americanization narrowed the emblems and acts identifying true patriots. These programs did not simply act upon immigrants, but simultaneously altered public understandings of nationalism. The importance granted the visual and performative display of patriotism is paramount to grasping this shift. Once public enactment and exhibition became seen as central to teaching and affirming allegiance, nearly all Americans were asked to engage in activities guaranteeing their love of country.

Rhetorical Shifts in Public Culture

To describe how Americanization impacted public culture, I rely on the tool of rhetorical criticism. Traditionally, the study of rhetoric is an inquiry into persuasion, the means by which a rhetor addresses an audience. In contemporary rhetorical scholarship, the study of public address often analyzes how discourse shapes culture. In many ways, to examine what is persuasive or what is rhetorically powerful is to engage with those machinations that produce and change a larger culture. Mary E. Stuckey expresses this understanding well, writing, "A people's identity, much like that of their nation, is largely imagined, based less on historical or geographical inevitability and more on the power of rhetoric to form and focus allegiances."[10] The study of Americanization as a rhetorical enterprise suggests its tactics were not simply a set of appeals directed toward an audience of immigrants. Instead, analyzing Americanization efforts suggests that the composite effect of these rhetorical endeavors was to reshape the visual character of nationalism.

In the early decades of the twentieth century, Americanization worked by identifying how citizens of this nation must act, think, and ultimately feel. Americanization pedagogy did not simply supply lessons in becoming a citizen, but identified a set of standards for marking patriotism in all Americans. Robert Hariman and John Louis Lucaites suggest culture is comprised of the "manner in which speech, writing, the arts, architecture, entertainment, fashion, and other modes of representation or performance cohere to structure perception, thought, emotion, and conduct."[11] Public culture, as they note, "defines the relationship between the citizen and the state."[12] Rhetoric as a vehicle for the creation and re-creation of public culture works by articulating a set of rubrics for what is valued and prescribing a normative precept for the acts of citizens. Rhetoric shapes public culture both broadly, for the culture writ large, and narrowly, for individual citizens.[13]

In this way, the various discourses and practices of Americanization acted as rhetorical pedagogies. Classically, as part of the trivium, rhetorical pedagogy taught students to exercise prudent judgment and reasoning through oratory. In the ancient world, rhetorical training enabled pupils to take advantage of opportunities by responding appropriately to any public occasion.[14] Ronald Walter Greene points out that modern rhetorical pedagogy is not simply how citizens are tutored in the oratorical or compositional skills required of democratic life, but is primarily how subjects are encouraged to recognize themselves in relationship to a larger public.[15] Thus, students are trained in public speaking, argumentation, and the like not simply to hone their oratorical skills, but to constitute a self and a place in the larger democratic public.

Certainly, Americanization education did not regularly offer instruction in public address or argumentation, but it was still a rhetorical pedagogy insofar as it aimed to create new subjects for the republic. From the nineteenth century forward, Americanization education commonly centered on naturalization, English literacy, American history, and national customs. In the early decades of the twentieth century, the availability of new media—films, photographic textbooks, stereoscope cards, and more—alongside the systematization of Americanization education dovetailed to emphasize the need to dazzle students if only to win their affections, if not their naturalization. Reading the rhetorical pedagogy of

Americanization, then, requires the critic to consider the visual, aesthetic, and even performative dimensions of these exercises. The rhetorical lessons at stake in Americanization were not designed simply to teach civics to immigrants, but to allow immigrants to see themselves as Americans. Greene's assertion that rhetorical pedagogies enable subjects to recognize themselves as "subjects of, by, and for a public" suggests that Americanization highlighted those formal performances and markers that counted as American and encouraged students to enact those rituals.[16] In this way, Americanization education relied on visual and aesthetic elements—features that can be productively explored through an examination of their rhetorical impact.

To be sure, rhetorical pedagogies act as vehicles for the transformation of public culture. Greene writes that rhetorical pedagogy "hopes to assemble subjects who desire the discourses of a public as much as a public craves new subjects for its discourse."[17] Rhetorical pedagogy teaches individual students, but also reflects and shapes the larger desires of the public. Likewise, Americanization acted on both students and the larger body politic. Angela Ray crafted a similar point about the educational purposes of the lyceum movement, writing that "mutual-education societies and the sponsored public lectures of the nineteenth century educated the population about who they were and what was important to them."[18] For her, these lessons "created a body of shared ideas and shared experiences, shaping a sense of nationhood through communal participation."[19] Americanization as a rhetorical pedagogy is unique in that its ends required a recognizable change in the pupil to combat larger cultural imputations. In the simplest sense, this pedagogy encouraged the public to view immigrants as desirous of American belonging. In a larger sense, the pursuit of Americanization sought to create a set of standards by which all residents could be seen as patriotic. Thus, the drive to Americanize immigrants supplied a normative framework through which nationalism could be discerned.

The early years of the twentieth century are crucial for understanding how patriotism became reconfigured through particular visual displays and forms. A number of historians have already demonstrated how some patriotic traditions—the observances of Independence Day, the designation of a national anthem, and the Pledge of Allegiance—were all created during this period. These scholars indicate that patriotism was heightened during the Progressive Era and that these practices operated as a form of chauvinism, even nativist reclamation.[20] Many of the rituals of nationalism today understood as hallowed duties were in fact institutionalized during the early decades of the twentieth century. Several nationalistic organizations attempted to reduce the purported pollution of immigrant traditions by cultivating decidedly American conventions. These groups drew inspiration from previous eras and customs to promote American symbols and performances as essential to demonstrating patriotism. Altogether, these shifts constituted new nationalistic rituals and traditions.

As a case in point, the Fourth of July became a more sober nationalistic observance during this period. In the nineteenth century, middle-class celebrations of the Fourth proved dramatically different than working-class, often immigrant, festivities.[21] Reformers sought to suppress rowdy parties on Independence Day in favor of more demure community commemorations.[22] According to Mary Lou Nemanic, the working class of Minnesota's Iron Range was prone to drunken parties with highly dangerous fireworks.[23] Citing deaths, injuries, and irreverence, a number of organizations encouraged all observers to participate in more worthy activities, including picnics, festivals, parades, and speeches.[24] Celebrations for the Fourth of July adopted a number of customs that transformed the holiday for the entire nation. David Glassberg notes that the Playground Association of America and the Russell Sage Foundation were integral players in creating a "Safe and Sane July Fourth" curriculum that could "reform the conduct of civic holiday celebrations."[25] These organizations incorporated ethnic traditions and play activities to persuasively cultivate a "wholesome" holiday.[26] While of course these activities attempted to manage the ribald working class, these same initiatives altered the holiday for the general public. As Glassberg contends, the "play spirit expressed in public celebrations also represented to recreation workers a powerful medium of mass persuasion capable of molding and remolding the collective identity and personality."[27] Reformers used Independence Day to affirm appropriate forms of patriotic enthusiasm and national commemoration.

Similarly, the gravity afforded one of the main rituals of Independence Day—singing what is now deemed the national anthem—multiplied during this period. Of course, "The Star-Spangled Banner" had long been a revered tune. But esteem for this song during the war years marks the symbolic changes in displaying patriotism. President Wilson authorized Francis Scott Key's "Star-Spangled Banner" to be played at executive events in 1916. In 1917, the army and navy designated the song as the official anthem for military services.[28] Shortly thereafter, in 1918, the tune was sung at its first professional sporting event, the World Series between the Chicago Cubs and the Boston Red Sox.[29] Congressional representatives began introducing legislation to adopt "The Star-Spangled Banner" as the national anthem in 1910. Though Congress would not enact such a change until 1931, as Marc Leepson notes, over forty bills advocating for the song would be introduced over the next two decades.[30] Certainly, many other patriotic tunes were quite popular during this period. Yet, the push for official legislative recognition of "The Star-Spangled Banner" is but one small measure of how congressional representatives authorized official performances of patriotism.

Emphasis on specific nationalistic performances extended to the public-school classroom as well. State-based legislation substantially increased the teaching of civics and patriotism. As Cecilia O'Leary notes, by 1913, twenty-three states required public schools to fly the flag.[31] The war years intensified nationalistic rituals performed in schools, and soon "nationalists upped their demands for national conformity, making the daily pledge of allegiance by every student and in every public school the normative expectation."[32] Many expressed concern that the pledge's wording should be changed to specify American patriotism above all. Against fears that the recitation of the pledge by immigrants could create a covenant with a European homeland, nationalistic groups such as the Woman's Relief Corps averred that the pledge include the phrase "to the United States of America."[33] With the understanding that the public school was a laboratory for nationalism, educators remodeled the classroom into a place where rituals of patriotism were standardized and routinized.

This period indeed witnessed the veneration of sanctioned acts of Americanism. Glassberg contends that civic officials in the early decades of the twentieth century labored to transform "expressions of holiday exuberance" into carefully controlled celebrations.[34] His point is that the culture metamorphosed during this period from sectarian traditions to homogenized demonstrations. O'Leary concurs and argues that government officials and leaders of private groups created an unprecedented demand for patriotism.[35] Importantly, both of these scholars draw attention to ritual and pageantry as tutoring participants in appropriate conduct and as publicizing American values. Thus, alongside the broader Americanization movement, all Americans were encouraged to enact particular performances of loyalty. In the face of a growing and ever more heterogeneous population, heightened xenophobia generated numerous efforts to fashion an identifiable national culture.

While historians have amply illustrated how patriotism changed during the Progressive Era, analyzing Americanization education through a rhetorical lens supplies a richer understanding of the shifts in public culture. Specifically, reading Americanization education as rhetorical pedagogies suggests that this period transformed not just how citizens celebrate America, but how Americans recognized one another. Patriotism and nationalism were certainly of paramount concern during this era, but the emphasis on display and defined performances of patriotism modified how residents interpreted and responded to the ostensible patriotism of themselves and others. In other words, national culture changed not simply by accentuating patriotism and defining American values, but by creating a set of visual and performative markers against which people were assessed.

I contend that Americanization changed public culture by articulating a visual logic of Americanism—a set of rubrics for measuring citizens. When scholars studying public culture refer to its visual logic, they typically mean the principles the audience uses to decode a particular visual artifact—the modes of reasoning applied to establish the meaning or function of an image. For instance, scholars will suggest that audiences use a visual logic to understand photographs as representations of the real world.[36] In this volume, visual logic refers to the common ways audiences read individual patriotism and loyalty as tethered to performance and display. Patriotism became configured as an emotional quality that must nevertheless be imbibed through spectacle and displayed on the bodies of residents. In this way, it is not enough to say that patriotism or Americanism mutated during this period. Rather, this book specifies how the metrics of evaluating patriotism and Americanism also changed.

Demonstrating patriotism required specific visual, aesthetic, and performative proofs. As articulated broadly across the social, the discourses and practices of Americanization changed public culture by defining the ways patriotism could be exhibited.

The unique features of nationalism on display can be explored productively by considering the twists and turns of particular tropes and figures of representation. That is, the structure of Americanization as a rhetorical pedagogy operated on a visual logic, one that can be discerned by analyzing the figural connections between the seen and unseen. Rhetorical figures and tropes are particularly useful in explaining and defining representational practices. They offer a way to understand how visual modes of representation are meant to signify particular qualities. Americanization educators aimed to inculcate patriotic practices that both elicited the students' emotions and generated public evidence of metamorphosis. Americanization strategies thereby mirrored the way scholars often treat rhetorical style—language or ornament that illuminates a quality not readily seen by audiences.[37] The ornament of patriotic display betokened emotional fidelity. More generally, rhetorical forms are ways of organizing communication to create shared meaning. Using the work of Kenneth Burke and Janet Lyon on rhetorical form, Bradford Vivian writes, "The form itself acquires an institutional character, or ethos, through ritualized performances that conditions the legitimacy and appeal of its 'imperatives.'"[38] As such, the codification of sanctioned performances of patriotism enabled the public to apprehend the forms of performance and display most readily communicating loyalty and patriotism. Indeed, these happenings attempted to represent the interior affection of the citizen in a way that made sense to others.

Rhetorical criticism often relies on tropes to explain the way a rhetor uses evocative tools for persuasive effect. Tropes help to explain the organizational structure of representation. Borrowing from Raymond Williams, Hariman and Lucaites aver that "structures of feeling," particularly in their visual instantiation, are "articulated by a system of visual tropes that proliferate across a very wide range of visual displays."[39] Their point is to connect our most quotidian experiences—emotions—to those rhetorical mechanisms of representation: the tropes and figures that manage the meaning and function of human experiences. Expanding on these arguments, I maintain that the shifts of public culture during this period can be illuminated by analyzing the tropological or figural work at play. I detail my methodology in chapter 1, but for now it is enough to suggest that Americanization predominantly changed public culture by situating visual, aesthetic, and performative exhibitions of patriotism as indicative of internal emotions. I interrogate how Americanization experts structured the ways loyalty and patriotism became recognizable through particular styles and forms of representation.

Framework of the Book

My use of rhetorical criticism to explain the lessons of Americanization aims to enrich the history of this period by identifying precisely how Americanization shaped national culture—by changing the visual contours registering Americanism. By contrast, consider that many contemporary historians contend that Americanization—whatever the lesson plan—was unsuccessful given its chauvinism.[40] Jeffrey Mirel insists that Americanization did not result in massive naturalization or broad assimilation. He argues that Americanization outcomes were complex, a negotiated balance between maintaining the immigrant's cultural traditions while developing an American identity.[41] For many academics, to study Americanization is to determine whether the project was successful by unearthing the number of individuals who naturalized, or by noting the cultural imperialism of melting-pot ideology.[42] While the material outcomes of Americanization are important, the focus of these studies fails to engage the role visuality played in the public anxieties that motivated Americanization. At the center of Americanization pedagogy is a profound concern about the recognizability of national belonging and identity. By focusing on whether Americanization resulted in naturalization or assimilation, current scholarship omits and therefore misses a broader understanding of how this movement fundamentally changed the nature of Americanism and, most importantly, how individuals recognized fellow Americans. Assessing whether Americanization worked therefore requires scholars to reconsider the terms registering success. In this book, I maintain that scholars can ascertain how national devotion became predicated on public displays of patriotism by carefully examining the visual and aesthetic pedagogies of Americanization.

Given my treatment of the visual and aesthetic through tropes and figures, this work helps demonstrate how criticism can use notions of style to explain the movements of public culture. My purpose in analyzing the visual logic of this period is to establish how Americanization quite specifically changed public culture not just for immigrants but for all citizens. Through a plethora of popular discourses and practices, exterior display and ritualistic performances of patriotism became linked to internal emotions. Interrogating the rhetorical mechanisms structuring the relationship between seen and unseen provides a new vantage on the Americanization movement—one that highlights how the visual logic of Americanization lessons organized the human experience of nationalism.

In this book, I also supplement rhetorical scholarship by examining additional ways rhetorical forms organize and shape human experience. In the simplest sense, this volume expands scholarship on the visuality of rhetorical figures. A number of authors have already considered how arguments, metaphors, ideographs, and other rhetorical schemes are deployed visually or graphically.[43] The analysis presented in this volume asserts that a number of rhetorical schemes previously treated as largely discursive or narratological can also manifest visually. In their visual use, these rhetorical figures often operate differently than in other modes of address. The pedagogical practices of Americanization suggested that immigrants must glimpse certain sights or exhibit specific qualities to be seen as Americans. Rhetorical forms thus shaped the nationalistic lessons of Americanization and thereby visual recognition of patriotism. Emotional dedication to the nation was not simply a narrative to which immigrants contributed, a value that students understood, or even a set of skills citizens enacted. Instead, Americanism also became an emotional fidelity imbibed and demonstrated by particular visual and performative acts.

The time period I consider in this book spans from the early years of the twentieth century into the 1920s. I begin with the dramatic increase of immigration in the early twentieth century and the concomitant fear of new immigrants as poisonous to national culture. I close my analysis with the rise of immigration restriction acts in the 1920s that changed the public's understanding of how Americanization worked. For many scholars of immigration, the first two decades of the twentieth century are the height of Americanization activity. During this period, progressive workers sought to acculturate immigrants using increasingly organized, and purportedly scientific, methods.[44] This is also the period in which educators were productively grappling with the power of the screen and other novel approaches to education. Against the fear of new immigrants and, later, the horrors of war, the spectacular efficiency of visual and aesthetic education for immigrants took on considerable importance. Much of my analysis focuses on the war as the event that crystallized the mission of Americanization and led to its significant expansion. Certainly, Americanization continued beyond the war years and the restriction legislation of the 1920s. As Mirel rightly notes, Americanization education remained strong into the 1950s.[45] Yet, while visual teaching tools continued to be used for the purposes of assimilation, the tenor of the approach differed from previous decades. The urgency was no longer acute, and the necessity of visual aids became relegated to simply another method of instruction. By attending to Americanization education in the early twentieth century, scholars glean a better understanding of how visual and aesthetic pedagogies solicited national emotions and how public displays of patriotism became codified.

In the bulk of this book, I analyze the pedagogies of governmental and prominent social agencies conducting Americanization work. The vast majority of the historical sources I engage address a national audience. The programs and curriculums I study were designed for widespread implementation and often spoke to an imagined national public. Nevertheless, as Mirel notes, Americanization programs were centralized in three epicenters: Chicago, Cleveland, and Detroit.[46] While I typically focus on the larger national public at stake, the analysis is nevertheless somewhat constrained by the goals of those sites producing Americanization curricula. My analysis is also limited by the aims of Americanization educators who typically sought to teach "new" immigrants from Southern and Eastern Europe. This is not to suggest there were not Americanization programs instructing Japanese Americans, Mexican Americans, and others. In Western regions, these audiences were central to the Americanization mission.[47] But, significantly, these audiences were often excluded from larger public discussions on the possibility of Americanization. As several historians have suggested, Americanization discourses and practices marked a racial hierarchy that identified who could dream of the possibility of American belonging.[48] I attend to this notion in the chapter on immigration exclusion, interrogating how the visual logic of Americanization created a rubric for categorizing subjects within this hierarchy. While regional and other differences may have changed the contours of individual Americanization programs, I illustrate in chapter 1 how Americanization became more organized and nationalized during this period. Even if Americanization catered to specific regions and to those immigrants who were seen as capable of assimilating, the national changes Americanization precipitated still engendered a palpable rubric against which these effects were measured. Put simply, Americanization was broad enough in scope and widespread enough in public talk to facilitate major shifts in understanding patriotism.

To grasp how rhetorical discourse impacts public culture, the critic typically must engage a multiplicity of popular discourses and practices. It is rarely enough to study one speech or one educational tactic if the scholar is to arrive at any meaningful conclusions. To craft my claims, I often cut across the period, moving from presidential address and newspaper accounts to regional experts and specific programs. I do so both to offer the reader a general understanding of Americanization as well as to document in greater detail the stakes of these public conversations and the ubiquity of the claims involved. In each chapter, I not only analyze a multitude of popular texts, but also situate those texts against the cultural conditions to which they were addressed. My purpose is to examine the rhetorical functions of Americanization beyond the student audience to illustrate how the principles shaping these lessons fashioned the registers of nationalism.

Throughout this volume, I engage Americanization pedagogy that was visual, performative, or aesthetic in orientation. I briefly discuss textual and other kinds of sources, but my concentration is on those materials employing the spectacular, ritualistic, or evocative to redress concerns about immigrants. My arguments, then, attend to understudied and new evidence from the period. I do so with a visual critic's eye toward interpretation so as to demonstrate how Americanization defined nationalism.

For instance, I analyze scouting groups that have received scant scholarly consideration for their Americanization work. My choice to explore the Americanization work of scouts sprang from the idea that much of their work publicized the group's reputation as patriots—a virtue not yet secured during this period. Studying these organizations provides a unique vantage on the visual orientation of this publicity and its doubled effect on both immigrants and Americanization agents. This doubled effect is useful in considering the relationship between larger changes in public culture and Americanization lessons. In general, the visual and aesthetic texts I engage illuminate the means through which these representational practices changed the visual contours of patriotism.

In the coming chapters, I detail how the discourses and practices of Americanization constituted a visual logic of Americanism by attempting to manufacture patent signs of allegiance. Each chapter analyzes one method of Americanization and the visual logic at stake in the representational practices of the lesson. I analyze both the visual and aesthetic principles of lessons as well as how students were asked to display their emotional commitment. I argue that both are forms of representation codifying the way nationalism was to be imbibed and exhibited. These rhetorical pedagogies were not simply an attempt to change the pupil, but produced familiar forms of patriotism for the larger body politic. Often, these visual and performative approaches—films, photographs, housing designs, parades, singing—relied on certain modes of representation. What the student or public saw on the surface was designed to evoke and represent nationalistic affection.

Each chapter also defines the rhetorical structure of the various forms of Americanization pedagogy to illustrate the overarching visual logic of period patriotism. I demonstrate this logic through rhetorical forms, including prolepsis, synecdoche, metalepsis, and prosopopoeia. In my view, Americanization lessons used the principles of tropes to imbue Americanization with the authority of recognition. By rendering Americanism through particular visual forms, immigrant audiences were promised a welcoming national home, and the larger public was pledged a fortified state. Clearly, the audiences reading performances of Americanism may not have been able to name the rhetorical trope or even the logic of representation at stake. Yet, for scholars and those seeking to understand the impact of immigrant education, these schemes help to explain the relationship between representation and patriotism that animated the pursuit of Americanization. To be sure, my purpose is to provide neither an exhaustive account of the various media used for Americanization, nor all of the rhetorical figures or tropes entailed in this pedagogy. Rather, my approach is to highlight some of the significant aspects of visual and performative representation at stake in Americanization.

The book is organized by attending to the purported *telos* of Americanization pedagogy. After a chapter detailing the problems faced by Americanization agents and my specific methodology, the first two analysis chapters interrogate those visual and aesthetic lessons used to instruct immigrants in emotional nationalism. Following this, chapter 4 focuses on those celebrations meant to demonstrate the success of Americanization by publicly displaying immigrants as patriots. Chapters 5 and 6 highlight how Americanization changed public culture and the exhibition of allegiance. The advantage of this organization is that it demonstrates how Americanization lessons labored to transform both students and the general public. These chapters thus proceed by attending to the momentum of Americanization: to teach students to desire Americanization, to teach the public to recognize successful Americanization, and to teach the country that Americanization was a lesson for all.

While the first half of this volume focuses on the codification of Americanism in meaning and exhibition, the second half highlights the slippage between figure and referent to interrogate the paradoxical visual logic of Americanization. That is, while visual and aesthetic Americanization education attempted to correct mismanaged national attachments, the presumed need for public affirmation sustained the anxieties surrounding the project. Visual proof could never fully satisfy public concerns about homeland fidelity. Thus, I am not suggesting that Americanization accomplished its assimilationist goals. Indeed, scores of historians indicate the ways Americanization failed, and the resistance ethnic groups leveled against many Americanizers.[49] Yet, what remains underdeveloped in historical and cultural scholarship on this era is the extent to which, and how, Americanization nevertheless organized the visual field delimiting the patriot. In other words, the chapters that follow attend to Americanization as a rhetorical pedagogy that articulated a desire to produce an American as a recognizable subject. Even if this desire remained unrealized, its enunciation nonetheless generated the terms against which individuals were judged.

Ultimately, this project insists that the Americanization project was successful in demarcating the qualities that counted as American. Examining the rhetorical structures of this movement highlights a visual logic that bears consideration for understanding the legacy of Americanization. The concluding chapter therefore unpacks the visual logic of Americanization and its importance for understanding the period. While Americanization may have failed to dramatically expand naturalization, these programs and pedagogical practices still organized how the sentiments of patriotism became recognizable to the general public. Yet, the bounty of national culture proffered by the Americanization movement is not simply relegated to the annals of history.

To better understand our current vision of nationalism, it is imperative to analyze the period in which patriotism became marked as a public good. Today, as in previous eras, public figures deem immigrants a threat to national identity and prosperity. Often, assessments of immigrants' patriotism are based on simplistic visual inspections. Lamentations on ostensibly foreign dress, calls for excluding certain peoples from immigrating, and claims that immigrants mask their nefarious disloyalty remain headline news. These contemporary arguments highlight anxieties regarding national culture and the proper exhibition of patriotism. While patriotism is still touted as an emotional quality available to all, the paradoxical nature of displaying nationalism alongside nativist claims undercuts who can be seen as an American. Indeed, the circumscribed registers of Americanism are apparent in the patriotic pomp of our own era.

Whether we recognize it or not, we are reminded of the legacy of Americanization every June 14 when the president of the United States officially proclaims the national commemoration of Flag Day. The legal proclamation urges "the people of the United States to observe Flag Day as the anniversary of the adoption on June 14, 1777, by the Continental Congress of the Stars and Stripes as the official flag of the United States."[50] Yet, the occasion is more pointed in its patriotic purpose. As the National Flag Day Foundation clarifies, Flag Day teaches the values of "Americanism" and the necessity of patriotism.[51] Celebrants in Waubeka,

Wisconsin—the town that birthed the National Flag Day Foundation in 1946—might raise the flag, sing the national anthem, pledge allegiance to the flag, watch a parade, or listen to a musical salute to the armed forces. While today Flag Day is often observed as a lackluster occasion, we inherit its rituals and commemorations as cardinal to our understanding and exhibition of patriotism. The first two decades of the twentieth century birthed a number of practices akin to Flag Day—events and rituals designed to sway the nationalistic attachments of citizens such that they could not help but wear their patriotism with bravado. Interrogating the rhetorical structures of representation bequeathed by Americanization pedagogy can help us navigate the visual field organizing what it means to be an American.

CHAPTER ONE

Public Culture and the Americanization of Immigrants

At the turn of the twentieth century, the United States faced one of the most dramatic transformations to its national identity. From the 1890s to the 1920s, nearly 23 million immigrants, largely from Europe, would constitute what Mirel deems "one of the largest migrations in human history."[1] While the United States had long been a nation of immigrants, the vast numbers of arrivals from Southern and Eastern Europe presented a significant shift from previous generations. For some, this momentous change was cause for disapprobation. Leonard Dinnerstein and David Reimers explain that, often fleeing "horrendous conditions" of poverty, immigrants came with "high hopes, unprepared for the coolness with which so many Americans received them."[2] These so-called "new immigrants" were often cast derisively, with differences in faith, customs, and appearance as the basis of critique. For many, new immigrants were fundamentally unlike most Americans and therefore threatened the character of the nation.

The nation metamorphosed during this period, and these overwhelming alterations generated a number of concerns about both national identity and composition. Alongside the Great Migration of black Americans, changes in the populace of Western states, and increased urbanization, the rise in immigration became seen as a monumental problem. The issue took center stage in the growing arena of mass communication that served, as John Durham Peters and Peter Simonson suggest, as new modes of "social organization."[3] Within these conversations, the basis of belonging amid such radical developments continued to vex the construction of national identity. Groups, individuals, and agencies with their own political and ideological commitments generated ample deliberation on the meaning of Americanism—discussions that shaped the contours of how new immigrants were understood.

Americanization responded to and helped shift the debates surrounding national identity. Congressional debate and legislation as well as mass media sources played a part in the rhetorical construction of immigrants as a problem, and the associated understandings of national identity that grounded remedies to these issues. The war was a turning point for the Americanization movement, motivating organized and scientific approaches to redress the presumed differences of new immigrants. Progressives and others labored to speedily transform immigrants into Americans to ensure preparedness for the coming conflict. Americanization during the war years was overwhelmingly concerned with loyalty, an emotional quality that was difficult to secure, let alone verify. Given this focus on the emotional foundations of nationalism, Americanization agents devised ways to enable immigrants to prove their loyalty. Spectacle and performance organized the visual logic of Americanization and set the tone for how immigrants could demonstrate patriotism.

The Differences of Immigrants

In many ways, the rhetorical construction of new immigrants was the result of the contest brewing between differing interpretations of national identity. This debate established how legislative and educational solutions to the presumed problem of immigration would proceed. John Higham suggests that during the 1880s, new immigrants "lived in the American imagination only in the form of a few vague, ethnic stereotypes."[4] Springing from a nebulous distrust, anti-foreign sentiment was "discharged with special force against these new targets so that each of the southeastern European groups appeared as a particularly insidious representative of the whole foreign menace."[5] As new immigrants became a more known quantity in the early twentieth century, nativist pronouncements against foreign threats increased dramatically. Nativists often proclaimed immigrants a hindrance to national progress, with immigration restriction as the natural solution. Progressives touting Americanization rebuked nativist sentiment and solutions. While Americanization advocates nevertheless understood immigrants as a problem, they believed in the auspicious future promised in the civic and emotional education of immigrants. In these ways, the battle between nativist, ethnic nationalism and progressive, civic nationalism set the stage for Americanization.

Nativist interpretations of national identity espoused ethnic nationalism to contend that real Americans were of a particular racial or ethnic stock. By the time the first surge of new immigrants from Southern and Eastern Europe became a public concern, nativism was already an entrenched ideology. In the late nineteenth century, nativist legislation had already succeeded in codifying racial hierarchies into law: the Chinese Exclusion Act passed in 1882. Andrew Gyory asserts that while nativism had declined significantly after the Civil War, the Chinese Exclusion Act generated a nativist agenda for future immigration policy. For Gyory, nativist arguments garnered votes by positing Chinese labor as jeopardizing American jobs, and asserting Asian immigrants as members of an inferior race.[6] These contentions were rhetorical tools used to mobilize the electorate via a crass model of racial hierarchy. For new immigrants at the beginning of the twentieth century, nativism likewise grew alongside those popular and legislative pronouncements declaring them dangerous. As Higham's work explains, nativism thrived in times of scarcity and conflict by positing immigrants as political and economic impediments to national prosperity and identity.[7]

In many ways, the key shift in the threat construction of new immigrants was the 1911 publication of the Dillingham Commission report. President Theodore Roosevelt appointed the commission after a series of congressional machinations stymied a 1907 mandatory literacy test.[8] Spearheaded by Senate restrictionists Henry Cabot Lodge and William P. Dillingham, the group was charged to "make full inquiry, examination, and investigation . . . into the subject of immigration" and to make recommendations for federal policy.[9] Daniel Tichenor argues that the work of this commission was "unprecedented" even in an era of "social engineering."[10] Taking three years, over one million dollars, and hundreds of staff to produce, the final report was a forty-two-volume comprehensive investigation of immigration.

While much of the data in the report was raw demographic information or statistical facts, historians argue the evidence was manipulated to promote restriction and exaggerate the racial inferiority of certain groups.[11] One of the most palpable rhetorical devices in this regard was the *Dictionary of Races or Peoples*, authored by economist Jeremiah Jenks and anthropologist Daniel Folkmar. The classification scheme identified dozens of different races based on purportedly scientific information, including a people's "languages, their physical characteristics, and other such marks as would show their relationship one to another."[12] The dictionary was fabricated from a number of ethnological publications, most notably William Z. Ripley's 1898 *The Races of Europe* (maps from Ripley's text were reproduced in the dictionary). The *Dictionary of Races or Peoples* and Ripley's work demarcated three overarching European races to uphold Northern and Western Europeans as superior to all others. According to this interpretation, Nordic and Teutonic races were preferable to the Mediterranean stock of new immigrants, who were described as patently different than the American people.[13] Using these operational definitions, the Dillingham Commission report staunchly supported immigration restriction.

In the report, immigration restriction was premised on the idea that members of certain races could not successfully become Americans. New immigrants were depicted as less fit for citizenship given their countries of origin, poverty, English illiteracy, unskilled labor, and natural criminality. For instance, while the writers acknowledged that no recent émigrés had caused any serious public health concern, they nevertheless positioned new immigrants as arriving from places with "dangerous and loathsome contagious diseases."[14] Likewise, the report on immigration and crime admitted that new immigrants were not necessarily more prone to crime than others, yet commission staff wrote that "simple assault is relatively more frequent as an offense of alien criminals of the newer immigrant races than of those of the older."[15] Throughout the forty-two volumes, distinctions between older immigrants and new immigrants were dissected thoroughly, even if some commission members understood those disparities as based on economic or situational variables. Restriction-minded public officials used the report to warrant their own policy mandates, including literacy tests and national-origin quotas.[16]

The eugenic bases of nationalism espoused by both Ripley and the Dillingham Commission were articulated across popular culture such that new immigrants became seen as racially incompatible with contemporaneous Americans. Beginning in the teens and continuing into the 1920s, a series of best-selling popular books denounced the supposed lesser peoples of Southern and Eastern Europe, Asia, and those of African lineage.[17] For Jerome Karabel, Madison Grant's 1916 *The Passing of the Great Race* popularized eugenics and lent "legitimacy" to immigration restriction policies.[18] Grant condemned black Americans as a "serious drag on civilization" and suggested that "Mongoloid" peoples were of the "lowest races of man."[19] Yet, for Grant, one of the biggest threats to the national composition of the United States was the onslaught of immigrants from abroad who have "lowered and vulgarized" the "whole tone of American life, social, moral, and political."[20] According to Grant, new arrivals would breed out the best in "native" American stock and pervert the nation.[21] Eugenics came to guide the categorization and assessment of immigrants and others.

Race-based critiques of new immigrants were bolstered by a series of cultural appraisals on the supposed problems encumbering their assimilation. Popular and even scholarly discourses of the period took great pains to distinguish new immigrants from others. Desmond King has amply illustrated how stereotyped views of new immigrants were fueled by racist understandings of their limited intellectual potential and inherent lesser qualities.[22] Even those divorced from explicit eugenic ideology nevertheless described new immigrants as impeding the nation's progress. For instance, sociologists began to study the criminality of immigrants by comparing these new arrivals to black Americans and others living in socioeconomically depressed areas.²³ Though these studies often blamed petty crime on poverty or urban living, they nonetheless capitulated to the dominant narrative of race hierarchy and cultural devolution. Accusations against new immigrants tended toward outright bigotry buttressed by eugenic dogma.

Nativist understandings of nationalism infiltrated public culture such that only Nordic, or later Anglo-Saxon, races could successfully become Americans. Mirel names nativist commitments "ethnic nationalism," typifying those who argued that immigrants and others were "*racially* incompatible with a country created by Nordic settlers and shaped by Nordic ideals and values."²⁴ Legislative endeavors and mass-media publications promulgated eugenics ideology via the Dillingham Commission, Madison Grant, Lathrop Stoddard, and other popular discourses. Racial categorization became a powerful rhetorical device to devalue certain peoples while glorifying an invented white, native stock. Consequently, immigration restriction advocates often used eugenic principles to promote and enforce legislative caste systems.²⁵ The racial bases of citizenship gained a major foothold in popular imagination.

Significantly, the decrees of the Dillingham Commission and other restrictionists generated considerable counter-advocacy. Diana Selig maintains that nativist and tolerant views of immigration "gave rise to each other" insofar as liberals responded "to anti-immigration sentiment."²⁶ Selig's work largely attends to the 1920s, but the same argument is true for the teens, particularly in relationship to the Dillingham Report. Even in the midst of compiling research, Franz Boas's work on the bodily form of immigrants contradicted the report's ultimate recommendations.²⁷ In congressional hearings held one year after the publication of the Dillingham Report, reformer Grace Abbott suggested that immigrants of all stripes could become Americans and that the nation could be positively shaped by their tenacity.²⁸ Abbott represented the Immigrants' Protective League, a group birthed as a corollary to the nativist Immigration Restriction League.²⁹ Further, the notion that immigrants could become Americans was a key theme of the 1912 election. As Hans P. Vought notes, "Roosevelt's Progressive party staked out a liberal position on immigration, largely due to the influence of former Commerce and Labor Secretary Oscar Straus and social worker Frances Kellor, who was the director of the New York State Bureau of Industries and Immigration and headed the New York branch of the North American Civic League for Immigrants."[30] The New York immigration commission that Kellor directed was what Matthew Silver calls a "pro-immigration foil" to the Dillingham Commission.[31] The rise in rhetoric promoting immigration restriction, then, motivated progressives to organize weighty opposition to these advocacies.

Progressive public discourses during this period countered ethnic nationalism by emphasizing the possibility that all residents could learn to become Americans through public education. Education in naturalization and cultural assimilation had long been a part of the American experiment in democracy, particularly during the second wave of immigration beginning in the mid-nineteenth century.[32] Reformers took up the mantle first assumed by settlement-house workers such as Jane Addams and Ellen Starr. There were certainly different views on how immigrants could be enfolded into the nation. Assimilationists often emphasized the need to engender a "union of . . . minds and wills" via public life.[33] Cultural pluralists adopted a "humanitarian" approach that sought to serve immigrants, suggesting that they need not assimilate by disavowing traditions but could acculturate on their own terms.[34] Mirel groups these various approaches to becoming an American under the heading of "civic nationalism," productively arguing that civic nationalists all believed immigrants could become Americans (through various approaches)—as opposed to those who espoused racial restrictionism.[35] Typifying progressive or liberal responses to immigration, civic nationalists worked in a variety of ways to ensure the United States would embrace all peoples.[36]

However, the rhetoric of civic nationalism was also beset by other understandings of nationalism. Eugenic racial typologies were pervasive enough that even progressive or liberal public advocacies often referred to the possibility of incorporation while tincturing that prospect through biologically based hierarchies. For instance, both Gary Gerstle and Leroy Dorsey depict Theodore Roosevelt's vision of civic nationalism as complex, touting some aspects of ethnic nationalism.[37] Roosevelt regularly asserted that all peoples, even those he deemed racially inferior, could work toward inclusion in the "great national experiment."[38] Thus, it is a mistake to assume that period discourses on immigration were ideologically pure.

As Mirel writes, categorizing responses in this manner fails "to capture the messy, at times contradictory, nature of people's ideas and actions."[39] While progressives often acclaimed the positive qualities of immigrants or promoted a more open immigration policy, they also relayed eugenic and similar racial typologies. Likewise Americanization advocates were typically progressive, yet they commonly depicted immigrants as inferior peoples, even if the conditions of their inferiority were anchored in culture or economics.

The promiscuous nature of public advocacy on immigrants was such that immigrants were positioned as a significant problem to be addressed—with various solutions proposed. Responses driven by ethnic nationalism routinely espoused immigration restriction or similar legislative solutions. Civic nationalists also regularly supported immigration restriction, albeit less stringent restriction, while principally insisting that nearly all immigrants could learn to become Americans. These differing viewpoints on immigration structured a whole host of conversations on foreign policy, labor reform, women's rights, educational curricula, and more. The vigor of that debate soon became elevated, and a whole host of new rhetorical tactics emerged that reshaped public discussions on national identity. Both ethnic nationalists and civic nationalists would grapple with a new aspect of national identity born from the modern era: how human emotions could be manipulated by the media during the tumults of war.

The War and the Question of Loyalty

Concerns about the threats immigrants posed to the nation escalated with the outbreak of war in 1914. While the United States would not enter the war until 1917, Christopher Capozzola argues that the war years witnessed "one of the twentieth century's broadest, most vigorous, and most searching public discussions about the meanings of American citizenship."[40] Wider debates about the basis of nationalism came to a head and motivated a keen public interest in immigrants as proto-citizens. For some, immigrants hindered preparedness and those with dual citizenship operated as enemy aliens in our midst. Immigrants from war-torn nations were described as impediments to a unified outlook on the war. As Robert Carlson notes, with "appeals for sympathy" pouring into the country "from both sides," legislators and the general public were acutely aware that the "National Mind [was] split on such issues as the advisability of United States military preparation, whether to favor one side or the other, and the wisdom of possible United States intervention."[41] As it became clear that the United States would not be able to avoid the conflict, President Wilson sought to create a "national consensus" on the war and organized a sweeping campaign to rouse prowar sentiment.[42] Public attention on the media's role in developing what David M. Kennedy calls a "commonality of mind," or national imagination, sparked concern that immigrants' emotions could be manipulated by news from the front.[43] Immigrants, especially German Americans, were viewed with deepening suspicion in what J. Michael Sproule deems the darker side of the wartime climate of "conformity, fear, and hate."[44]

Some of the vitriol directed at immigrants related to public anxieties surrounding military preparedness. Nancy Gentile Ford maintains that in the early teens it was widely acknowledged that the United States military was "ill-equipped to fight a major war against the massive armies of Continental Europe."[45] Immigrants, in particular, posed a unique problem for readiness. Stephen Vaughn notes that those planning for the war complained that five million residents were unable to speak English.[46] Military leaders confronted obstacles in organization and command when it was discovered that "Three million unnaturalized persons of military age were in the country. About half a million foreign-born registrants between the ages of twenty-one and thirty-one could not understand military orders in English."[47] Advocates pressed the urgency of war to proclaim immigrants as deficient soldiers.

Period mistrust of immigrants precipitated a number of legislative efforts to close the border for new arrivals, albeit temporarily. The combined need for reservists in warring nations coupled with nativist legislation in Congress "put a temporary end to European emigration."[48] Further, the 1917 literacy test passed over President Wilson's veto, facilitated by "the new concern about the depth of foreign-born loyalty."[49] Congress extended the "Asiatic barred zone" (save Japan) to incorporate parts of the Soviet Union, Afghanistan, Saudi Arabia, India, Sri Lanka, and more.[50] Despite these exclusions, perhaps even because of these legislative changes, the obstacles posed by the new mass of immigrants remained on the national radar as war clouds gathered.

Though President Wilson was slow to support United States involvement in the war, by 1917 participation was deemed a necessity. Once the United States declared war in April, xenophobic mistrust reached new heights. President Wilson used the Alien Enemies Act of 1798 to define all male German citizens aged fourteen and older as "enemy aliens."[51] Wilson required designees to register at post offices; nearly 250,000 did so.[52] Enemy aliens were not permitted to own "guns, radios, or explosives and were not allowed to live near munitions factories or military areas."[53] Law enforcement arrested over six thousand individuals who violated the act or who were considered radicals.[54] Of those arrested, over two thousand remained interned until the war's end.[55] German Americans were asked to renounce dual citizenship, and any celebration of German heritage was viewed with hostility.[56] These legislative acts contributed to fanatical pronouncements on immigrant disloyalty and a host of punitive and vigilante actions.

Justified by the new mission abroad, Wilson exhorted Congress to pass laws to police antiwar sentiment, particularly among immigrants. The resulting Espionage and Sedition Acts of 1917 and 1918 respectively radically reduced civil liberties.[57] In 1917, Wilson's postmaster general, Albert Burleson, deployed the Espionage Act to censor socialist and labor publications and successfully prosecute antiwar advocates, including members of the Socialist Party and the International Workers of the World.[58] Within this climate, immigrants from warring nations, most notably Germany, became seen as especially menacing. The Espionage Act had designated flying the flag of an enemy nation as an arrestable offense.[59] Foreign-language newspapers were monitored for subversive content and later required to submit English translations to the government.[60] Further, Wilson did little to combat, and in some ways even "abetted," vigilantism against German Americans.[61] He failed to publicly condemn such violence until the summer of 1918, a few months before the end of the conflict.[62]

By the late teens, this hyperbolic vision of nationalism resulted in the further demonization of immigrants and those who espoused leftist political views. As Ford writes, "Much of the emotion of the day was redirected into a Red Scare—an early twentieth-century witch hunt to purge the country of 'dangerous' radicals."[63] Following a number of anarchist bombings directed at prominent industry leaders and federal legislators, the new attorney general, A. Mitchell Palmer, orchestrated a series of raids resulting in thousands of arrests.[64] Those captured were often targeted by virtue of their political beliefs. Immigrants were particularly vulnerable during this period. Susan F. Martin avers that the "raids unquestionably reflected the deepening suspicion of immigration as a threat to the security of the country."[65] The Red Scare was a key marker of the period's building hostility toward immigrants, especially those of German ancestry.

As these legislative and social events make clear, this period was rife with rabid approaches to nationalism that entrenched xenophobia. Yet, animosity toward immigrants during the war only tells part of this history. Another aspect of nationalism significant to this period was spun from the conflict brewing between modern mass communication and the presumed manipulability of emotion. One of the more exceptional legacies of World War I is the speed and efficiency with which the federal government crafted a unified prowar sentiment. The Wilson administration used propagandistic mechanisms, such as the Committee on Public Information, and disciplinary actions, such as the Espionage Act, to shape broad support for the war as well as the public's understanding of Americanism. Stewart Ross admits that the corollary to marveling at Wilson's prowar machinery was the acknowledgment that "public opinion could be molded more quickly than ever before—in fact, at an astonishing rate when put to the test."[66] Once the prowar campaign began in earnest, commentators argued that immigrants could be easily swayed by mass media.

As the first bullets were fired abroad, many public advocates voiced concern that immigrants from Germany, Austria-Hungary, and other nations might pervert public opinion on the conflict. Early in the war, German American institutions and individuals defended the actions of Germany or encouraged American neutrality.[67] As Ross notes, propaganda from both Britain and Germany "flooded America with war 'news,' pamphlets, books, speakers, movies, all presenting one-sided versions of the origins of the war and the righteousness of their cause."[68] The presumption that immigrants could be easily persuaded by the media remained strong, with fears that German propaganda was infiltrating the popular press while German immigrant organizations were being used to "accomplish imperialistic aims."[69] The threat of German spies and the demonization of home-front radicals inflamed the public's fear of disloyalty.[70] Brenton J. Malin argues that the increase in new media at the dawn of the twentieth century, alongside the rise of urbanism, "created a range of anxieties about the speed and amount of stimulation—emotional, informational, and otherwise—that a person could handle."[71] Wartime demands for loyalty motivated discussion of the ways mass media impacted the nationalistic emotions of immigrants.

Public discourses focused on the emotional effects of media channeled aspects of both ethnic nationalism and civic nationalism. The emotional foundations of nationalism had long been considered the glue of American democracy, dating as early as Benjamin Franklin and Daniel Webster.[72] Immigrants during the early twentieth century presented a unique concern for emotional nationalism. Public recognition of modern media's fantastic power maintained that these modes of communication could conjure a racial or national consciousness—an idea certainly related to ethnic nationalism. Simultaneously, many invoked civic nationalism to proclaim that the insidious propaganda of the Central Powers—even German music, language, or literature—could teach Prussianism to unwitting immigrants. Apprehension about the role of mass media focused on what was being taught and to whom it was being broadcast. According to Andrew Burstein, in the fledgling republic, emotional nationalism built consensus and concealed the limitations of the nation.[73] The role of emotion in the Progressive Era was not simply to supply consensus but to generate heartfelt loyalty, a barricade against the onslaught of pernicious media.

In newspaper and magazine articles, the role of war imagery took center stage as many insisted that immigrants would feel sympathy after viewing or imagining the "horrors of war."[74] Many asserted that immigrants could not help but react to the carnage with sympathy and a desire to fight for their former homeland. In a 1914 article from the *New York Times*, an anonymous reporter cautioned against picture shows in the Lower East Side of Manhattan that screened old footage of European battles and military training. As the reporter warned, "Unless the local authorities take some steps to curtail the activities of some exhibitors, I am afraid we will have riots on the east side before the war is over."[75] Because these films "spared none the horrors of war," the author contended, New York officials might have to subdue riots. The story recounted how San Francisco authorities had already quashed a brawl between German and French reservists associated with similar footage.[76] In this instance, the reels did not show actual footage from the front, yet the power of the visual still affected audiences. Any projected image of fighting in the homeland might animate an uprising.

Media's ability to modify the sympathies of immigrants became seen as an obstacle to unity. The screen image and an individual's imagination were important vehicles in these discussions. Popular texts warned that reading materials and visual representations could shift immigrants' nationalistic emotions. Benedict Anderson posits a connection between the image and imagination: citizens may not know one another, but each nevertheless "lives the image of their communion."[77] The correspondence between the media's conjuring of a national public and the work of visualization creates an investment in the concept of the nation. During the early twentieth century, the concern was largely the obverse: the fragmentation of media engendered disorder. Immigrants engaged media sources that might fundamentally change their national outlook. Fears regarding the foreign language press, popular films, and more indicated that these sources might affect immigrants negatively, preventing their assimilation.

Many authorities argued that the mediated horrors of the war publicized in films, newspapers, and other forums elicited sympathy with immigrants' native lands, rendering American allegiances dubious at best, and at worst, treasonous. The popular idea that immigrants were here on a temporary basis and therefore not dedicated was exacerbated by news of the extradition of soldiers to their homelands.[78] War imagery threatened the capacity for first- and second-generation immigrants to remain loyal insofar as it supposedly reignited a love for the homeland. Revived emotions, then, were said to replace American allegiances and jeopardize the very stability of the union. Citing the circulation of familial letters carrying news from the front, in 1916 President Wilson contended that the war affected immigrants, noting, "Their affections are stirred, old memories awakened and old passions rekindled."[79] Wilson referenced the emotions of nationalism, admonishing his listeners to be more understanding of immigrant sympathy for native lands: "There is no country in the world, I suppose, whose heart is more open to generous emotions than this dear country which we love."[80] Wilson's proclamations suggested that the war, particularly via communicated messages from family, animated robust old-world allegiances by accessing the memories immigrants held of the former nation.

Experts warned that sympathy was an innate devotion coaxed to the surface by the mediation of the war. Some period texts dramatized the tensions between European nationalism and American loyalty generated by newspaper reports.[81] One of these accounts is Lida C. Schem's (pen name Margaret Blake) *The Hyphen*. Popularly understood as a detailed study of racial psychology, the novel's protagonist is Guido von Estritz, the son of a Prussian American and a Russian.[82] Brought to the States as an infant and raised by a German American couple, Guido believes he is of the same heritage as his adoptive parents. With the advent of war, Guido becomes enamored with the news coverage. He soon finds his sentiments on the war and on his own identity radically altered. At his mother's request, the adolescent Guido attempts to avoid discussions of war, yet despite his resistance, "War claimed him. It tugged at his heartstrings, it plucked greedily at his mind, it cried loudly for a hearing, for utterance, for discussion, for a brace of tongues."[83] Guido cannot resist this urge. Even though he rationally disagrees with the actions of the German Kaiser, his disposition on the war soon changes:

> Guido was terribly stirred. An intense excitement had taken possession of him. He was racing along through the moist embraces of the mist-laden air like a madman, unconscious of hour, goal or mileage. The motion of his legs seemed to be energizing his brain. A myriad thoughts pressed about him, clamoring for utterance. They reached out toward him like hands, like fingers. Like faces they peered at him through the mist.[84]

Ultimately, Guido determines that this feeling and excited state is natural. He hears the following lines, "We love as one, we hate as one," and resolves that there is a "collective soul of race."[85] In this story, Guido's loyalty seems out of his control; coverage of the war roused his racial consciousness and diminished his loyalty to the United States. Notably, Schem entitled this work *The Hyphen*, implying that difference itself created the conditions through which war could accomplish such profound change. Of course, the hyphen and hyphenated Americans were long used as derogatory terms for immigrants. But, in the Schem story and during the war generally, the hyphen signified both the gulf between two national homes and the space of invisible disloyalty that could erupt given exposure to certain media. The work of imagination forever modified Guido's national sentiment.

Amplified by the need for preparedness, immigrants became a focal point for concerns about loyalty. Public discourses proclaimed that the mediation of the war could destabilize the emotion of patriotism in the foreign-born. Despite vigorous conversations on the various foundations of nationalism, redressing the problem of immigration remained of central importance. The promiscuous relationships between ethnic nationalism and civic nationalism congealed around questions of loyalty and patriotism. The feelings of immigrants were often described as racially motivated, yet stimulated by public imagery. The complex interplay between these understandings of national identity and consciousness would play out in the discourses and practices of Americanization. Eliciting immigrant loyalty became the primary task for Americanization agents, who sought to tame the vicissitudes of the immigrant's heart.

The Americanization Campaign

The drive to ensure unity motivated a sharp increase in Americanization programs during the teens and early twenties. The Americanization movement was, as John F. McClymer puts it, "one of the largest social and political movements in American history."[86] The term "Americanization" gained currency as public and private organizations increased the number of educational programs for immigrants.[87] Carlson notes that Americanization became an "all-consuming passion" in the United States, with hundreds of governmental authorities, social agencies, and businesses attempting to naturalize immigrants and tutor new residents in the American lifestyle.[88] The goals for Americanization programs varied by the organization engaged in the work. For some, Americanization strictly focused on the acquisition of English, written literacy, and naturalization. For others, Americanization comprised education in the American way of life, including training in civic responsibilities and domestic education for women. The nature of assimilation depended upon the individuals or groups conducting Americanization programs. Some insisted that Americanization necessitated the complete rejection of one's ethnic or national culture and the full adoption of American standards.[89] Others argued that the immigrant's heritage was a gift that allowed for the continual evolution of the American way of life.[90]

As war loomed on the horizon, the United States coordinated a national campaign for Americanization that decidedly modified the national outlook for immigrants and immigration. A number of state-based programs became the foundation for these larger changes. Gwendolyn Mink notes that Grace Abbott and Frances Kellor were key figures in state-level structures of Americanization.[91] Each helped to incorporate Americanization programs into public schools. Kellor orchestrated adult and child Americanization curricula as chief investigator for the New York Immigration Commission and as founder of the Committee for Immigrants in America.[92] Abbott held a variety of public roles through her position at Hull House, her work with the Immigrants' Protective League, and her work on behalf of children's rights. She led Americanization public education initiatives in both Massachusetts and Illinois.[93] By 1916, both women "had helped organize a National Conference on Immigration and Americanization, marking the beginning of a concerted political effort to assimilate, rather than exclude, new southern and eastern European immigrant Americans."[94] The conference, alongside ongoing regional efforts, created the conditions in which Americanization would become a nationally organized campaign.

Kellor, in particular, was integral in changing the national understanding of Americanization. In 1915, Kellor established Americanization Day festivities—events that generated such demand for Americanization programs that the National Americanization Committee (NAC) was formed with Kellor at the helm.[95] According to Hartmann, the NAC pursued four goals: English literacy, naturalization, industrial efficiency, and the maintenance of American standards of living.[96] Although the NAC was private, it operated in tandem with the Bureau of Naturalization, the Bureau of Education, the Committee on Public Information, and the Council of National Defense. Kellor was appointed as liaison between the Bureau of Education and the NAC. In its now politically valuable position, the NAC coordinated and nationalized Americanization endeavors for various federal, state, and civic organizations conducting work among immigrants. President Wilson lent significant authority to the NAC's Americanization campaign, participating in many of its initiatives and promoting its agenda.

By systematically coordinating federal, regional, and local approaches, the NAC's campaign was remarkably successful in positioning Americanization as an urgent need. Kellor was trained as an industrial safety expert and her skills were put to good use for the NAC.[97] A devotee of scientific management, Kellor sought to approach the "problem of Americanization" with exacting precision.[98] Kellor insisted that the NAC's vision of Americanization supplemented the factory-based philosophy of scientific management with "citizenship management."[99] She elaborated, "Some of us believe that in this new spirit lies the hope of the nation."[100] Implementation of citizenship management for the NAC was broadly construed but often focused on labor and industry.[101] The NAC launched the "America First" campaign in 1915 that "standardized citizenship courses in all normal schools and night schools," publicized the need to prioritize Americanization, and strove to make its work part of the war-preparedness campaign.[102] From that point forward, the NAC often touted Americanization as essential to the war effort. Its vision of comprehensive Americanization became the touchstone that animated nationalistic groups, state-based initiatives, and ad hoc programs. As McClymer recounts from a 1919 *Chicago Tribune* article, "Only an agile and determined immigrant, possessed of overmastering devotion to the land of his birth can hope to escape Americanization by at least one of the many processes now being prepared for his special benefit, in addition to those which have surrounded him in the past."[103]

As systematic efforts and public outcry transformed Americanization into a near-compulsory demand, the methods of this type of instruction became of increasing interest. Drawing on public misgivings about the role of media and the need for stalwart nationalism, Americanization instruction sought to win the affections central to patriotism. Educators discussed at length the failures of memorization or rote methods of instruction and insisted that new approaches must be devised to stir the sentiments of patriotism in students. The terms these educators used shifted from "sympathy" and "spirit" to "emotion" and "patriotism." Nevertheless, each term indexed the need to instill Americanism as an emotional quality. For both adults and children enrolled in or engaged with Americanization curricula, nationalism was to be understood as an affection that bound a people together. Teaching methods were to inspire the feelings of patriotism and loyalty.

A clear example of the push for changes in Americanization teaching methods appears in Royal Dixon's 1916 *Americanization*. Dixon was the vice president of the League of Foreign-Born Citizens and editor of *Immigrants in America Review* and therefore intimately connected to the work of the NAC and Bureau of Education. For this Texan, patriotism was an intense emotion, an electric spell that bewitched the citizen: "Patriotism says that the idea of a man's country gives him a thrill; that he loves its soil, its sights, its sounds; it forever speaks to him, it beckons him back, it holds him; and he will, under the spell of patriotism, die for his country, knowing that his death is the most honorable of all human acts of nobility and sacrifice."[104] Dixon contrasted his definition to the failure of Americanization, why America had yet to speak to the "heart of the foreigner" and "enlist his fidelity" to the United States.[105] His answer was that the nation as a whole neglected to wield Americanization to thrill the immigrant: lessons in American citizenship did not provide the emotional and inspirational charge essential to love of country. Dixon insisted that Americanization education focus on "nourishing the spiritual consciousness of the American" with "patriotic method."[106] If that were successful, "Americanism would be no mere word,—it would be a power such as no body politic has ever known, if half the energy in it were exerted."[107]

As is evident in Dixon, Americanization as a rhetorical pedagogy commonly situated nationalism as shared emotional dispositions. These educators opined that if immigrants could feel the love of patriotism, they could learn to become Americans. The manifest hope of civic nationalism became routed through the emotional mechanisms of group consciousness. To become an American was to remain loyal to the United States above all and to become bound by the feelings of patriotism. For Dixon, a "new America" would emerge from the "conscious, directed campaign" of Americanization.[108] In this way, the nation could manage a heterogeneous population by building a common emotional base in the populace. As Dixon phrased it, a "national conscience [sic]" would fulfill the "destiny" of the nation once "the hearts of all her peoples beat with an indescribable, sublimely wonderful thrill at the very mention of her name—this will mean 'patriotism.'"[109]

The Americanization movement deployed the image and imagination as vital tools in cultivating emotional nationalism. To be sure, immigrants were not seen as lacking any patriotism, but for Americanization agents, their feelings for the American nation must consume them to thwart the possibility of divided ties. In some ways, this new vision of emotional nationalism can be understood as a form of civil religion, a faith in the United States.[110] Analyzing nationalistic discourses of this period, Vaughn avers that the Committee on Public Information deployed a secular religion that might weld the populace together.[111] Yet, emotions as the basis of nationalism during this period were a bit more complex. Americanization experts invested in education to corral a diverse population affected by the tumults of modernity. The lessons of Americanization used the image and imagination to generate an emotional bond to the republic.[112] The goal was to use formulized educational processes to direct the affective sensations of the screen to specific emotional outcomes. Thus, it was not simply that Americanization used emotional appeals, but rather it relied on visual and performative education to fashion unbreakable patriotic bonds.

The presumed need for emotional nationalism shifted the tone of Americanization pedagogy. Given that Americanization did not necessarily augment naturalization, it is telling that many Americanization lessons pursued abstract ambitions. Pointedly, throughout the discourses I study in this text, there was considerably less focus on naturalization or traditional civic practices. Rather, educators designed lessons capable of wedding immigrants to the nation. National identity and immigrant loyalty would thus be strengthened through emotional education prompting immigrants to truncate affection for the homeland. Many assumed other forms of national commitment would follow naturally from patriotic emotions. Emotional nationalism was to overcome the prejudices of nativism and open the pathways of inclusion. Yet, Americanization's focus on emotional nationalism simultaneously masked the structural limitations precluding full access. Despite proclamations that patriotism and loyalty alone could transform any immigrant, those same pedagogies rarely addressed ongoing disadvantages. An abstract pedagogy of patriotism dampened the outcry of nativists just as it disavowed material inequalities. Love of country was to bind the nation together and smooth the assimilation of newcomers into the status quo.

Methods of Americanization aimed to supply students with those astonishing experiences that could quickly redirect their patriotic sentiments toward the welcoming arms of the United States. Visual aids and performative rituals became key tools for this process. Americanization educators proclaimed that the mesmerizing work of the visual and ritualistic ensured that immigrants would learn efficiently. Ostensibly, much of this efficiency stemmed from the spectacular capacities of such engagement—the ability to cunningly shape the feelings of the student. Certainly, most educators maintained that using images and performances helped students concretize the language and customs of the nation.[113] However, for proponents of visual and aesthetic education, the student would easily remember the lesson because it elicited his affections. As Gladys Bollman and Henry Bollman (1922) argued of Americanization work, films and other dazzling displays imparted "higher ideals of citizenship," increased membership in English classes, and successfully illustrated "the best ideals of American life."[114] The "power of the screen" supposedly resulted in stronger Americanization outcomes.[115]

The national work of Americanization engendered the conditions through which this rhetorical pedagogy became not simply a lesson for individual students, but an understanding of citizenship management—as Kellor phrased it—that transformed public culture. Combating the fear that immigrants might undermine war preparedness, Americanization authorities invited students to love the United States above all. To accomplish such a task, they emphasized new approaches to education that relied on visual aids and performative rituals. Visual aids were useful tools in arousing and directing the emotional commitments of students. Yet, these individual lessons were also extrapolated for all citizens. The power

Dixon referenced marked a desire to instill a new mode of emotional nationalism that might transform immigrants and the nation writ large.[116]

Thus, the educational practices of Americanization precipitated a major shift in public culture such that patriotism was positioned as an emotional disposition with demonstrable impacts. Parades on Flag Day and Americanization Day did not simply display Americanized subjects before the public but also relayed those markers of Americanism deemed most valuable nationally. In so doing, the Americanization movement helped constitute a visual logic of Americanism—a set of representational structures coding the recognition of patriotism. Rhetorical investigation of these structures illustrates the grounds of a rather paradoxical understanding of nationalism: the tensions between the emotional basis of nationalism and concern for the patent differences of immigrants undermined the appearance of Americanism while prompting its continual enactment. The longing for emotional union could not mitigate concerns about immigrants as disloyal and un-American; instead, the visual logic of Americanization reified this very concern and propelled repeated displays of patriotism. Examining the tropological structure of this relationship allows scholars to better understand the work of Americanization.

The Tropes of Nationalism

One of the most difficult obstacles for Americanization agents was to prove the success of their teaching. They faced a number of challenges in this regard. Nativists insisted that immigrants could not be Americanized. For them, the most appropriate course of action was to close the border and maintain the supremacy of Nordic, American stock. Even most progressives argued that immigrants were not yet Americans and required further instruction to be afforded the full measure of citizenship. Meanwhile, the war generated anxieties about the emotional vicissitudes of immigrants and the need for an ardent patriotism within all Americans. Against these various viewpoints, Americanization educators devised ways to prove that immigrants shared in a common understanding of Americanism. Given broader concerns about disloyalty, Americanization agents labored to inspire the feelings of patriotism and to illustrate that such sentiments were legitimate and unwavering. Those demonstrations typically prompted immigrants to perform Americanism in publicly marked forms.

Americanization articulated a pedagogy for changing public culture through the work of emblems, visual aids, and performative rituals. The correspondence between image, imagination, and the transformation of public culture was key to Americanization lessons. Émile Durkheim asserted in 1915 that symbols and signs are constitutive elements of the social. He wrote, "The emblem is not merely a convenient process for clarifying the sentiment society has of itself; it also serves to create this sentiment; it is one of its constituent elements."[117] As with Durkheim, many scholars suggest that both sentiments and emotions are foundational to social organization and nation-building.[118] For Americanization agents, patriotism did not emerge from the ether. In keeping with Durkheim's discussion of the emblem, it worked via visual and performative lessons that structured the emotional foundations of nationalism.

By deploying visual and performative markers of patriotism, Americanization functioned as a rhetorical pedagogy of civic recognition. Teachers regularly used spectacular displays and public rituals to inspire allegiance in pupils. At the conclusion of Americanization lessons, public ceremonies and exhibitions were to demonstrate to both the student and the public that Americanization had successfully inculcated the emotional foundations of nationalism. The mechanisms for illustrating such success relied on common forms of patriotic representation. Repeating these displays across public culture transformed the registers of nationalism such that patriotism became codified into a set of particular practices. As a form of civics education, Americanization did not simply forward democratic practice through naturalization or public advocacy. Instead, this pedagogy solicited students' emotions and sought to create a model of Americanism for all.

To elucidate how these schemes of recognition impacted public culture, it is important to describe the visual logic that propped up the Americanization project. That logic is best explored through the tropological dimensions of representation. While today tropes, much like rhetoric generally, are popularly reduced to ornamentation, scholars have long understood tropes as particularly important tools for discovering structures of human expression and thought. For written and spoken language, tropes are the names given to the logic of representation such that metonymy is a relationship of condensation or displacement while metaphor can identify similarity or substitution. Ancient scholars such as Cicero and Quintilian used tropes to explain the pathetic appeal of the speaker's performance.[119] For Cicero, a trope of the body—including gesticulation, movement of the eyes, emphatic delivery, and more—"displays the movements of the soul, affects all mankind; for the minds of all men are excited by the same emotions, which they recognise in others, and indicate in themselves, by the same tokens."[120] In this vein, the orator's body was a particularly important vehicle of representation that required rhetorical finesse to hold suasory power. Noting the way Cicero dually treated tropes of the body alongside tropes of language, John Richard Dugan summarizes the relationship between tropes and bodies: "Cicero uses language as a trope for the sign-system of the body, and the body as a metaphor for the articulations and adornments of language."[121] Taken more generally, tropes are useful tools to both categorize and explicate the relationships between rhetorical style and persuasion.

For this project, tropes explain how immigrants were induced to perform as Americans, and the way these practices collectively generated the interpretive rubrics against which patriotism was assessed. In this light, tropes serve an ontological and epistemological function—a mode of representation that is repeated across culture such that it becomes a way of organizing and constituting human expression and knowledge. Thus, I use my own academic training to read the representational practices of Americanization through particular rhetorical figures. Doing so allows me to analyze how these practices transformed the public registers of nationalism. Here, tropes do more than describe the individual assignation of Americanism for particular immigrants; rather they are methodological terms that help interrogate the way Americanism became a publicly identified devotion. On Erik Gunderson's view, this was always the case with tropes of the body. The orator was not simply a "good man, speaking well," but a student tutored to adopt "a certain soul and a certain body, and thereby to become a good man."[122] Tropes thus access the visual logic of Americanization lessons both for the individual and for public culture.

I am not the first to apply tropological analysis as a method of analyzing the constitutive impact of individual rhetorical lessons on larger social formations. At least since Giambattista Vico, scholars have understood tropes to serve a world-making purpose. In *The New Science*, Vico describes tropes as modes of communication helping humans make sense of their surroundings.[123] The earliest human utterances named the world and supplied a moral valence through which to view that world. For Vico, tropes are the basis of social relations. As Vico scholar David Marshall contends, rhetorical tropes are not mere *techne*; they fashion "those realms in which meaningful public appearance is possible."[124] Later scholars have followed this vein of thinking, proposing various ways of understanding the world-making potential of rhetorical tropes. Paul Ricoeur, attempting to unite Aristotle's treatment of tropes in both the *Rhetoric* and *Poetics*, writes, "Metaphor is the rhetorical process by which discourse unleashes the power that certain fictions have to redescribe reality."[125] Kenneth Burke, Hayden White, Ernesto Laclau, and others present tropes as constitutive of language and meaning.[126] To access the foundations of public discourse, it is critical to interrogate, as Christian Lundberg maintains, "the specific economies that underwrite the circulation of texts and tropes at specific sites of economic exchange."[127] As such, a tropological reading of individual Americanization lessons provides a useful starting point for extrapolating the larger visual logic of patriotism.

One of the benefits of using a tropological method to analyze Americanization discourses is that tropes allow scholars a better understanding of the visuality of nation-building. While some may read tropes as primarily linguistic or language-based, a number of authors understand tropes as signs or modes of representation that include images, schemes, and more.[128] The way visual and performative signs of patriotism became codified during this period indicates that public culture was transformed by the imaginative capacity of signification—what Vico or Ernesto Grassi might refer to as "poetic consciousness."[129] In this way, tropes become an expanded methodological tool to grasp how visual and performative modes of representation allow for a productive ambiguity. The linguistic signs of "American" or "patriot" are, in fact, opened up by another field of tropological relations: the visual and performative symbols that attempt to emblematize those terms. It is the flexibility of visual and performative acts that both enables the work of Americanization to include immigrants, and demonstrates the productive paradox at stake in the project.

Indeed, tropological analysis enables the critic to focus on the tensions of meaning that inhere in all modes of signification. Ricoeur describes this function well, writing that the "'place' of metaphor" is "neither the name, nor the sentence, nor even discourse, but the copula of the verb *to be*."[130] He continues, the "metaphorical 'is' at once signifies both 'is not' and 'is like.'"[131] In metaphor, "identity and difference do not melt together but confront each other."[132] The trope of metaphor works by crafting relations of similarity based on difference. Holding similarity and difference in tension allows for new meanings and significations. Ricoeur is focused on metaphor, but the same argument can be applied to a number of other tropes. While not all figures and tropes rely on relations of similarity, they are still predicated on twisting and turning meaning and signification. Part of the task of this book is to add to the study of Americanization history by illustrating how the relationships between identity and difference structured (and in some ways continue to structure) the visual rubrics of nationalism.

The first two decades of the twentieth century amplified patriotism and nationalistic display, a trend that culminated in the heightened Americanism of the war years. Tropes are methodological tools that show what these nationalistic displays were meant to signify or do within public culture. Interrogating Americanization pedagogies through the lens of tropes accesses how, as Lawrence Prelli writes, "reality is constituted rhetorically through the multiple displays that surround us, compete for our attention, and make claims upon us."[133] Public culture was transformed by those symbols and performances designed to act upon the imagination of the populace.

Yet, tropes as analytical devices also help to flesh out the tensions that circumscribed the Americanization project and, as I will later argue, generated a paradoxical condition for determining Americanism. While immigrants were prompted to perform in very specific ways, these guidelines did not necessarily dominate their daily practices. Given that all performances are sites of struggle, it is important to remember that Americanization was a complex symbolic endeavor. To be sure, period rubrics associated with nationalism cannot be fully understood as symbol systems or even simple systems of representation. Symbolic analyses, such as that of John F. McClymer and others, have already suggested that

Americanization worked to "fix the public meaning of Americanism."[134] This social-constructionist or symbolist perspective correctly identifies the codification of Americanism, but misses the idea that these symbols remained ill-fitting forms of representation. It would be incorrect to suggest that Americanization organized representations of loyalty such that immigrants could perform Americanness and thereby become seen as Americans. Instead, a tropological approach illuminates the ways contingency continued to haunt the project of Americanization. While Americanization authorities sought to create a stable meaning for Americanism, "contingency is the invariable scene of rhetoric."[135] Tropes signify only by capitalizing on the contingency of any rhetorical act. The tropological logic of Americanization was such that the relationship between figure and referent productively exploited the catachrestic potential of representation—the idea that all names and symbols are ill-fitting. If immigrants were to be seen as Americans, the symbol of American had to be opened up for resignification. However, the slippage between figure and referent simultaneously undermined such a possibility and created a paradoxical condition—signs of patriotism (at least for immigrants) were haunted by the invisibility of national affections. Identity and difference remained in problematic tension in the discourses and practices of the period.

In some ways, the visual logic of period patriotism emerged from broader understandings of the visibility of immigrant differences. Analyzing popular sources from the late nineteenth century, Shawn Michelle Smith has artfully demonstrated precisely how photographic practices and eugenic ideology articulated how Americans ought to look.[136] For her, bodily appearances were linked to internal "essences."[137] In the discourses and practices of Americanization, the same form of visual reasoning continued to underwrite discussions of period nationalism. Americanization agents forwarded a larger rubric in which patriots were assessed by marked differences. Yet, burgeoning discussions of Americanization as a form of emotional education redirected this visual logic in important ways. Within this cultural rubric, seeing did not result in believing.[138] Thus, Americanization agents often battled general apprehensions about the invisibility of emotion while simultaneously relaying schemes of recognition predicated on exterior validation. These paradoxes of representation can be productively excavated through tropological analysis.

Americanization appeared at a time in which national identity was changing dramatically. Immigrants became seen as a threat to nationalism, particularly as the war amplified concerns regarding loyalty. The coordinated movement for Americanization fashioned a new outlook on national identity centered on loyalty and patriotism. Particular performances of Americanism were necessary to elicit and display the faithful feelings of the subject. To understand the complexities and paradoxes that both plagued and motivated the Americanization crusade, critics must unearth the tensions of meaning and national identity juxtaposed in its discourses and practices. Rhetorical criticism facilitates an understanding of the Americanization campaign beyond jingoistic ornamentation or ideological content. Instead, rhetorical criticism can help scholars understand the visual logic of Americanization and the means through which nationalism was forever changed.

CHAPTER TWO

The Visual Pedagogy of Americanization

———•◆•———

In 1919, Raymond Crist, the director of citizenship in the Bureau of Naturalization, appeared before a House committee hearing on proposed changes to naturalization laws. In his opening statement, Crist suggested that the true import of his testimony was to praise the recent education initiatives of Americanization: "There is, however, a far greater subject which I should like to present to the committee for its most careful consideration. That subject is the all-absorbing, Nation-wide question rather loosely referred to by the term 'Americanization.'"[1] For Crist, effective Americanization altered the hearts and minds of the unnaturalized. He explained, "Americanization work starts with the work of transforming the mental attitude of the permanent foreign resident population in this country and developing a higher intelligence throughout the millions composing that mass of politically undigested human beings."[2] In keeping with Crist's claim that education should be a key consideration for naturalization laws, participants in the hearings detailed the methods of instruction used successfully across the country. For these experts, English illiteracy and ambivalence stymied effective instruction in naturalization. In this light, visual aids and other demonstrative teaching methods widened educational opportunities for newcomers by encouraging pupils to transform their attitudes toward Americanization.

According to Crist and many others, images possessed pedagogical value given their ability to stir nationalistic sentiment through concrete visualization. They worked both practically and imaginatively. At one point in his testimony, Crist lauded motion pictures as especially valuable tools for successful Americanization:

> It [the English language] can be put in visual form, and they [immigrants] can have the United States Government visualized to them in its relationship to them in every classroom in the United States. That visualization would mean the advancement of the best interests of the country. The elements of the Government that are directed particularly to the betterment of the individual will be visualized through these motion pictures. There are now a good many activities being demonstrated by the Department of Agriculture, and we could make use of their films. We will show to these people who have come from central European countries, many of whom are a purely agricultural people, that this country offers them places where they can get back to the earth and feel that they have at least gotten to a land which offers them a vocation with which they are thoroughly familiar.[3]

Here, motion pictures aided Americanization through their demonstrative and idealistic capacities. This teaching tool materialized the English language and governmental processes. Yet, film also enabled the viewer to envision the United States as home—as a place to find the comforts of the homeland. Crist maintained that visual methods marshaled "a latent desire for citizenship" into a keen understanding of what citizenship might beget.[4]

While Congress failed to pass the bill these hearings considered, Crist's discussion highlights how experts hypothesized the persuasive power of visual aids for immigrant viewers. Visual aids stirred the feelings of the audience and substantiated the benefits of American life. Crist drew on the pedagogical insights afforded to him by Americanization programs of the war years. In the midst of international conflict, experts averred that Americanization must be broad in scope, speedily enacted, and resoundingly effective. Visual aids and performative teaching methods helped achieve these ends. While some scholars contend that visual aids were used to combat English illiteracy, their employment was more often predicated on their ability to animate the human body.[5] Ultimately, such visuals supplied an affectively dazzling experience that could wed immigrants to the United States.

Analyzed rhetorically, a number of Americanization pedagogies and visual aids were designed to arouse the affective foundation of emotional nationalism. With the understanding that an affective charge could be routed toward particular emotions, educators deployed photographs, stereoscope slides, films, and more to provide a spectacular experience that might deliver students to patriotic adoration. The first step in this process was to excite pupils, to stir in them a longing to engage in the process of Americanization. Thus, the bedrock of Americanization's rhetorical pedagogy was the ability to motivate robust participation. The use of visual aids and patriotic rituals were thought to do just that, evoking an affective response in students that might induce cooperation. The lessons designed for individual students imagined an intimate relationship among image, affect, and emotion. Thus, the first premise in the visual logic of Americanization relied on a presumed correspondence between sensory apprehensions and a subsequent emotional nationalism.

The rhetorical figure of prolepsis helps identify the affective foundations of emotional nationalism. At root, the rhetorical pedagogy of Americanization sought to create new citizens by opening their capacity for emotional connection. The visual and embodied experiences of Americanization were understood as especially helpful tools for that process. Visuals ostensibly created longing for national union. Prolepsis is a figure of anticipation—a trope used to identify the relationships between our knowledge of the present and the possibilities of the future. In linguistic form, the warning from a parent "Do that one more time and you are grounded" is proleptic in that it forecasts what will follow from bad behavior. In Stoic and some Roman philosophies, prolepsis was a mode of tacit knowledge guiding anticipation for what follows.[6] In the visual lessons of Americanization, prolepsis identifies the move from mediated perceptions to anticipation for national kinship. Visual and other similar lessons supplied a perceptual and temporal lesson in emotional nationalism. Stereoscope slides, posters, films, and photographs depicting images and scenes of the American landscape provided vicarious stimuli that might prompt eagerness for the future and thereby encourage student investment in the process of Americanization.[7]

Visual Education and Affective Stimulation

Americanization educators often declared emotional nationalism as the glue of a heterogeneous nation, particularly one managing a massive shift in national composition. For these advocates, the benefit of visual and performative teaching tools was their ability to rouse the affective registers of students. Period discussions of affective stimulation were indebted to larger interest in emotional education and crowd psychology. In popular and scholarly discourse, the affective commotion of media for immigrants, children, and women had already been established. For instance, a rising tide of psychologists and film critics argued that the visual charge of some films would create delinquency in minds supposedly too feeble to resist the spell.[8] Despite some admonitions against popular films, especially crime dramas, some educators investigated the promise of visual media in the classroom. Once funding for vocational education and naturalization courses increased substantially in the early twentieth century, adult immigrants became a target for visual education.[9] The animating potential of the image became the ground upon which these advocates debated the success of visual aids as pedagogical tools. To usher students toward the common bonds of emotional nationalism, Americanization teachers relied on the vivacity of visual aids.

Broader investment in psychology, particularly among teachers, set the stage for an upsurge in pedagogical discourse on affective stimulation and emotional education.[10] The term "affect" was distinguished from "emotion" in these discourses. It referenced a state of agitation and excitation stirred by certain stimuli. Affect provided a gateway to emotions. In the United States, popular interest in affective stimulation and emotions emerged from the publications of William James and Carl Lange in the late 1800s, which separately devised an understanding of emotional states as predicated on bodily sensation.[11] The 1899 publication of James's wildly popular *Talks to Teachers* familiarized educators, and the general public, with what came to be called the James-Lange theory of emotions.[12] Through one of the earliest articulations of what is now called affect theory, the public learned that emotions are unnameable without identifying certain embodied sensations. Paul Stob suggests that James's instruction in psychology enabled teachers' greater "professional esteem" and an enhanced public image.[13] In effect, emotional psychology became an important teaching tool and a point of consideration in wider public discussions of human motivation.[14]

Still another set of popular discourses sprang from academic accounts of crowd psychology. More generally, public concerns regarding film indicated that crowds could be led astray by the influences of a demagogue or films with malicious plots.[15] The affective excitation of audiences reportedly opened up the potential for manipulation. Indeed, much of these discussions projected audience response onto the object: the film fomented the affective and attitudinal dispositions of the audience.[16] Pointedly, the creation of a group consciousness typically depended upon affective stimulation as foundation.[17]

Given the popular uptake of these psychological theories, many experts began to apply these insights in the classroom, especially by employing increasingly available visual aids. While the nature of implementation varied, images and other arresting media became seen as integral to shaping the student's emotions.[18] Affective responses to media cued emotional shifts. The popularity of what came to be called moral or emotional education was such that by the teens, its usefulness in the classroom was virtually unquestioned. In 1918, the superintendent of schools in Decatur, Illinois, and a prolific author on pedagogy, James Ozro Engleman, referenced a nascent understanding of crowd psychology and displayed significant elements of the James-Lange theory. Engleman declared that the latter was "nearly universally accepted by psychologists and thoughtful teachers"; the theory should "become familiar to every teacher in the elementary schools, and every parent as well."[19] For Engleman, "moral education can never be divorced from an education of the emotional life."[20] He prompted teachers to use the theory to specific benefit: "Very few psychological principles can be observed with greater profit, either in the wise discipline and treatment of a child, or in the self-control of an adult who tends to be dominated by his coarser emotions."[21]

For immigrants in particular, the image purportedly supplemented their lack of experience with the English language, American life, and the joys of democratic government. Engleman insisted that well-crafted emotional education for immigrant students required visual appeals:

> We need from time to time the fervid appeals to our imaginations made by such men as Jacob Riis and such women as Mary Antin before we can thrill with passionate interest in our democracy. The intelligent immigrant sees and teaches us the superiority of this liberty-loving "Promised Land" over the less favored despotisms of the Old World, and in so doing gives us a basis for a still finer type of patriotism.[22]

Here, the ground of patriotism rested on the thrills of visual appeals. Passion and patriotism were an outcrop of visual titillation. Once aroused, the immigrant would not only become a patriot, but "teach us," other citizens, the advantages of democracy. As is clear for Engleman, many educators during this period became invested in the relationships between stimulation and emotions, and theorized how the classroom could cultivate particular feelings, especially for students whose emotions were seen as base. Images began the process of Americanization by animating the student's embodied enthusiasm and by generating an implicit understanding of the nation and its practices.

It is the stimulating function of visual Americanization tactics that can be dissected via the rhetorical concept of prolepsis. For Stoics such as Chrysippus or Sextus, prolepsis was a form of preconception, a human propensity that gives rise to certain ways of seeing the world. Henry Dyson argues that Stoic prolepsis operated as tacit knowledge brought about by observation and experience. Children, for instance, "might form the prolepsis of an elephant through regular, direct experience of these animals, whereas others would not have the requisite experiences."[23] Everyday sense perceptions allow children to reason what an elephant is, what she will do, and their own relationship to the animal. In most of Dyson's examples, prolepsis is necessarily imagaic. It is an apprehension of the senses, typically ocular, that informs human reasoning of "basic natural kinds and moral properties."[24] Visual Americanization lessons work as a form of proleptic stimulation—these lessons provide the foundation of seeing the world as Americans. Visual stimulation through mediated images supposedly accomplished what direct observation generated for inferential reasoning. Visual media as proleptic worked affectively, as a charge that was "psychologically functional in the formation of presentation and impulses," but not yet available to ruminative reflection.[25] Prolepsis thus helps to explain the structure of Americanization as a rhetorical pedagogy—creating an emotional bond among students began by stimulating the senses.

Americanization Education through Slides, Posters, and Films

The earliest attempts to use visual media for the education of immigrants occurred shortly before the initial battles of World War I. During this period, educators relied on stereoscope and lantern slides as easily accessible visual aids for tutelage in the English language and in naturalization courses. As the Americanization movement gained momentum, enthusiasts embraced other available tools. Posters and films joined slides and photographs in the schooling of immigrants. Americanization authorities justified their use of these visual aids on the embodied stimulation they provided. Images were claimed to be compelling not simply because they overcame illiteracy in English, but primarily because these instruments engrossed the pupil and encouraged her to feel the lesson with her entire body. In the methods of visual instruction designed for immigrants—including stereopticon slides, posters, and films—the first step in Americanization pedagogy required elevated senses, primed to understand the sights and rituals of Americanism as other Americans ostensibly did. These modes of education functioned as proleptic forms in that they supplied the affective charge and common perceptions central to that priming.

STEREOPTICON SLIDES

Given the limited availability of a variety of visual aids, many teachers relied on stereopticon or lantern slides for Americanization instruction. The Syracuse school district is an exemplary program for understanding how these slides were used—it benefited from one of the most developed visual education programs in the country, the New York State Visual Instruction Division. Speaking at an Americanization conference in May 1919, Principal H. D. Rickard of Putnam School detailed how Syracuse's school district employed stereopticon and lantern slides for night classes.[26] Rickard observed the need for English instruction to teach students to "assimilate the American spirit of freedom and gradually conform to the American ideal."[27] Yet, he noted that too often this goal had not been met. Lesson plans were haphazard and instructors did not often have access to the best teaching tools, including visual aids. For Rickard, the solution to this predicament was to adopt available instructional devices emphasizing the individual student. He praised stereopticon slides as helpful in this regard. The slide represented a concrete object that the student could understand and that captured his "interest."[28] As with many uses of stereoscope slides, the image was seen as powerful because it formed a common understanding of the American ideal. Its sensory stimulation not only grabbed the audience's attention but also supplied the implicit knowledge key to Americanism.

For Rickard, the benefit of stereopticon slides was their sensational qualities. Images piqued the student's interest. Here, the role of imagaic prolepsis was pure anticipation, capturing the attention of the student and assuring him that something worthwhile would follow. Just as classical scholars described prolepsis as reasoning from sense perception, here the projected image in a darkened room vivified the audience's expectations. As Rickard wrote, "the attention of the whole room is concentrated upon an 8-foot square. Concentration means progress."[29] He emphasized the value of lantern and stereoscope slides as located in their capacity to engross the audience. Once the teacher could excite the class with the projected image, she could more easily instruct students. For Rickard, the help of affective images inspired the "spirit of true patriotism and loyalty toward his adopted country."[30] In this way, the image was valuable not simply for its practicality, but because it fascinated the audience.

The proleptic work of visual aids during this era used the intimacy of viewing mass-produced stereopticon slides to tantalize the audience. The stereoscope was a tool designed primarily for leisurely viewing, a vista through which privileged viewers could access other places and peoples.[31] Jonathan Crary describes the affective work of stereoscope viewing, writing that "The experience of space between these objects (planes) is not one of gradual and predictable recession; rather there is a vertiginous uncertainty about the distance separating the forms . . . the absolutely airless space surrounding them has a disturbing palpability."[32] Put simply, it feels real and yet unreal simultaneously, providing an arresting experience for the viewer. For Rickard and the many who responded to his presentation, the experience of the stereoscope and slides was integral to the education of immigrants. These experiences offered students a mode of study that rendered their full, embodied engagement vaguely real, even if the viewer recognized the artifice of the images.

Rickard referenced stereopticon slides as engendering a national consciousness. Stereoscope slides were thrilling media that could evoke a group or national sentiment through affective stimulation. His modern deployment of proleptic knowledge situated anticipation as longing begat by visual provocation. The exciting, fantastic image suggested the inference that the nation was just as impressive. Rickard closed his address by denoting images as powerful pedagogical tools for inculcating American virtues:

> Let us eradicate the question of hyphenated loyalty by teaching the truth concerning the American ideal. . . . In the words of Royal Dixon, "The new America will be permeated by a patriotism so strong and loyal so as to destroy all racial and religious prejudices. Here will be welcome every form of religion and sect, every color and every race will be at home, and 'Do unto others as you would have them do unto you' will be the motto of all." In the sky of liberty a new constellation will appear and its name will be America—many peoples, but one nation.[33]

Significantly, Rickard's description here seems divorced from the original discussion of concrete teaching methods that began his presentation. Yet, his argument was that Americanization should "hasten" the development of Americanism. The image was bestowed with the ability to create the possibility of, and speed the process of, Americanization. It aided Americanization by making the experience exciting, a feeling that generated anticipation for one's future in the nation. National consciousness was the outgrowth of the image's spectacular appeal.

In addition, the visual provided not simply tacit knowledge of certain lessons but also relayed the intangible qualities of Americanism. As one teacher commented on Rickard's presentation, "I just want to say that there are wonderful opportunities in the slide for teaching history to foreigners, making them understand why we love America, why America stands for the greatest things in the United States, and our glorious history will rank with the history of their nations."[34] This comment strangely placed America as an ideal within the United States, but the slippage is noteworthy. Her argument seemed to suggest, in keeping with Rickard's address, that the visualization of America as an ideal provided an implicit understanding of the virtues of the nation, the reason for resolute love, and the glory of the country's history. History can be taught via a multitude of methods, but her insistence that the slide espoused a more robust form of national love indicates the significance of the visual's arresting form. As an object imbued with considerable rhetorical power, the visual stimulated a common base from which to communicate American values.

The praise afforded visual lessons was predicated on interpreting the audience as unlearned or as dull in their imaginative capacities. For Rickard, by simply gazing upon the facile image, the student would aspire to the sentiments of patriotism. He acclaimed slides as providing an apt form of demonstration: "In every stage of work the picture helps the pupil to grasp the idea quickly, and its value can not be overestimated. If it gives an actual view of one of the many experiences with which the foreigner must deal in his daily life, it will add much . . . interest and will arouse an enthusiasm which otherwise might lie dormant."[35] Rickard insisted that teachers guide students through easily intelligible images to cultivate their "enthusiasm" for enculturation. Notice that this discussion situated the audience as particularly naive or ignorant given that it assumed immigrants were unable to feign interest without the image. The argument positioned immigrants as an intellectual underclass that must be tantalized while being groomed for appropriate modes of citizenship.

Given this understanding of the audience, this use of prolepsis as a rhetorical pedagogy centered on embodied stimulation. Without the image, the student's enthusiasm would otherwise "lie dormant."[36] Here, proleptic anticipation was assuredly a visual tactic, a rhetorical pedagogy only available via the mass production of images. Reasoning from the stimulation of the visual spawned an eagerness for the process of Americanization. The image provided a sign from which students might infer the possibilities of the future. Once the commotion of the visual could evoke such perceptions, the remaining lessons would be easier to teach.

Yet, for most educators the visual as simple stimulation was inadequate to the task of Americanization. In other lessons, the rhetorical strategy of proleptic training relied on both corporeal arousal and specific imagery to build a common visual reasoning among immigrant pupils. The tactic pitted educational visuals against popular distractions. Here, the crowd would not be stimulated toward prurient interests but toward stalwart nationalism. To wit, Americanization educators opined that certain sights would evoke the virtues Americans shared. Rural vistas and a focus on the future were thought to spur a shared orientation to the nation.

FORD EDUCATIONAL WEEKLY SERIES

The Ford Educational Weekly Series was a group of films developed in 1916 and distributed at minimal cost to nationwide theaters until the early 1920s.[37] Like the mission of industrial productivity promoted by the NAC, the Ford Educational Weekly series sought to Americanize workers for increased yield. Of course, Henry Ford's use of scientific management in his factories transformed the workplace by employing efficiency protocols to speed the pace and output of labor. The use of efficiency to attract and sustain immigrant viewership similarly motivated the production of the Ford Educational Weekly film series. The films promoted and operationalized efficiency on the spectacular appeals of the moving image and the nation's wondrous sights. The work of these images deployed prolepsis as sensory stimulation and the perception of common locales. The affective stimulation of the films progressed from the mere arousal typifying popular responses to the James-Lange theory of emotions and crowd psychology. Instead, affective stimulation generated a cooperative way of seeing images such that all audiences would feel a similar charge. Mass media was to teach a universal conception or feeling—the affective arousal of media substituted for perceptions naturalized by American viewers. The image served as a prosthetic for supposedly natural experiences; students would learn to see and feel as other Americans.

The Ford Weekly series was incredibly popular and therefore an important film series for grasping some of the broader visual strategies of Americanization. The series reached between four and six million viewers and often provided subtitles in a number of other languages.[38] Ford and the Young Men's Christian Association (YMCA) were the two largest producers of Americanization films during this period. While the YMCA often used a teacher to guide the lesson of the film, the Ford series wholly relied on film to efficiently impart the lessons of Americanization to industrial workers, schoolchildren, and other audiences.[39] Ford's ultimate goal was to supply a visual lesson plan that would prompt viewers to become more productive workers and loyal Americans. As written by Lee Grieveson, "Ford and other advocates for the utility of cinema, like those in the flourishing visual instruction movement in the early 1920s, prized moving images for their mobility and communicative efficacy in relation to the young, working-class, and immigrant audiences who were in particular need of 'education' in the ways of industrial modernity and liberal capitalist civility."[40]

Ford predicated the effectiveness of film on the way its spectacular imagery efficiently transformed pupils. Ford's substantial investment in Americanization programs, most prominently represented by the company's English school, often employed visual aids. Most of these visual pedagogies assumed that students would be quickly converted through fantastic theatrics. Similarly, the films developed for the Ford Educational Weekly series attempted to Americanize viewers through enchanting images dancing across the screen. Ford advertisements in a number of pedagogical journals promoted the series in this manner:

> Motion Pictures speak in all languages. Every mind in the world touches all other minds in the "movies." Translation is not needed. And a motion picture is so easy to show! Insert a film—press a button, and

life is pulsating before the eyes of a school. Signing of the Declaration of Independence on the wall helps. But *the thing itself* in a motion picture—not "words" or wall pictures—gets a story across to the mind of a pupil—no matter where born, or how old or how young, in *one-tenth of the time*, and with *a thousandfold dent* on his memory.[41]

As this advertisement proclaimed, movies were effective teaching tools insofar as they dazzled the audience with a "pulsating" image. Moving images animated the eyes and minds of pupils, no matter their differences. The medium of film worked precisely because it created a similar bodily response in all viewers. Given that the motion picture "touches" the minds of the audience, it quickly expressed the lesson with more memorable results. Analyzed for the purposes of Americanization, then, Ford's films relied on the supposition that moving images communicated successfully given the charge audiences felt during the picture and the deep impression on their memories from that interaction.

In those films related to the project of Americanization, Ford emphasized America's most impressive tableaux.[42] The pictures often displayed sweeping vistas of the country and modern machinery at work in factories.[43] Both scenes attempted to excite viewers—the affective charge that so many believed corroded the morals of immigrants in popular films. Yet, such imagery also endeavored to change the way audiences looked at filmic images. The scenes identified what aspects of the nation were worthy of immigrant attention. The goal was to focus concentration such that immigrants might invest in these images as Americanization agents desired. As written in an advertisement from a 1919 edition of *Popular Educator*, "If you want pupils to stop mental loafing—to wake up—to take on a genuine interest in study—to grasp facts in a fraction of the time it now takes them to do it, and to retain those facts ten times more easily—introduce the Ford Educational Weekly—*visual education*—into the curriculum at once."[44] These films promised that the stunning medium of film could evince patriotism by boasting the nation's most astonishing qualities and garner "genuine interest" where it was due.

Unlike the basic stimulation model of affective appeal espoused by Rickard, the proleptic rhetorical pedagogy in the Ford Weekly series was a two-pronged approach. First, these films provided arresting affective media to attract the interest of the student, to squelch mental loafing. Films were imagined as especially successful for Americanization because they mystified. Prolepsis in this first use indexes the affective inputs of Ford's Americanization lessons: the embodied, sensory routes through which physical and cognitive attention could be gained. The second function of prolepsis marks the common sights or knowledge required for later reflection and discovery. With Ford, those images provided tacit knowledge of the nation's majesty. The goal was not to change immigrants primarily through these films—after all, Ford offered numerous programs to its own workers for the processes of naturalization and assimilation and therefore understood Americanization as a long process.[45] Instead, the goal was to encourage audiences to see these images as energizing. The films were to motivate full participation in Americanization by showing thrilling images. They were the first step on the assembly line of Americanization. Once Americanization lessons were treated akin to factory processes, efficient and able mechanisms of assimilation would ensure long-term success.

AMERICA FIRST POSTER

To wit, the work of proleptic common imagery evident in the Ford Weekly series can also be seen in the America First poster, wherein the imaginative potential of such affective stimulation comes to the fore. As part of the America First campaign, the Bureau of Education, in conjunction with the NAC, created a nationally distributed poster that invited immigrants to enroll in night courses. The poster's design illustrates how Americanization experts commonly understood the suasory capacity of the image for immigrant pupils, particularly laborers. The poster is a significant exemplar as the only poster designed for the America First campaign. It was one of the most widely seen visual documents of the Americanization movement. While private organizations designed other recruitment tactics and the period is known for its propagandistic posters, this poster was essential to the NAC's mission in laborer education and resoundingly praised for its rhetorical finesse. The campaign was a triumph and H. H. Wheaton, the bureau's campaign organizer, received "prompt requests for posters, coming from all parts of the United States and even from abroad"—a demand that "very shortly exhausted the supply."[46] The poster's rural hometown imagery highlights the way proleptic allusion supplied the affective foundation for emotional nationalism.

Up against the presumed need for war preparedness, the Bureau of Education and NAC developed the America First campaign to bolster Americanization missions. Wheaton contended that immigrants were often unaware of available resources they might use to learn English and begin the process of naturalization.[47] More broadly, the campaign concentrated on industrial laborers as central to the war effort. For the NAC, this campaign was to focus on industrial relations, often suppressing the Americanizing work of trade unions. According to Alex Carey, the NAC received "popular support and public funding" from industry leaders who "had long sought for a program against radicalism among immigrant workers."[48] The Bureau of Education distributed over 150,000 America First posters advertising night schools across the country.[49] Popular authors justified the campaign on the idea that English literacy created better employees. As written in the *American City*, "Many manufacturing plants reported increased efficiency in their immigrant employes [sic] when the latter had learned English."[50] The goal of this poster, then, much like other aspects of the campaign, was to encourage immigrants to continue their education so as to become faithful workers.

To achieve that ambition, the poster used imagery that might instill common sights and ideas in its audience. The work of proleptic common perceptions is key to this rhetorical pedagogy. These images aimed to supply a shared understanding of American idealism via the power of the lithograph. In a 1916 issue of the *Annals of the American Academy of Political and Social Science*, Wheaton explained the psychological rationale of the visuals appearing in the poster. He wrote, "For its psychological effect upon aliens and local communities an 'America First' poster was distributed during the fall and winter, 1915–16. Attractively lithographed in red, white and blue, it bore upon its face the unusual invitation in eight languages."[51] Wheaton situated the poster as successful given its "psychological effect." His discussion initially was nonspecific, simply noting the relationship between attractive coloring and the use of foreign languages. Wheaton continued by arguing that the poster was persuasive because its imagery referenced the common sights of the nation. In particular, images of Uncle Sam and other American scenes lent "the poster a touch of patriotism and fellowship."[52] Speaking before a more general audience, Wheaton averred that the poster "appealed to the imagination of the country."[53] Through the power of visualization, the imagery in this poster did not communicate a specific end, but implied abstract sentiments of patriotism and communion.

From a rhetorical perspective, the poster's effectiveness was based principally on its use of imagery to build a shared orientation to the nation. The poster taught a proleptic mode of visual inference. The illustrations highlighted what perception of the nation immigrants should grasp, what visuals could and should animate them. For instance, the medium-scale full color lithograph depicted Uncle Sam welcoming a farming immigrant to his new home (see figure 1).[54] This version of Uncle Sam was quite different from the popular war posters ordering onlookers to the recruitment station. In the foreground, Uncle Sam shakes the laborer's hand and opens his left hand to the other scenes in the poster. The figure welcomes the audience and highlights the nation as a gracious place. Behind the two men are illustrated aspects of a picturesque American town. The background shows a large two-story home and a schoolhouse with a waving flag. Centered in front of these buildings is the scene of an immigrant receiving his naturalization papers. The imagery drew upon the myth of small-town America to emphasize the spirit of belonging emblematized by that allusion. For laborers targeted by this poster, the use of rural imagery was key. Given that the vast majority of immigrant laborers worked in urban settings, these references highlighted the rural mythos of the nation. The choice was strategic—it provided a colloquial set of images that might inflect the virtues of Americanism presumably absent in the newly urban population of the early twentieth century. A large Victorian home, the public school, and the pickaxe indexed a nostalgic vision of the American Dream. The feeling of belonging implied by rural imagery was consecrated in the midground and foreground of the poster—in naturalization and the welcoming Uncle Sam.

OPPOSITE: Bureau of Education America First poster in black and white. Courtesy of the Library of Congress, Prints and Photographs Division, photograph by Harris and Ewing [LC-DIG-hec-03080].

These images were likely divorced from the known reality of most immigrants. The point was to use the exciting possibilities entailed in the visual imagery to orient the audience's understanding of the nation. Here, the role of affect in emotional education was similar to that theorized in group psychology. Those who studied the attitudes of the crowd averred that "the group is grounded in a common object of identification which establishes equivalentially the unity of the group members."[55] Groups and publics are shaped by shared experiences and common modes of identification. In the early twentieth century, that shared state was attributed to a specific object, namely, the media. For Americanization educators, the imagery of the poster became a kind of affective stimulus to bind the people together. It was an external object to which students' emotions corresponded. As Sara Ahmed writes of such object orientation, the "social bond is binding insofar as feelings are deposited in the same object, which may then accumulate value as happy or unhappy objects; a group may come together by articulating love for the same things, and hate for the same things, even if that love and hate is not simply felt by all those who identify with the group."[56] The poster deployed patriotic imagery, intimate scenes, and small-town vignettes to stir the feelings of Americanism. The lesson adopted a proleptic form in that it attempted to create a shared orientation to such imagery—it marked what Americans should feel about the nation and its ideals. These images circulated across hundreds of public places and thereby sought to secure the affective orientation of viewers toward nationalistic imagery. The poster labored to direct audience members' thinking and feelings about the nation and their future place in it.

In this instance, the viewer's affective orientation was to invest in the optimism promised in the American ideal, to become attached to the possibilities entailed therein. Pointedly, workers were the primary audience for this poster. Laborers were invited to begin the process of Americanization by sharing in the feelings and imagery of the American people. Given the placement of this poster and other America First materials in areas frequented by industrial workers, the practical impact of this poster attempted to ensure that industry titans would find more loyal and efficient employees. As noted by the experts above, once the immigrant felt at home and was a legal citizen, his industrial productivity would increase dramatically. This is not to suggest that these images were not fantastic, even escapist. Yet, their primary purpose was to create better workers by eliciting Americanism as a shared understanding of these ideals and an optimism that steadied their pursuit.

Imagaic prolepsis in this poster progressed such that it had a psychological effect more complex than mere animation or even common identification. Poster designers employed abstract imagery to generate a shared understanding of the virtues of Americanism. The poster's affective power moved from corporeal response to a cognitive function wherein these images generated a vague optimism or hope. For ancient rhetorical teachers, prolepsis connected perception or universal understandings to reasoning. Proleptic conceptions supplied the basis for processing what would happen next, of applying philosophy to the natural world. Indeed, the Stoic understanding of anticipation likely influenced Gérard Genette's description of prolepsis in narrative, wherein the trope marks an "anticipation of as yet unrealized episodes or events."[57] The American ideal promoted by the Bureau and the NAC aspired to a cooperative way of seeing. Much of this strategy banked on the feelings the selected imagery inspired. The purpose was to link the present apprehension of these images to enthusiastic anticipation. Visual prolepsis thus forecast the future, pleasurable disposition of the worker as predicated on her adoption of the sensibilities of Americanism. While not all appeals to immigrants would focus on their feelings in this manner, the national campaign for Americanization seemingly centered on the emotional nationalism of laborers and all immigrants as key to codifying national identity. Visual education often began, then, by trying to change the way immigrants saw certain sights and to direct the abstract sensation of those sights toward specific modes of feeling and reasoning.

The visuals identified here—educational slides in New York, the Ford Educational Weekly film series, and the America First poster—positioned visual imagery as unparalleled in its power to transform immigrants. Each of these endeavors used the visual to motivate pupils to pursue official channels of enculturation. Such motivation was the result of the way the visual elicited excitement in the viewer. In this way, the rhetorical form of the message worked proleptically, through sensory stimulation and a shared set of particularized perceptions. Once those became repeated across Americanization pedagogical sites—stereoscope slides, films, posters, etc.—the articulation encouraged immigrants to invest in the bright future promised by educators. Of course, such a strategy makes sense given that the primary audience included workers with little time for night classes. Yet, the use of anticipation in these media operated by insisting that the future was brought into being from the feeling inspired by the visual. For the Stoics, learning the principles of philosophy allowed for the "articulation, systematization, and correct use of our prolepsis as standards."[58] Thus, while Americanization sought to use the excitation of the visual to form a common understanding of the nation among immigrants, that animated state was directed by the content of the lesson plans. In other Americanization materials, the lesson plans managed the affective stimulation of visual aids to far more specific outcomes.

Photographic Textbooks and Prolepsis

One of the most fully developed and schematized set of educational materials geared toward Americanization was a series of textbooks published in the early 1920s by the American Viewpoint Society (AVS). A subset of Boni & Liveright publishers, this group organized an editorial board in 1921. The board consisted of professors at esteemed universities and public-education administrators. A substantial number of these men created curricula to combat English illiteracy, generate opportunities for the assimilation of immigrants, and support vocational programs. A 1921 article from the *New York Times* described the agenda of the AVS as educators who sought to use the tools of "progressive journalism" to "provide the average American with the means whereby he could learn the fundamentals of citizenship."[59] The AVS promised a series of cheaply distributed, illustrated textbooks on civics and health, and accompanying educational films. While evidence indicates that the films did not materialize, the board published nearly a dozen illustrated books and briefly operated the *Journal of Educational Sociology* as well as the *Junior-Senior High School Clearing House*.[60] Each book noted that the AVS was "authorized" by the U.S. Department of Labor to produce books for citizenship classes and to further the department's citizenship training work.

Given the wide array of expertise and experience represented in this group, the techniques employed in these volumes epitomize the pinnacle of visual education for the purposes of Americanization. In some sense, these volumes represent the culmination of visual education principles popularized in the teens and early twenties. The foreword to most AVS textbooks indicated that at least some of these textbooks were designed for citizenship training work among children and adult immigrants, and that the mode of instruction was tailored to this purpose.[61] Each volume used a similar method with images intended to illuminate the grandeur of the United States—the images were to "tell their own story"—while the accompanying narratives explained the topical lesson.[62] The formats of the books relied on images to attract the viewer, but ensured that textual captions and content directed the audience toward particular ends. In short, the AVS aimed to rhetorically direct the sensational aspects of the image to progressive educational outcomes. To do so, the AVS sequenced the images and the accompanying captions to efficiently demonstrate the bright future that lay ahead once immigrants merely desired Americanization.

The visual and textual strategies deployed in these textbooks received rave reviews as critics lauded their potential for cultivating Americanism. Reviewers commended the visual teaching method and its usefulness for Americanizing the immigrant and the American-born alike. In the *Journal of Social Forces*, one commentator suggested that *We and Our History* by Albert Bushnell Hart was "well-designed" for "use in citizenship training work."[63] In the *School Review*, W. G. Kimmel contended that the graphs, charts, and photographs in *We and Our Government* by Jeremiah Whipple Jenks and Rufus Daniel Smith proved "valuable pedagogical aids" to the "adult in the Americanization school" and the young pupil.[64] Other reviewers praised the "vivid reactions" and captivation "aroused" by these volumes.[65] Critics heralded these textbooks as exemplary visual aids, a benefit that made them especially unique for use in civics classrooms and the tutelage of the adult immigrant.

Importantly, while the vividness of visual education was mentioned as an advantage to these volumes, reviewers also remarked that the accompanying use of captions and specific lessons tempered the images.[66] Thus, these books proved commendable teaching tools given that the textbook guided the affective charge of visual aids into educational outcomes. Mary O. Cowper in the *Journal of Social Forces* noted that the "rich illustrations" of the volume did not "detract from its sound principles and methods of presentation."[67] One reviewer commented that these books "exhibited a thoroughgoing application of the principles of visual education" by presenting the material in three different modes: pictures, captions, and text proper.[68] W. G. Kimmel averred that while most visual education materials were not yet adapted to proper classroom use, through "a series of pictures arranged in motion-picture sequence" the collection followed "advanced pedagogical thought."[69] These critics extolled the method of these volumes as that which rendered spectacular images educationally valuable through the disciplinary mechanisms of captions and content.

The praise for the guiding features of these textbooks indicates a significant difference in the use of prolepsis as a rhetorical pedagogy from less-developed forms of education. In the educational materials discussed thus far, prolepsis identifies the way visual education employed sensory commotion and selected imagery to prompt shared understandings of the nation. In these textbooks, prolepsis shifts such that these sensory inputs directed an orientation to one's future as a member of the nation. The guiding features of the textbooks transformed mere titillation into a particular outlook. This shift is in keeping with the ancient pedagogical use of prolepsis to correct false reasoning and to transform the nature of human experience. According to Glidden, a psychological reading of prolepsis situates proleptic conceptions as the criteria for truth—what we see verifies what we know.[70] Dyson builds on this argument to suggest that prolepsis shapes our recognitional ability.[71] Reading Chrysippus, he argues that prolepsis was a pedagogical device shaping sense perceptions by "articulating each conception" to reasoning such that sign-inferences are redirected for those who lack the requisite sensory inputs or who reason incorrectly.[72] Prolepsis as a form of apprehension can be strategically repeated and systematized so as to generate a particular understanding of how to read what is presented. In the lessons supplied by the AVS, Americanization education worked by encouraging students to infer an optimistic understanding of the future via the visual and textual evidence displayed. Prolepsis in these works organized the sensory, affective experience of the textbook such that the future enabled by Americanization seemed a bright probability.

AFFECTIVE INVESTMENT: IMAGES

With the exception of one children's book, each of the AVS textbooks exhibited over five hundred images within its pages.[73] Of this set of five hundred, three different kinds of imaging strategies appeared. First, a sketch by Hanson Booth, a prominent magazine illustrator, preceded each chapter (see figure 2). Second, a dual set of running images flanked the pages of the chapter proper. The running images used a mixture of formats, including photographs, sketches, cartoons, diagrams, and document facsimiles. Third, at the beginning of most chapters, the authors employed a text box relating the lesson of the chapter. The rhetorical purpose of these imaging practices was to stitch the immigrant's affective investment within the temporal momentum of history. The images implied a particular mode of proleptic reasoning from which the student would envision herself as part of the nation's future.

Much as the reviewers noted, the AVS selected a multiplicity of photographs, diagrams, and sweeping vistas of the countryside to elicit a vivid response from the viewer. As with the Ford Educational Weekly series of films, the rhetorical composition of those images endeavored to create an affective commotion in the viewer, a sense of wonder or astonishment at the nation. A clear indication of this goal emerges in a set of images portraying the evolution of a natural waterfall to its use as a power source. In a section of *We and Our History* explaining how federal, state, and local governments provide care for the people, the viewer is entreated to engage a photographic sequence on the left side of the textbook depicting modern but ordinary labor in farming. The images themselves are slices of life, illustrating rural activities such as irrigation and harvest. On the right side of the page, the top image is the most prominent in this layout, showing a magnificent waterfall from the vantage point of the pool below. Following this impressive photograph are two photographs of hydroelectric generators at waterfall sites. Together, this succession of images invited the viewer to marvel at a nation so adept at moving rapidly from the humdrum of the agrarian life to

"European Immigration. No nation that ever existed has been so hospitable to newcomers as the United States." Sketch by Hanson Booth from A. B. Hart, *We and Our History* (1923).

harnessing the magnificent power of a waterfall for hydroelectricity. The composition here translated Romantic Sublime images—the power of nature—into images touting the supremacy of American modernity.[74] If the images used in this textbook were thought to arouse dramatic reactions, then here, the wondrous strength of nature is transformed through the sequence of photographs to a modern spectacle of the country's energy creation. The desired outcome in the viewer was similar to the aim of artists during the Romantic period: to marry the awestruck state inspired in the viewer to the splendor of their new nation. Once again, these types of images relied on a proleptic rhetorical scheme insofar as the imaging sequence attempted to manage the emotions of the audience. By juxtaposing images of rural life against modern machinery, the photographs rhetorically cultivated adoration.

The number of photographs in these volumes and their layout operated on a temporal progression that further stitched the immigrant's affective investment to the momentum of history. The sequence of these images asked the immigrant viewer to locate himself as an integral figure to the nation's past and as part of the drive pushing toward the modern future. At key intervals in the construction of the text, images specifically geared toward immigrants appear: from portraits of famous foreign-born citizens and photographs of stereotypical types of immigrants to images of individuals working diligently in industries and as members of the armed services. Images specifically meant to appeal to immigrants appear so frequently that the figure of the immigrant as integral to the nation's future often propels the sequences. In a chapter on the Constitution in *We and Our Government*, the book offers several images, including a Booth sketch of the Statue of Liberty, a group photograph of children of immigrants, and a shot of foreign-born soldiers. These images are interspersed between pictures of key moments in history, contemporary legislators, and illustrations of constitutional provisions. The evolution of the images begins a narrative journey inaugurated by the torch of freedom.[75] The immigrant becomes the key rhetorical figure that exemplifies these ideals by his appearance in the temporal progression of national history. The immigrant is welcomed by the torch of freedom, carries that freedom to the next generation, and shows devotion through military service to his new home.

Yet, the concrete future is conspicuously absent from the images in the text itself. Rather, the sequence of the images moves rapidly from past to present, prompting the viewer to imagine the marvels of the future. The audience is offered one visual space to reflect on the anticipation the text provokes: the futuristic sketches by Booth that launch the majority of chapters. After the reader propels herself through the set of historical and contemporary images reaching toward a possible future, the next chapter often begins with a chimerical sketch provided by Booth. By virtue of the arrangement, this drawing becomes the visual location where the viewer ponders the coming years. Interestingly, Booth's ethereal style prompts this type of reflection. For example, his charcoal drawing accompanying the chapter on "Emigrants and Immigrants" from *We and Our History* directs the viewer to meditate on the future (see figure 2). In the lower corner of the image is a small boat crowded with somber figures. The water near the boat is darkened, while the open sea beyond lightens to almost the pure page. In the distance, the viewer can make out the faintest sketch of a city skyline. The composition in this image entreats the audience to picture a brighter future just ahead and to labor toward that end by relinquishing the gloom of the past. If the observer were to mirror the expressions of those figures in the boat, she should wistfully yearn for the world to come. Many of Booth's images employ this same artistic strategy. The overarching effect is that the reader understands the imagistic lessons of the text as suturing her import to national history—past becomes part of the present and is quickly transformed into the future. Yet, the future here still remains open. The vague images do not yet direct the viewer to a particular end.

The future orientation of these textbooks was a strategic choice organizing the affective expression solicited by the images. Consider for a moment the rural imagery of the America First poster, wherein immigrants were invited to love the nation because it beckoned to the "old" world, the past as a mode of understanding the new nation. Similarly, nationalistic groups of the period such as the Daughters of the American Revolution, the Sons of the American Revolution, and the National Society of Colonial Dames aimed for a return to a glorious past. As Kristin Hoganson argues, an "imperialist nostalgia" dominated their Americanization tactics wherein immigrants were seen as limited cultural resources for that return.[76] In the AVS series, the work of proleptic perception was to guide the student's affective register such that his understanding of the future banked on anticipation. In much the same way that Brian Massumi writes that affect can supply a direction, a tendency toward futurity, the rhetorical pedagogy of prolepsis prompted anticipation for what follows Americanization.[77] Prolepsis encourages the viewer to use reasoning to determine what comes next; these images indicated a prosperous future. The temporal orientation of the lesson was further directed by the relay between image and text.

DIRECTING THE VIEWER'S ANTICIPATION

The anticipation of the images is one of the most powerful rhetorical features of these textbooks. But, just as the reviewers remarked, that splendor was anchored by carefully crafted pedagogical lessons. The images reigned supreme, but to create particular ends, the stimulation had to be controlled. The editors and writers at AVS disciplined the viewer's excitement through ample captions and particular content lessons. As the foreword of *We and Our Government* made plain, Donald Stewart, the editor of the series, arranged the pictures and captions to emphasize the main ideas of the chapters in a "simplified and concise" fashion.[78] The effect was to solicit a desire in the reader: he should yearn for the future by fashioning himself as a progressive, learned citizen of this nation.

The guiding features of AVS textbooks channeled the proleptic anticipation supplied by the images to a positive outlook on the future. For ancient literary critics, prolepsis was key to motivation; sense perceptions guided the reader or viewer.[79] In many classical references to prolepsis, anticipation was based on wanting to know the end of a story or a particular mode of inference. Dyson indicates that Stoic teaching methods attempted to direct proleptic conceptions toward desired ends by instructing students in reasoning from sensory apprehension.[80] In the AVS textbooks, futurity remained the focus of the textbook by specifying what Americanization would beget. Yet, that outcome was often ambiguous, a rhetorical strategy that ultimately positioned longing for a happy ending as the sign of proper motivation toward Americanization.

Visual and textual mechanisms frequently routed the affective sensation of the visual toward a yearning for the future. Such a future was rarely specified, but rather the proper place of Americanization motivation was to aspire to a life beyond mere citizenship. In *We and Our Government*, the chapter on "American Citizenship" begins with a Booth sketch showing over a dozen individuals huddled together with their suitcases (see figure 3). The sketch itself functions in much the same way as other Booth drawings. The juxtaposition of light and dark conceal the figures in the back, while as the subjects come closer to the viewer's presumed location, Booth incorporates much more light. The figures in the image emphasize the direction of the light by looking toward the perspective of the viewer, toward the source of light indicating a brighter future. The most prominent figure in the drawing is a woman gazing off to the right of the page. By her side, her small son grasps her skirt. Her hopeful gaze and young child all punctuate the same message as the lighting: an auspicious, albeit vague, future welcomes immigrants to this nation. The caption distinguishes the nature of that future and locates the source of the light for viewers. It reads, "American Citizens of the Future, Citizenship is the highest and greatest gift of the nation."[81] The caption uncovers the light/dark archetypal veil of the Booth drawing, steering the affective sensation of the image toward the need for citizenship.

To escort the viewer toward the promise of citizenship, the textbooks would often prompt students to look away from the doldrums of the past. In so doing, the disciplinary features of these books taught students how to read certain images. The rhetorical features of these lessons, then, deployed prolepsis by articulating sensory perceptions to particular outcomes. For example, in *We and Our Government*, three images show people standing in line with their suitcases, a crowded downtown street, and two men sitting together at a table. The captions profess that "WHEN A PERSON COMES TO THIS COUNTRY," he or she should avoid living all the time in the "FOREIGN QUARTERS OF THE CITY," and rather begin "mixing with Americans" to "make friends" and "be more successful in GETTING A JOB."[82] At first glance, the capitalization of key phrases accents the simplest of messages: become an American and you will easily find employment. Read more generally, the textual lesson accompanies the image to

"American Citizens of the Future." Sketch by Hanson Booth from J. W. Jenks and R. D. Smith, *We and Our Government* (1922).

demonstrate how to decode the photographs. If one were simply to look at these urban, ethnic neighborhood shots, the lesson of Americanization might be lost. Instead, the guiding features of the textbook entreat viewers to see these sights as undesirable, as a replication of the past that obscures the bright future promised in most of the other photographs and sketches of the books. The captions make plain what is not as readily visible in the images proper.

Unlike other visual Americanization pedagogies that typically centered on simple affective stimulation, AVS textbooks promoted civic responsibility as a comprehensive understanding of the nation and government. In the foreword of *We and Our Work*, Johnson lamented the fall of great empires as attributable to an unlearned populace. He maintained that the true bulwark against this fate was an educated public. This theme emerged in all the volumes written under the banner of the AVS. The ultimate point of these textbooks was to motivate the reader to pursue knowledge that might otherwise be considered boring or obtuse. AVS volumes vigorously promoted the use of this new knowledge through multiple modes of civic participation: from heeding laws and voting, to maintaining sanitation and working efficiently. Further, the AVS did not shy away from political disputes—all volumes encouraged differences to be adjudicated via official mechanisms—but relied on knowledgeable citizens as the defense maintaining the nation-state.

Despite this complex understanding of citizenship and earnest belief in the learning potential of immigrant students, the lessons of the textbook nevertheless attempted to manage students' understandings of democratic life. The AVS repeatedly explained to readers that through responsible citizenship, newly naturalized citizens could easily navigate the difficulties of their current home and create a true sense of belonging. Within AVS textual narratives, the immigrant was asked to pledge himself to Americanization activities to consecrate the joyous future. The use of prolepsis here was to transform the stimulation provided by the textbook to the ends of citizenship. Yet, the future nevertheless remained quite vague. Even with full knowledge of the government's workings, the best outcome of citizenship was abstract. Prolepsis as a form of strategic rhetorical pedagogy, then, used images and directing features to prompt the pursuit of happiness as the *telos* of Americanization.

In *We and Our Government*, Jenks and Smith argued that intelligent participation in civic affairs guaranteed that citizenship would achieve happiness for all—an *"enlightened democracy."*[83] For these authors, egalitarianism emerged in "American democracy" as "organized in order that the opinions and policies of the citizens may find free expression."[84] Citizens with a complete knowledge of the political system, and a noble character committed to improving the community ensured the "happiness and safety" of the people.[85] So long as citizens remained well informed of their rights and responsibilities, they would better their communities and foster their own happiness. In *We and Our History*, this sentiment reemerged as the need for studying history. The authors contended that citizens should be thankful to study the progress of history. Yet, they cautioned "that study would be thrown away if it did not make us rejoice anew that we are citizens and dwellers in so great and so happy a land."[86] Here, much as in the visual sequences of the texts, happiness is the result of enlightened citizenship. It is an emotion that arrives as a result of the new citizen's civic knowledge. Once the new citizen understood how lucky she was to exercise rights, she would experience elation.

The conjoined relationship between responsible citizenship and happiness is similarly evident in the dialectical tensions between text and images. Photographs and facsimiles depicting the legal procedures of naturalization from petition to oath illustrate the process while the captions focus on the responsibilities required of those worthy enough to become citizens. After explaining that only "WHITE PERSONS" or those of "AFRICAN NATIVITY" are able to naturalize, the captions extol the need for "good character" and to "know, obey, and support the law."[87] Here, the racial hierarchy of immigration law comes to the fore, in that only certain populations are seen as capable of assimilation so long as they are ideal citizens.[88] Photographs and captions after this set of photographs change dramatically, inaugurated by the snapshot of newly naturalized World War I soldiers smiling and waving their certificates in the air. Consecutive images depict ceremonial celebrations of the flag with far more joyful, smiling citizens within the photographs than in the previous naturalization photographs. In this succession of images, the proper care of the flag becomes emblematic of the contentment entailed within the responsibilities and rights of citizenship. This sequence suggests to the reader that by naturalization, the newcomer would become a citizen of this progressive nation and also experience the feelings of joy shown by the smiles of those citizens in the photographs. For the AVS, the temporal progression of images promised that citizenship would assuage any hardship, disaffection, or antipathy. These images and their captions attempted to situate the ideal of citizenship as future happiness.

The AVS aimed to inspire immigrants to become educated citizens who could use the official systems of the United States to redress concerns. The editors and writers presented a spectacular array of images that might inspire immigrants to see the nation within those pictures anew. The visuals were to affectively impact the viewer, generating a kind of intensity that would change her orientation to the subject. By harnessing the spectacle of the image, the AVS hoped to direct the powerful condition of seeing magnificent and modern visuals to the promise of happiness. The affective charge of the visual was directed to a particular outcome—the manifest hope of happiness. Together, the lessons attempted to solicit a desire in the viewer to enact enlightened citizenship through education. In these ways, AVS textbooks heavily leveraged anticipation and futurity to encourage the first steps of Americanization.

More generally, the promise of happiness in these textbooks operated as a form of longing, a rapt scene of desire structured by the rhetorical work of proleptic anticipation. The lessons insisted that happiness would result if students engaged in the process of Americanization. The purpose was to engender motivation. Yet the ambiguity of the future and the *promise* of happiness evaded concrete outcomes and tangible benefits by focusing solely on emotional potential. Such outcomes were not lost on ancient scholars, who maintained that the psychological effect of prolepsis can lead to increased emotional involvement over rational processing.[89] For the AVS, students were asked to live in a present state of longing in order to reach toward happiness.[90] This proleptic move attempted to manage the affective charge of the visual with a temporal lesson on the advantages to come. As a rhetorical pedagogy, the lesson bears potential but also considerable risk. As Zizi Papacharissi writes of affect's in-betweenness, such "liminality renders individuals powerful and potentially powerless at the same time because of its ephemeral and transient nature."[91] The role of anticipation and longing in the process of

Americanization thus bore possibility but at its core remained a tenuous enterprise. Indeed, the tension between the hope of reshaping nationalism as an emotional commitment was plagued by the need for an external object that stimulated such shared dispositions.

The Drive toward Americanization

Taken together, these pedagogical materials illustrate how visual media were thought to sway immigrant pupils. Against the fear that those new to the United States would remain un-American and threaten the ideals of the nation, Americanization experts turned to the visual to overcome the immigrant's naiveté and supposed mental deficiency. For those like Rickard and Wheaton, the visual was a pedagogical tool that could quickly illustrate the lesson at hand and overcome the problems of limited English literacy. Yet, the primary value of visual teaching tools was their capacity to enthrall the senses and arrest attention. To craft the stunning experience of the visual into educational outcomes, Americanization authorities styled the image with rhetorical features that would deliver viewers to the affective foundations of specific emotions. Put simply, the affective sensation of the visual was to provide the bedrock of emotional nationalism.

In this chapter, the rhetorical figure of prolepsis defines the movement from affect to the possibilities of emotion. In a significant sense, prolepsis is the ancient name that marks the translation of sensory perception to common modes of reasoning, albeit preconscious or precognitive. For ancient scholars, prolepsis identified the natural correspondence between everyday sights and moral reasoning, or the modes of knowledge that could be extrapolated from common sights and sounds. Yet, here the work of prolepsis as a trope of affect is more instrumental. In the midst of a radically changing nation, Americanization educators sought to locate a new form of nationalistic education that might overcome overwhelming divisions among the populace. They relied on mass media to create and systematize those experiences generating patriotism in all citizens. Once students felt the charge of the screen and witnessed spectacular vistas, that charge might be directed toward particular ends. In this way, modern media became a surrogate form of proleptic sensation, a gateway for inculcating a directed form of emotional nationalism.

Yet, to change the masses, each student must first be stimulated by the splendors of the screen. These individual lessons were structured to corral the affective charge of the visual. The point was to guide affective commotion to an "emergent futurity," a hopeful vision of the "as if" emblematized by the promise of happiness.[92] Longing for a bright future became a temporal pivot point for Americanization discourses and practices. The act of looking upon arousing images of the nation intermingled present affective responses with a bright future. The student could use modern media to feel the charge of patriotism and its specific imagery to imagine her potential as patriot.

The screen image was a motivational device, a teaching tool that might overwhelm ambivalence or antipathy. Progressive educators did not commonly imagine these modes of education as forced assimilation. Instead, the use of the visual sought to elicit immigrants' attachment to the United States. At the heart of such advocacy was the notion that the corporeal effects of viewing—the pleasure of looking, the excitation of a novel experience, and the rapt attention commanded by the screen—would move immigrants by virtue of the feelings inspired in that interaction. Thus, while these visual aids were helpful to literacy, the primary goal of Americanization pedagogy was to use the embodied sensations delivered by the image as a motivational tool. Americanization promised immigrants happiness via the pleasures of peeking into the future. Pointedly, the immigrant was to see her joyous future as sutured to the nation. The desire of these educators became translated onto the image as an object that could potentially perform a miracle. Energizing images might actualize a desire to invest in the nation and its possibilities. Yet, much like any object of desire, the image was a projection of a shared fantasy, an object that displaced the complex material realities of assimilation. In other words, the fantasy of visual education insisted that the persuasive force of these encounters would fashion a resolution to the persistent obstacles of a heterogeneous nation. Images would create the fledgling connections of emotional nationalism.

While some of the visual aids used for Americanization focused on citizenship as the adjudication of political and other differences, most visual and performative methods of Americanization favored abstract feelings of Americanism. These Americanization enthusiasts invited students to yearn for the comfort of national belonging. To do so, lessons catered to one particular goal: inculcating the emotions students should feel as Americans. To wit, the aspects of group consciousness espoused in the psychology of affective and emotional response worked by suggesting that certain lessons would not simply stimulate students, but concretize their emotional dedication to the nation. Yet, in most of the lessons analyzed here, students were not yet delivered to concrete emotions. Instead, the visual pedagogies of the Syracuse School District, Ford, America First, and the AVS primarily focused on the first step: affective prolepsis. Other lessons centered on the American lifestyle and community as concretizing the emotions of nationalism.

CHAPTER THREE

The American Lifestyle through Housing Reform

———•◆•———

In a 1917 issue of the journal *Housing Betterment*, the editors reprinted a section of Governor Martin Brumbaugh's annual message to Pennsylvanians. At one moment in the address, Governor Brumbaugh proposed a statewide housing code to preserve the health of the populace. As the governor affirmed the responsibilities of the state toward residents, he hailed proper living conditions as requisite to the production of stronger citizens. In particular, he heavily promoted these standards for the populace of ethnic neighborhoods, stating, "We are not Americanizing our new-coming immigrants if we allow them to live in what is often termed the 'black spots' where they fail to obtain that home life so essential to the making of a true American citizen."[1] For Brumbaugh, particular forms of housing would engender better citizenry. The National Housing Association published the magazine in which Brumbaugh's address appeared. The organization was integral to the creation of municipal housing codes designed to facilitate assimilation.² Much as with this group, the goal of housing reform more generally was to create ideal constituents.

As Brumbaugh noted, for many Americanization experts, the major hindrance to the ideal American home life was the home and community of the immigrant. These enclaves ostensibly allowed immigrants to live separately from the rest of the American citizenry. Discussions of the home and neighborhood were used to identify and place the nationalistic affections of immigrants. Each represented the feeling residents held for their former nation and new homeland. For some reform authorities, the poverty of ethnic neighborhoods and the squalor in which immigrants lived decelerated the integration of residents. The negative feelings inspired by such conditions pushed residents to long for the comforts of home and thereby the homeland. For less sympathetic experts, the ethnic colony or the keeping of old-world standards indicated residents' inability to demonstrate practical and emotional commitments to the United States. Immigrants who merely re-created the old world in the new failed to exhibit their love for America.

Transforming the homes and communities of immigrants was thought to instill appropriate levels of patriotism. If the residence and community could inspire a shared set of nationalistic emotions, experts promised each might be a site of Americanization. This work used two significant methods: reimagining the layout and use of the home, and revamping community life. Considered together, these endeavors reconstructed the spaces and peoples experts contended were un-American. Practitioners reworked these locales by situating the aesthetic principles of their architecture as rhetorical lesson plans in the emotions of American citizenship. In this way, the meaning of the American lifestyle was largely based on shared feelings and nationalistic attachments. Kinship was to be found in the happiness and contentment of Americanism. Altered homes and communities supplied proof of these patriotic emotions. Housing reform thus posited the American lifestyle as an aesthetic shift—the visible display of one's familiarity and intimacy with American sensibilities.

The reformation of the home and community of immigrants presented a synecdochal relationship between the amenities of the American home and the emotions entailed in citizenship. Synecdoche is a figure of substitution, where the part stands in for the whole or the whole stands in for the part.³ In housing reform efforts, educators deployed a synecdochal relationship between the modern home and neighborhood and the feelings of nationalism. The home became the synecdochal manifestation of residents' emotions and their potential alignment with the larger understanding of emotional nationalism. The house and neighborhood were treated as locales that could deliver immigrants to the proper emotions of Americanism: the contentment and happiness entailed in living in an American home and the community of feeling shared among neighbors. Whereas the grounds of emotional nationalism in visual pedagogy were predicated on affective sensation, the work of Americanized housing sought to concretize the specific emotions Americans ought to feel. That is, these designs gave form to the emotions of nationalism. Americanization lessons focused on housing reform did not simply prompt anticipation, but aimed to materialize the emotions of contentment and happiness. Experts argued that once immigrants could share such feelings with their neighbors, assimilation would be assured.

Applying the figure of synecdoche to space illuminates the rhetorical pedagogy of housing and community reform. Michel de Certeau writes that synecdoche "expands a spatial element in order to make it play the role of 'more' (a totality) and take its place."[4] Synecdoche "replaces totalities by fragments (a less in the place of more)."[5] De Certeau's example is the image of a bicycle that stands in for a whole street. In housing reform discourses and practices, the home and neighborhood became symbolic fragments of the immigrant's emotional state while simultaneously situating that fragment as relative to emotional nationalism writ large. Thus, the work of Americanization housing reform sought to inculcate national emotions through particular types of housing and neighborhood configurations, while such lessons simultaneously imbricated these sites as visual evidence of internal feelings. In this way, the home and community were publicly imagined and materially changed in ways that further constituted the visual logic of Americanism: external markers (e.g., the home) indicated internal states.

The Ethnic Colony

Many Americanization experts maligned the immigrant neighborhood and home as significant obstacles to Americanization. These criticisms centered on two key concerns. First, given that residents of ethnic neighborhoods supposedly built colonies of the old world in the new, these neighborhoods were seen as impediments to assimilation. This claim assumed that when immigrants lived together, the grouping of foreign bodies prevented them from blending with those Americans who would aid in their assimilation. Second, ethnic neighborhoods and the homes within them were often seen as overcrowded and poorly maintained. Experts alleged that the decrepit state of these sites extended a longing for the comfort of the homeland. The ethnic neighborhood was thus marked as a locale that allowed immigrants to retain emotional ties to the old country and disengage from the process of Americanization. The synecdochal relationship between the home and the emotions of immigrants can be identified here. The home supplied a marker of immigrants' true feelings and a place for Americanization experts to redress disaffection. Authorities asserted that redesigning homes and neighborhoods reformed the emotions of immigrants.

Those concerned with immigration matters christened the ethnic neighborhood a "colony" and bemoaned the effect of this outpost on its residents.[6] The colony was seen as the manifestation of the old world in the new. Such neighborhoods purportedly precipitated un-American living by the concentration of peoples from one home country. Naming these locales "colonies" suggests that immigrants merely imported the old world into the United States. In effect, these districts were often seen as settlements of other nations. For some, this condition prevented immigrants from seeking naturalization and assimilation.

The supposed impediment presented by the ethnic colony is evident in the words of former president Theodore Roosevelt. Notorious for his disdain for hyphenated Americans, Roosevelt faulted the ethnic colony for labor unrest and the disunity of the populace during the war.[7] In a 1915 speech to the Knights of Columbus in New York, Roosevelt stated,

> The foreign-born population of this country must be an Americanized population—no other kind can fight the battles of America either in war or peace. It must talk the language of its native-born fellow citizens, it must possess American citizenship and American ideals. It must stand firm by its oath of allegiance in word and deed and must show that in

very fact it has renounced allegiance to every prince, potentate, or foreign government. It must be maintained on an American standard of living so as to prevent labor disturbances in important plants and at critical times. None of these objects can be secured as long as we have immigrant colonies, ghettos, and immigrant sections, and above all they cannot be assured so long as we consider the immigrant only as an industrial asset. The immigrant must not be allowed to drift or to be put at the mercy of the exploiter. Our object is not to imitate one of the older racial types, but to maintain a new American type and then to secure loyalty to this type.[8]

Roosevelt rhetorically ensconced the colony as the expression of immigrants' attachments to another country: to another "prince, potentate, or foreign government." The colony stood in for their distanciation from American ideals. Roosevelt insisted that a new type of Americanism would protect not only immigrants but also the war's labor supply. Given that he was speaking to the Knights of Columbus, who regularly countered anti-Catholic nativism, Roosevelt's arguments undercut nativist claims by implying that all immigrants could learn to become true Americans.[9] Yet, he insisted that immigrants must become Americans. New arrivals could not meaningfully change the qualities of Americanism. In the end, Roosevelt called for the development of an identifiable "American type" and suggested that immigrants must be loyal to that type. The assertion intermingled the performance of the colony resident with nationalistic ideals and affections. Speaking English, naturalization, and the exhibition of allegiance were evidence of internal Americanism—a task that must be accomplished in wide measure to secure loyalty to such a "type."

For others invested in Americanization, the ethnic neighborhood proved problematic in that it impeded the cultivation of emotional nationalism. While some advocates blamed immigrants for creating slums and suggested they were moral contagions, progressive reformers worried that the neighborhoods where poor immigrants could afford homes produced a malaise that pushed residents to long for the old world.[10] In 1916, Grace Abbott maintained that while most immigrants adapted from the "village life at home" to the "complex industrial life" of the city, for some, "a tragic moral collapse or general demoralization of family standards results from the inability of the immigrant to adjust his old standards to the new."[11]

For her, these maladjusted circumstances particularly erupted in the "so-called foreign colonies" where residents did not feel that their homes were akin to their dwellings in the old world, nor were they fully American.[12] Abbott called for those engaged in "intelligent community planning" to gather "sympathetic knowledge of the life and hopes" of the people in these neighborhoods.[13] As Abbott illuminates, the ethnic community was rhetorically marked as a problem because it inspired the wrong feelings in residents. As such, the colony became the synecdochal representation of homesickness, marking feelings of longing hindering assimilation. These colonies sustained an aching for home while simultaneously precluding residents from building a new, American home.

Still other experts diagnosed the problem of slum living as a structural concern that nevertheless impacted the patriotic sentiments of residents. In 1918, sociologist Henry Pratt Fairchild opined that the awful housing conditions of immigrants resulted from "the social and economic relations of society."[14] He argued that the slum proved injurious to Americanization. As he wrote, "No poorer training school for American citizens could be devised. Not only is the life prejudicial to health and morals, and destructive of ambition, but it precludes practically all incidental or unconscious contact with the uplifting influences of American life."[15] While Fairchild noted that structural factors explain why immigrants appeared less clean than native-born Americans, he nonetheless insisted that these conditions encumbered Americanization by trampling the morale of immigrants. The ethnic neighborhood thus proved problematic insofar as indigent circumstances dampened the spirit of Americanism. To live in such a locale meant that the immigrant could not cut the heartstrings binding her to the homeland. In effect, the ethnic colony prevented the conditions encouraging Americanization.

Experts lamented that the ethnic colony curtailed immigrants' interactions with American citizens. Many Americanization authorities contended that immigrant interactions with true Americans could fashion a community based on shared sentiment. A telling example of this logic appeared in a 1913 article by Simon J. Lubin, president of California's immigration commission. Lubin, a former settlement worker, argued that the key to better citizenship rested on "an exchange of ideas" that could "impress more deeply the spirit of the community and to modify it for the better."[16] In particular, he called for an exchange between immigrants living in colonies and heterogeneous populations, for the "free flow of ideals, ideas, customs and habits," especially a "common language."[17] Lubin maintained that the best form of Americanization operated by intermixing immigrants with those who could teach the customs and language of the area. If immigrants could be induced to connect with properly assimilated citizens, they might discover the same feelings as fellow patriots.

The ethnic colony was described as an obstacle to assimilation. It was a synecdochal fragment representing the affections immigrants held for their former nations. The poor state of this neighborhood and its so-called insulating effects were believed to prevent Americanization by imbuing residents with patriotic malaise. As prominent author and newspaper columnist Frederic Jennings Haskins complained, "So long as it [immigrant communities] crowds into colonies and holds itself aloof in communities that never feel the touch of American customs and ideas, how can we expect it to become like us and a part of us?"[18] He called for the distribution of immigrants "widely throughout the country" so that those new to the nation might undergo "the digestive juices of American influence."[19] Like Lubin, other Americanization experts, community planners, and progressive reformers retooled the home and neighborhood as technologies for assimilation and democratic participation. Immigrants were to live in places that could catabolize the undigested foreign body into one more identifiable as American. The synecdochal relationship between home and feelings supplied the visual logic of housing reform: internal emotions were inculcated and diagnosed by external features. These reform discussions declared the home and community as classrooms that could teach residents how to feel as Americans and as outward demonstrations of particular sentiments. In these ways, the home stood in synecdochally for the possibilities entailed in Americanization, and ultimately the positive emotions new Americans ought to experience.

Reimagining the Home and Neighborhood

One way Americanization experts began to address the supposed problems of the ethnic colony was to promote new community planning and housing designs.[20] While very few of these schemes were implemented wholesale, advocates promoted city and architectural planning as a stronghold against supposedly un-American influences. Thus, housing reform positioned effective tutelage in Americanism as based in visual and aesthetic principles. The design of the home delivered residents to concrete emotions. Specifically, authorities touted design principles as able to shape the emotions of residents by materializing the contentment and happiness entailed in the American lifestyle. For instance, a 1916 contest orchestrated by the National Americanization Committee (NAC) and Chamber of Commerce (COC) invited architects to draft homes for immigrants. In the winning designs for this contest, the synecdoche between the American home and joy was affirmed. The pleasures of living in an American home represented the happiness of nationalism. In this way, the home became imbricated in the visual logic of Americanization: it was a material marker evidencing immigrants' dedication to (or deviation from) emotional nationalism.

Importantly, the rhetorical pedagogy of housing reform often displaced immigrants' notions of home and comfort with a set of housing and lifestyle standards preferable to Americanization authorities. That is, while Americanization pedagogy encouraged immigrants to feel at home in their new nation, that goal was undercut by the notion that old-world or other lifestyles were patently demeaned. Conduct associated with the ethnic colony or other stereotypes of immigrants were referenced as the antithesis of American living. Americanization required the rejection of old-world comforts and an emotional embrace of American conveniences. As with the larger push for emotional nationalism, housing reform declared positive emotions as the natural outgrowth of modern amenities and particular designs. If immigrants could be located as Americans within these residences, proper American emotions were ostensibly assured.

For laborers, the overarching political work of this contest was to supply an aesthetic palliative that might soothe the workforce and repel radical influences. The first two decades of the twentieth century experienced a boom in the emergence of company towns constructed to circumvent unionization and control the living conditions of laborers.[21] During the war years, housing for industrial workers was of paramount importance to entice the finite labor supply to work for the war effort.[22]

Building on the recent popularity of company towns (despite a number of major catastrophes), reformers during the war years changed the environs of workers. Given the limited resources available during World War I, most proposals for the redesign of neighborhoods and housing forwarded entire communities funded by industry elites.[23] Rehabilitation of the laborer's accommodations typically sought to minimize the supposedly radical impulse of unionization and instill the American lifestyle.[24] As such, industrial community and home design during these years aimed to create efficient and happy laborers that might better serve the needs of business.

An important program for housing reform in this vein emerged from the NAC and the national COC. In the spring of 1916, these organizations jointly funded a contest inviting professional architects and planners to design several different styles of homes for laborers—small and large single-family homes, duplexes for families with lodgers, boarding houses, and railroad bunk–style lodging. Prizes ranged from $100 to $600 for winning designs.[25] The contest was widely supported by political, social, and business leaders.[26] Helen Astor, wife of John Jacob Astor's progressive heir, hosted a luncheon to announce the contest.[27] Print promotions appeared in *Immigrants in America Review*, trade journals, and the *New York Times*.[28] While the contest could apply to workers in general, promotions for the competition singled out recent immigrants as central to the end goal for this challenge.[29] Through better housing designs, contest officials hoped to acculturate immigrants to the American way of life, especially those who labored in "munitions towns."[30] Given the federal backing for this contest and its noteworthy benefactors, the winning designs epitomize the aesthetic principles of Americanization architecture.

Part of the impetus for this contest sprang from those public conversations suggesting laborers would re-create the ruinous ethnic colony within company towns and lodging. Justifications for the contest began by noting the unsanitary conditions in which laborers' families lived, particularly those who were employed in war manufacturing. In one article on the contest, Frances Kellor noted an NAC and COC study of "two hundred and fourteen small industrial communities" and the unlivable conditions residents endured.[31] Her description of these towns mirrored those discussions of the urban slums in which immigrants often lived:

> From fifty to one hundred men lived in each "stable-like" house, lacking privacy of any kind. Waste water and refuse were thrown all around the house. Toilets were open privy vaults, dirty and seldom cleaned. In another town the two-family type of house prevailed, and families kept boarders. In one three-room apartment a father, mother, daughter and baby, and six boarders occupied small and dilapidated rooms. The family and boarders used the same kitchen sink for washing purposes and the same tumble-down outhouse. Boarders and family mixed promiscuously—the conditions making privacy impossible. In still another place, small shanties, made of old wood and tin, housed small groups of immigrant workmen. No windows made ventilation impossible. Cooking facilities, garbage collection and disposal, and drainage were unknown.[32]

Kellor likened immigrants living in such conditions to animals. They lived in stables, in filth, without proper disposal of human waste. Kellor continued by asserting that families mixed "promiscuously" with boarders, hurting privacy. She alluded to indiscriminate mingling as a failure of character. While in other arguments, Kellor placed responsibility clearly on the owners of company towns, here she blamed immigrants themselves.

To prevent such squalor, reformers maintained that the new company town should supply particular design features. Much like broader discussions of the ethnic colony, contest organizers suggested that employers must provide better housing conditions to improve the emotional states of disaffected residents. Kellor highlighted dismal living arrangements as problematic for Americanization. As she averred, "You cannot really Americanize the immigrant who is badly housed. Americanization has for its object the establishment of one language, one citizenship, and one loyalty to America."[33] According to the NAC, immigrant workers could not improve their conditions themselves insofar as "a large percentage of these workmen are immigrants who have no way of creating American standards for themselves."[34] Employers were urged to provide better accommodations to enable uplifting sensibilities. As written in *Immigrants in America Review*, the end goal of this contest was to "bring home to employers the fact that improved housing means better health, stronger men and women and community happiness, resulting in greater contentment and efficiency."[35] The warrant for Kellor's argument insisted that efficiency and contentment were the effect of happiness. Here, the emotions being pursued are specific: happiness solicited residents to enact "American standards of living."[36]

In this contest, happiness was to soothe workers, to circumvent their disaffection and potential radicalization by unions. During this period, NAC member Frank Walsh had already accused the organization of focusing on employer benefits rather than the Americanizing work of trade unions. He charged the NAC with creating "'docile subserviency.'"[37] Thus, happiness here was not necessarily a benevolent goal, but rather a palliative that sought to better workers' living accommodations, if only to secure a more obedient workforce. In *The Promise of Happiness*, Sara Ahmed asks scholars not to consider happiness as an end point, but to discover the work that happiness does. As she contends, the aspiration to happiness is routed through the "regulation of desire."[38] Happiness is "what you get in return for desiring well."[39] Happiness in this contest was the synecdochal materialization of the feelings of nationalism—the workers' happiness and contentment with the American lifestyle. If immigrants were to desire well, they would find gratification with the American lifestyle and home.

In this way, the home was the synecdochal materialization of happiness, situated as the concretization of the residents' feelings for the nation. For contest planners, enacting "American standards of living" would produce positive emotions and thereby better the wartime labor force.[40] Even though the winning designs were never constructed, the rhetorical work of these pronouncements turned on the same visual logic manifest in discussions of the ethnic colony. Whereas the colony was the outward expression of disaffection, the Americanized company town and home were capable of reforming the workers' feelings. In each case, the home stood in for the individual's emotions. The American home thus represented synecdochally, as Hayden White writes, "some *quality* presumed to inhere in the totality."[41] The work of this trope is integrative, for White, wherein the aggregate is "qualitatively different from the sum of the parts."[42] In this light, the home communicated the joy of the American lifestyle and promised an emotional basis from which a loyal workforce might be secured.

The focus on happiness as the basis of nationalism routed the affective stimulation of the visual to concrete ends. Whereas in the last chapter, I illustrated how visual stimulation heightened emotions, in these discourses and practices, the materialization of happiness in the American home aimed for efficiency and contentment. Amid a dwindling wartime labor supply, the contest prompted industry titans to consider how workers could best be enticed to work harder for their company and simultaneously resist radicalizing union influences. The professional and high-society audience targeted for this initiative would be quite familiar with the recent failures of company towns, including the labor unrest at Pullman.[43] By contrast, this contest aimed to breathe new life into the company-town movement by shifting away from Pullman's draconian models to towns that produced effective and loyal workers through positive emotions.[44]

Happiness as the quintessential emotion of American nationalism was seen as critical to the success of Americanization writ large, and for the workers addressed by the NAC and COC in particular. As Frances Kellor wrote, "The health and happiness and good citizenship of this country are very vitally nurtured by decent housing, and the opportunity is squarely before the business men of America to abolish that double standard of living which has so long been a source of the race riots and labor troubles of the country, and which obstructs Americanization to-day."[45] For Kellor, health and happiness were part and parcel of good citizenship; these feelings and actions were nurtured through decent housing. The contest focused on workers as those who could be reformed by a comfortable lifestyle. The NAC and COC contest represented the home as the key material piece of American life that could produce health and happiness. The home symbolized the promise of America—one that without the elimination of double standards in housing would remain broken. If immigrants inhabited comfortable accommodations, their health, happiness, and good citizenship would follow. The synecdochal connection between the emotion of happiness and broader assimilation appeared throughout the leading designs.

In the January 1917 issue of the *Architectural Review*, all winning designs (out of 370 submissions) were presented with accompanying rationales for their effectiveness. A number of authors and architects within the issue accented the need for designs that promoted clean living conditions. These circumstances were thought to instill the proper spirit and feeling of patriotism. For example, in his introductory article, E. T. Hartmann, the secretary for the Massachusetts Civic League, a community reform organization, described those hygienic features of the home that might induce immigrant workers to adopt American standards. He wrote,

> There should be a bath and two set-tubs, with running water wherever available. Their absence adds to filth and disease, and makes also for unnecessary labor and house-hold drudgery. Patriotic Americans will work for these things, to the end that we may be proud of Americans as well as of America. The day is coming when we will be ashamed to have split our throats and marched our legs off at the nod of those who make the flag an emblem of tyranny, and religion a mockery, while all the time ignoring the things of health and comfort,—the things which alone make an intelligent and modern democracy possible.[46]

In this passage, Hartmann insisted that Americanization is only possible once the "things of health and comfort" are provided. According to him, these qualities enabled "intelligent and modern democracy." His warrant is causal in that simply providing the tools of hygiene would ostensibly create healthful living. The work of inculcating modern democracy was to be accomplished by architects and contractors in Americanization—these are the "Patriotic Americans" he suggested should work for "these things." Earlier in the essay, Hartmann admitted that immigrants are "glad to take what may be had at the lowest expense," and therefore architects should not "allow [them] to fall victim to such conditions."[47] Such claims maintained the notion that design, not housing codes or structural changes, transformed living standards. For Hartmann, Americanization began by providing health and comfort. Americanized design inspired feelings that combated anti-patriotic sentiment: "those who make the flag an emblem of tyranny, and religion a mockery." The feeling supplied by the immigrant's lifestyle facilitated national unity.

Other authors commended designs with gardening or green spaces, as such sites were thought to fertilize contentment. These designs often drew on the myth of agrarian serenity popularized by the garden city movement. Garden cities were comprehensively planned, low-density communities where industry, suburban homes, and agriculture were interwoven into a vision of balanced communitarianism.[48] Gardening was seen as an essential element in these cities as it supposedly produced "social tranquility."[49] The vision of tranquility inspired by the garden city movement clearly appears in contest discussions of garden and outdoor recreation space as supreme Americanizing forces.[50] For Kellor, gardening provided an Americanizing activity insofar as the cultivation of the land simultaneously nurtured a love of country and dedication to an employer. As she wrote, "They [Americanization agents] discovered that the man who has a house and a garden stays for the garden, and that next to the job-stake the home-stake in America is the big, vital, Americanizing influence."[51] She maintained that when industrial communities provided good housing and gardening space, the evils of boarding disappeared, "family life improved, and the workmen [were] made contented."[52] Here, the synecdochal work of the garden was to relay contentment. The lessons of Americanization were not abstract affective feelings, but rather distinct: happiness and satisfaction. The garden and green spaces were seen as smaller manifestations of the pleasures of American life.

The synecdochal work of the home as evidence of residents' national affections would become materialized in the architectural stylings of these homes. Drawing on the designs and layouts popularized in England's garden cities, a large number of the homes drafted for this contest were styled as cottages, regardless of their size. In *Building the Workingman's Paradise*, Margaret Crawford argues that the winning designs for the NAC and COC contest favored distinctly American cottage styles. Crawford notes that one of the judges for the contest, Grosvenor Atterbury, designed Indian Hill, an industrial town near Worcester, Massachusetts. As she acknowledges, Indian Hill's cottage style is remarkably echoed in the awarded designs.[53] Atterbury's cottages for Indian Hill were clearly Americanized with more colonial markers. The homes intentionally rejected European, particularly Germanic, traditions.[54] Similar principles appeared in the NAC and COC contest. For example, the judges stated that Murphy & Dana's plans for a single-family house used a gambrel roof to achieve a "cottage effect."[55] High-hipped, sloping roofs and arched doorways or windows provided a similar aesthetic in most of the other honored designs. In these discussions, the style of the home was situated as emblematic of its Americanness. That style was positioned as a demarcation of residents' nationalistic emotions.

For many commentators on the awarded designs, the cottage was a home preferred by Americanized citizens. The claim entrenched the synecdochal connection between the home and inhabitants' nationalistic affections. As E. T. Hartmann observed of the designs, "The cottage, detached or semi-detached, is better than the tenement. As one student of the subject puts it, 'The single-family house stimulates a better home life than the tenement, and gives the occupants more of the sense of really belonging to the community and of having a personal stake in it.' The small house is preferred by genuine citizens."[56] For Hartmann, smaller houses ensured stronger health and morals for immigrant families. Genuine citizens would always prefer a smaller house given that it enhanced insular family life. The synecdoche at stake in this reading was made plain by Frances Kellor, who wrote, "The most conspicuous evidence of this anti-Americanism is to be seen in housing."[57] She continued, "patriotism and loyalty and love for America" could not be found in housing that demoralized and sapped enjoyment from its residents.[58] In this line of reasoning, and as White highlights in the aggregative quality of the synecdoche, the home was to create happiness and national affection while it simultaneously served as evidence of such emotions.

Ultimately, the objectives of the NAC and COC were to enable employers to attract high-quality immigrant workers and to use happiness as a tool for generating a loyal workforce. Given wartime shortages, none of these houses were built. Nevertheless, the contest represents a variety of similar efforts during this period to design company towns.[59] What proves distinctive about this contest is how organizers imagined the aesthetic and material qualities of these homes as proof of residents' positive feelings for the nation. The American home operated as a synecdochal rhetorical form—the particular instantiation of the broader emotions of American life. In the previous chapter, the focus of visual education as a type of abstract, affective stimulation pointed to the possibilities of the future through Americanization. Here, the home is a concrete space that stands in for the larger contentment of American life, and a sign of inhabitants' familiarity with and aspiration to those feelings. The home thus moves away from abstract affective stimulation to materializing specific emotions. In this instance, happiness and contentment facilitated patriotism. The industry professionals who backed this contest pursued these emotions in order to bolster efficiency, asserting that once workers felt positive emotions, they would be more productive.[60] But, the visual logic at play operated on an evidentiary relationship between internal feelings and external markers. Other Americanization efforts in housing reform would aim for a similar synecdochal logic, but often through the pursuit of shared sensibilities as opposed to simply positive emotions.

Americanization of the Ethnic Neighborhood

A number of settlement and social-work activities, community centers, and public school programs sought to Americanize ethnic neighborhoods by deploying visual and aesthetic lessons in American citizenship. Typically, this tutelage implied that if immigrants could interact with Americans, they would model their practices. Residents would come to see their homes and communities as locales in which they could perform as Americans. Work along these lines within already existing neighborhoods ranged from classes in naturalization to social events. In these imitative and participatory lessons, the goal was to deliver pupils to a community of shared emotions. The synecdochal logic of these reforms suggested that the community and its sympathetic attachments stood in for the larger bonds of emotional nationalism. As with the discussion of happiness in the NAC and COC contest, the goal was more pointed than simple stimulation. Americanization through neighborhood practices was to manage the specific emotions of immigrants.

A principal method of Americanization used expert personnel to teach residents models of Americanism. Joseph Mayper, former head of the Americanization division within the Bureau of Education, provides an apt example of this kind of tutelage. Mayper asserted that prior to reform work, the residents of Barren Island, New York, lived in poverty and squalor. To address these concerns, the New York City Department of Health engaged in an aggressive plan of neighborhood rehabilitation that included a hired nurse, a milk station, home visitation, recreational facilities, a reading room, gardening instruction, grievance adjudication, and a central space for education and consultation with health officials.[61] Mayper insisted that the success of this plan rested on providing imitative instruction. He described how the "graphic demonstrations of treatment" provided by the Department of Health nurse proved of tremendous "educational value."[62] Mayper detailed one vignette in this regard: the nurse arrived at the home of a woman suffering from illness. Her neighbors had been called to attend to her, but stood there "impotent without direction."[63] The nurse quickly put the women to work "opening a window . . . mopping the floor . . . bringing a clean nightgown . . . getting some warm water . . . fitting up another bed with clean linens."[64] In this excerpt, the nurse was valuable because she was able to instruct immigrant women in the right course of action.

Repeatedly, Mayper underscored how demonstration and imitation were key to fashioning Americanism, and in particular the shared sensibilities and emotions of American life. As he wrote, "The improvement of Barren Island in sanitation, education, beauty and other conditions which could in any way conduce to the health, morality, happiness and general good citizenship of its residents was sought."[65] Here, practical and imitative lessons provided a conduit to health, morality, and happiness. In a similar fashion to Kellor, Mayper positioned health, morality, and happiness as related to the physical conditions of the neighborhood. If residents could appreciate the cleanliness, educational opportunities, and beauty of their communities, that valuation would lead to a "high type of American citizenship."[66] The relationship between visual and corporeal demonstration was to model good praxis and evince the joyful emotions, qualities, and aesthetics of civic life.

Other lesson plans were far more explicit in their pursuit of fellowship to heighten happiness and expedite Americanization. In a 1918 book, Christian minister and accomplished author Henry Ezekiel Jackson extolled the virtues of the schoolhouse as a makeshift community center. For him, central gathering sites instilled a sense of belonging in community members.[67] He extended this logic for immigrants in particular: "If they are ever to feel that they belong with us, the right hand of fellowship must be extended to them. The neighborhood spirit alone can create in them the spirit of America."[68] Significantly, Jackson's use of pronouns presumed that "they," immigrants, would interact with "us," Americans, to learn the proper neighborhood spirit. In keeping with this view, Jackson suggested that particular community-center activities encouraged the emulative interactions central to Americanization:

> The means employed are various—games, folk dances, dramas, chorus singing—which require the subordination of self to coöperative effort, dinner parties, where the people break bread in celebration of their communion with each other as neighbors. These activities not only render a service to the individual by promoting his happiness and decreasing his loneliness, they discover in the community unsuspected abilities and unused resources.[69]

For Jackson, the activities of the community center supplied a spiritual sense of belonging and promoted happiness over loneliness. The goal, then, of these collective activities was to join people together such that immigrants felt wedded to the community and bolstered by the jubilance entailed.

For these progressives, happiness was contagious via participation in community life. Once immigrants felt a sense of belonging to their communities, interacting with one another would breed positive commitment and elation at the prospect of collective activities. Notice that Jackson situates certain activities as replicators of happiness so long as the self is subordinated to collective effort. These activities created a place from which to draw shared emotion and a sense of purpose. National emotions thus resulted from shared interactions premised on the effacement of self in favor of group consciousness. The work of happiness was to create a cooperative commitment to the group—so long as that group demonstrated the spirit of Americanism.

The extent to which Americanization banked on the shared emotions of nationalism is revealed in an influential volume funded by the Carnegie Corporation. Directed by Allen T. Burns, a former superintendent of Boston schools, the Carnegie volumes amplified progressive views on assimilation articulated during the war by insisting that immigrants must feel happiness or a shared spirit in order to become Americanized. In *America via the Neighborhood*, John Daniels argued that reformation of the ethnic community could be accomplished by urging residents to participate in public gatherings. He contended that communities could Americanize residents—even those born as American—through participatory events that inspired a "community of feeling."[70] When communities came together for loan campaigns, school events, settlement programs, or similar activities, they developed the loyalty and democratic engagement central to Americanism. For Daniels, these practices evoked positive emotions and transmitted national sentiment. As he wrote, "The neighborhood is infused with new sympathies, new ideals, and new motives for action."[71] He advised using community activities to engender positive emotions and hone the group consciousness of Americanism.

Daniels cautioned that certain activities proved more successful than others in this regard. Throughout this volume he commended neighborhood events that rested on aesthetic and visual experiences. For instance, he lauded the overwhelming patriotic displays of a middle-class Bohemian[72] community on Long Island; musical and theatrical societies as naturally inspiring positive feelings of loyalty; and school programs where children put on pageants and invited their parents. Throughout these examples, his greatest acclaim was reserved for events at which residents communed for positive or patriotic ends. Quoting a U.S. Treasury official, Daniels agreed that community participation produced American loyalty: "From these many peoples from many climes, now all under one flag, we now have an outward and visible sign of that inward and spiritual Americanism which is evidenced by our country's motto, 'E Pluribus Unum.'"[73] For Daniels, participation was not simply part of nationalistic practice, but evinced democracy through aesthetics. That is, participation both formed the community of feeling Daniels desired and visibly demonstrated loyalty. Once immigrants interacted with Americans at joyous events, Daniels averred that immigrants would feel the same spirit. The shared emotions of the community represented synecdochally a broader emotional nationalism.

The need for common sympathies continued in other volumes wherein the synecdochal work of happiness was the glue binding individuals to a larger sense of emotional nationalism. In his 1920 dissertation completed at Columbia University, educator Isaac Baer Berkson analyzed the efficacy of contemporary methods of Americanization. He opened his study by suggesting that the recent war engendered the need for "proper adjustment" of newcomers to the "life of America."[74] Heavily employing the work of his teacher, John Dewey, Berkson rejected those theories of assimilation in which ethnic group members were molded to fit American standards. From this premise, Berkson asserted that Americanization ought not erase all differences, but rather America must cultivate a novel nationalism based on a "spiritual plane."[75] As he wrote, "The immigrant must be made to feel American; it is not sufficient that he strive in an objective way or mechanically for ends which can be identified as American. For it is such whole-hearted emotional identification with the body of citizens which is at the basis of a lasting allegiance."[76] For Berkson, feeling as though one were an American became the synecdochal part standing in for emotional identification with the nation.

Yet, Berkson did not simply point to shared feeling as the foundation of emotional nationalism; instead he indicated that Americanization must cultivate happiness to work. Throughout the volume, he praised participatory practices as imbued with the joy of democracy. While Daniels espoused mimicry, Berkson opined that any form of community participation would evoke the shared emotions he pursued. Democracy, on his own account, "is so touched with deep emotion" that "its real essence is spiritual."[77] It reaches up to "attain the heights of the spirit."[78] Referencing the tenets of humanism, he argued that modern nations "worship. . . . Progress and Happiness."[79] Though he noted the religious principles of this secular theology, he nevertheless wondered if community participation might help immigrants locate "their highest expression of happiness."[80] In this way, Berkson premised democracy's aspirational work on the self-evident truths of the Declaration of Independence. Whereas life, liberty, and the pursuit of happiness animated the colonists, for Berkson, the modern era's democratic praxis should aim for a group consciousness in which liberty and happiness were maximized. Rhetorically, Berkson's argument situated positivity as the basis of a shared national consciousness. For him, a joyous disposition was foundational to an inclusive and robust democracy. The synecdoche thus tied happiness to national unity. If one could feel happiness, then one was imbricated within the shared emotions of the nation.

Americanization experts developed a number of lessons in the American lifestyle that aimed to reform residents of the so-called ethnic colony. Community centers, schoolhouse events, and home instruction are just a sampling of the methods these authorities employed to access the hidden enclaves of immigrants' hearts. These tactics reframed the home and community as Americanizing spaces, inviting immigrants to see these places as communities in which they could find happiness. Part of that happiness banked on locating a community of feeling—a place of belonging and shared sensibilities. Communities of feeling and the emotions they espoused were synecdochal in that they stood in for Americanism. In all, these methods of teaching Americanism were not simply practical lessons, but rather insisted that positive, emotional attachment to the neighborhood and country were the primary outcomes of the lesson plan. The neighborhood was to create emotional experiences that were both internal to those who felt them and shared by both the neighborhood and the nation. Overall, the point was to use the imitative and aesthetic practices of the neighborhood to build a relationship between the sights, practices, and feelings of home and the larger emotions of nationalism.

The Americanization Aesthetics of the Home and Neighborhood

Americanization experts situated the home and community as classrooms for the tutelage of immigrants. With the right design or teacher, these spaces could inspire particular emotions in residents. Once immigrants felt contentment or happiness, their patriotism was clinched. Architects of the NAC and COC contest argued that the Americanizing residence engendered a comfortable and prosperous life for laborers. The home's design was thought to cultivate familiarity with the feelings of Americanism by the serenity it afforded. The rhetorical work of the home was to engender a salubrious life allowing for an emotional attachment to the United States. For those practitioners that aimed to improve standing homes and neighborhoods, the goal was to evoke happiness in residents through mimicry and the contagion effect of group consciousness.

Ultimately, the synecdochal logic of these tactics positioned the neighborhood and home as able to change the emotions of immigrants, and as corresponding evidence of immigrants' emotional states.

The work of synecdoche helps to explain the specific rhetorical work of housing and community reform on emotional nationalism. In visual education pedagogies, Americanization began by arousing an affective charge, a hopeful orientation to the future wherein Americanization promised a new vista. In housing design and reform, Americanization was to materialize those abstract feelings into particular emotions. Namely, contentment and happiness emerged as the glue affixing residents to home and thereby to nation. De Certeau suggests that synecdoche can be used to expand a spatial element by allowing it to stand in for a totality. In the discourses of housing design and reform, the work of synecdoche is spatial, visual, and aesthetic. It is spatial in much the same way as de Certeau admits: a concrete space that elicits and represents the totality of the nation. It is also visual in that Americanization authorities used immigrants' lifestyles and accommodations as evidence of their internal emotional states. While squalor produced malaise, American housing created joy. Yet, ultimately, the most important Americanization mission of housing design and reform was aesthetic; the work of the beautiful home or community was to inspire those emotions that might fortify nationalistic attachments. The promise of housing design and reform was to teach residents how to desire the right kinds of American emotions.

Rhetorically, housing reform materialized the emotions of nationalism. Immigrants could better embody the feelings of Americanism through the lesson plan of the home. Americans lived in comfort and happiness. Yet, the synecdochal logic of these discourses and practices tethered the creation and verification of those emotions to visual and aesthetic display. The figural work of the home gave form to the emotions of modern American life. The home became the concrete manifestation of abstract feelings. Yet, giving form to these emotions was a goal for external audiences that may not have actually materialized for residents. That is, given the idea that these homes and neighborhoods were to displace former lifestyles and attachments, the idea that happiness and comfort could be so easily created was largely an ambition for Americanization authorities. Thus, the rhetorical work of reading the home as evidence of an emotional change was predicated on the demands set forth by Americanization protocols and not necessarily an achievable outcome.

Indeed, the circumscribed role of participation evident in the discussions of housing and community reform highlights the political force of these changes. Participation in these discourses and practices was not necessarily related to acts of governance such as voting and public deliberation, but rather couched as a purely aesthetic experience. In his reading of Machiavelli, Thomas Docherty argues in *Aesthetic Democracy* that there are distinctions between participating and inhabiting as it relates to the aesthetics of democratic practice. While the former is typically understood as the exercise of civil rights, the latter involves an "intimacy with a public space or public sphere" to establish the "legitimacy" of citizenship.[81] In the discourses of Americanization housing reform, participation meant inhabiting certain homes and shared public spaces so as to ensure that immigrants learned the emotions of Americanism. Here, democratic participation was intricately connected to the world of appearances, being present in spaces and with peoples that were presumed to have an Americanizing influence. The aesthetics of participation thus became a question of form—of immigrants publicly acting in ways that appeared as American. Design and housing reform aimed to *show* immigrants how to live as Americans, while it encouraged them to *illustrate* their own submission to the American way. Housing reform thus promoted American living, but divorced the aesthetics of democracy from the rights entailed in democratic governance.

In these reform discussions, aesthetic instruction shifted the emphasis of Americanization pedagogy. Immigrants were invited to live as other Americans purportedly did: in single-family homes, with modern amenities, kept to a certain set of hygienic standards, while actively involved in their neighborhoods. Significant to these discourses is the traditional notion of aesthetics—that which is beautiful, corporeally pleasing, or arousing of the divine. Aesthetic markers were instrumentalized into identifying visible forms of emotional nationalism. The American lifestyle was reconfigured as a set of conspicuous signs indicating one's emotional dedication. Immigrants learned to recognize these signs through the design of ideal homes and communities and the tutelage of the home teacher or Americanization agent. These spaces and models marked those performances that counted as American. Likewise, these signs rendered visible immigrants' commitments to Americanization. Living as an American was an outward expression of the immigrant's internal dedication to national ideals.

In a larger sense, the qualities of Americanism often became flattened in Americanization pedagogy. While the progressive drive for shared emotions sought to counter nativist bases of belonging, the aesthetics of happiness limited what Americanism could be. Instead of embracing cosmopolitanism, as many progressives did, nationalism was relegated to appearing as though one belonged. Immigrants were encouraged to embody lifestyles that suited preconceived notions of acceptance. Moreover, in housing reform discourses, the overwhelming focus on lifestyle occluded any discussion of traditional civics. This is not to suggest that all Americanization programs worked in this way. Authors for the AVS, for instance, promoted democratic participation as essential to assimilation and national improvement. Yet here, and in the vast majority of visual and aesthetic Americanization pedagogies, the metrics evaluating Americanism were rather elementary. What immigrants felt was determined by where they lived, who they lived with, and how they lived. Americanism became predicated on a superficial synecdoche: outward appearances stood in for national belonging.

Yet, the work of the synecdochal rhetorical form—indeed all forms—is always a bit perverse. Such duplicity is certainly at work here. The slippage between the part and the aggregate works to arrest the ambiguity entailed in the emotional mechanisms of Americanization. Yet, artificial representations of emotions—the immigrant's home, community participation—could never fully appease concerns about disloyalty. The synecdoche remained a strained trope. That is, housing reform was based on what Ahmed would call the immigrant's melancholic attachment—his inability to extricate the bond to the motherland.[82] The Americanizing home attempted to displace that melancholic attachment precipitated by the ethnic colony with another, more joyful attachment—the happiness of the new nation in place of the dead object. For outsiders, the pull of the homeland undermined protestations of Americanism. For immigrants, the luxurious and comfortable feeling of the American lifestyle came at a steep cost: discarding one's lifestyle and considerable connection to the homeland. Given that the work of Americanization was never quite complete, the specter of that attachment continued to haunt immigrants.

While Americanization agents endeavored to assuage public anxieties about the sentiments of immigrants, such moves could never fully erase the very perversity that supposedly required Americanization. When immigrants displayed signs of living as Americans, Americanization authorities exclaimed these performances as demonstrative of their desire to become patriots. Experts intimated that the aesthetic experience afforded by implementing the American lifestyle would result in a drive to further the process of Americanization. Yet, Americanization rested on a peculiar visual logic. On the one hand, those immigrants who acted as Americans promised authorities that Americanization worked. On the other hand, visible signs of Americanization could never dispel more general concerns that immigrants' feelings could be easily swayed. Emphasis on superficial signs of nationalistic emotions accented the ambiguity at play. As such, the visual logic of Americanization could not provide unassailable guarantees of a successful outcome. This ambiguous relationship is especially exemplified in Americanization parades and choral ensembles popularized during the war. These resolutely public displays of patriotism labored to render the passion of patriotism visible in immigrants, yet simultaneously amplified the inability to verify the feelings immigrants held.

CHAPTER FOUR

Displaying Americanization in Public Celebration

———•◆•———

In Philadelphia on May 10, 1915, President Woodrow Wilson addressed a group of four thousand newly naturalized citizens. While Wilson delivered the address mere days after the sinking of the *Lusitania*, he did not reference the attack by German U-boats, the nearly twelve hundred dead. Wilson asserted that the day's celebration of naturalization emphasized the rebirth of the American spirit and the need for loyalty. Noting the promise of immigration for the United States, Wilson said,

> This country is constantly drinking strength out of new sources by the voluntary association with it of great bodies of strong men and forward-looking women out of other lands. And so by the gift of the free will of independent people it is being constantly renewed from generation to generation by the same process by which it was originally created. It is as if humanity had determined to see to it that this great Nation,

founded for the benefit of humanity, should not lack for the allegiance of the people of the world.[1]

Wilson posited immigrants as key to the nation's renewal and exceptionalism.[2] The nation drank "strength" from these new arrivals, whose allegiance invested in the "gift of free will." Amid broader concerns that the specter of war animated homeland sympathies, Wilson deemed the arrival of immigrants to the United States as evidence of the country's bright future—immigrants invigorated the promise of democracy. Although Wilson emphatically praised immigrants for the blessings they bestowed upon their new nation, he reminded these new citizens, and the larger audience of fifteen thousand, of their responsibilities: "You cannot dedicate yourself to America unless you become in every respect and with every purpose of your will thorough Americans. You cannot become thorough Americans if you think of yourselves in groups."[3] Thus, while Wilson acknowledged that one's "nation of . . . origin" was "sacred," he nevertheless insisted upon undivided allegiance to the United States.[4]

The event at which President Wilson spoke was designed to inspire the kind of loyalty he described. Organizers fashioned the ceremony with a heavy dose of patriotic pageantry. Distinguished guests included city and state officials, lawmakers, armed services officers, and other noteworthy representatives.[5] American flags adorned twenty pillars installed for the event.[6] Patriotic bunting was draped from the ceiling and fashioned into a fan shape over the choir.[7] And, most notably, newly naturalized citizens faced a "wreath thirty feet in diameter" that read "in electric, lighted letters: Welcome to a government of the people, by the people, for the people."[8] For Americanization experts, celebratory events such as this motivated immigrants to feel the ideals of Americanism. As written in *The Survey*, the purpose of these festivities was "to welcome the naturalized, to invite the unnaturalized, and to give both, together with their families, a true conception of the meaning of American ideals and institutions as well as a sense of participation in them."[9] Patriotic celebrations, then, welcomed new citizens while broadcasting the significance and "meaning" of "American ideals and institutions." Americans were to be loyal and render visible their dedication to the United States. These celebrations did not simply honor immigrants or new citizens, but were carefully planned rhetorical events designed to sway the nationalistic attachments of all attendees.

The notion that these patriotic exhibitions were fashioned for naturalized citizens, their families, and other audience members bespeaks the importance of public display to Americanization. These festivities labored to exhibit the efficacy of the project to the public. The Philadelphia celebration was merely one of hundreds of patriotic festivities planned to commemorate the naturalization of citizens and to publicize patriotic virtues. For instance, the Committee for Immigrants in America promoted July 4, 1915, as National Americanization Day.[10] Hundreds of cities organized Americanization Day pageants and parades like the event in Philadelphia. As Edward Hartmann wrote, "No section of the country failed to respond to the rallying call; even New Orleans in the deep south held a most successful celebration."[11] While in the last two chapters I detailed the rhetorical work of Americanization lessons for its principal students, this chapter attends to the way public celebrations used rhetorical exhibition to demonstrate the success of this pedagogy. Positioned as evidence of Americanization's workability, patriotic pageants, parades, and singing provided an opportunity to render visible immigrants' commitment to the nation.

Although public celebrations have long been significant to cultivating patriotism, the way these celebrations emphasized distinct markers of allegiance is important for grasping period nationalism. In crafting a display that demarcated the loyalties of immigrants, parade and choral organizers simultaneously codified Americanism as a set of tangible signs. Particular patriotic exhibitions were selected repeatedly in a fashion that narrowed the possibilities of demonstrating patriotism. Further, these public pageants highlighted the need for public recognition of immigrants' changed dispositions. Americanization was devoted to galvanizing emotional nationalism, instilling a certain kind of patriotic adoration in subjects. These celebrations invited the public to focus on external signs to prove that immigrants had, in fact, ingested the emotional requirements of Americanism. Thus, parade designers rhetorically crafted these pageants as events through which Americanism could become recognizable to immigrants and the general public.

However, illustrations of allegiance remained problematic given the difficulties of demonstrating internal emotions. The trope of metalepsis is useful in explaining the contradictory mechanisms of visual proof. Metalepsis is an extended or doubled figuration—for example, when a common trope or maxim (e.g., the early bird catches the worm) is used in a new way (e.g., I've got to catch the worm tomorrow). The layering of the trope distances or stretches the connection between figure and referent. As literary scholar Daniel Fischlin argues, metalepsis "implies a resistance against literality . . . a trope or figure transgresses and defers its initial significance."[12] As a visual figure in Americanization celebrations, metalepsis identifies the strained evidentiary association between public exhibition and emotional nationalism. Certainly, these festivities were not solely visual occasions insofar as they also involved sound, participation, and more. Yet, attending to the visual display of immigrant bodies at these events indicates the paradoxical status of evidence in the pursuit of Americanization. These pageants situated the immigrant's patriotic performance as proof of his drive toward assimilation. Patriotic rituals publicly marked the immigrant's devotion as they did for other Americans. However, used in this new way, the very same visual display generated a peculiar status for immigrants: the pressure to perform as Americans simultaneously denoted immigrants as outsiders playing Americans. As such, the strained nature of metalepsis can well inform wider understanding of the rhetorical work of parades and choral ensembles. The figural presentation of the immigrant's body is displaced by the contradictions at the heart of the project. Patriotic rituals did not secure the immigrant's status as an American, but instead highlighted the differences between American and foreigner.

Americanization pageantry attempted to show the project's efficacy, yet simultaneously highlighted the vicissitudes of proof. I call this phenomenon the paradox of visibility. Despite the progressive turn to more sympathetic methods of enculturation, authorities were concerned that the loyalties of immigrants remained unverifiable. Broader discourses on nationalism as an infection set the stage for understanding emotional nationalism as an internal quality that could nevertheless be displayed on and through the body. Given this nationalistic outlook, parade organizers emphasized the exhibition of patriotism to render emotional changes visible for the public. These occasions invited audiences to see the patriotic acts of immigrants as proof of Americanization's success. Still other celebratory events—namely, choral ensembles—show how this evidentiary association was strained: the need for public assurances of loyalty drew attention to the foreignness of the immigrant at the same time as she labored to prove her dedication. Here, I'm interested in how these rhetorical tactics amplified the disparities between loyal Americans and immigrants, entrenching the general anxiety that no amount of Americanization could weld the disparate populace into a unified whole.

Nationalism as Infection

A paradox of visuality plagued Americanization. Popular authors and speakers warned that simply appearing loyal could not guarantee one's national ardor, while public exhibitions of patriotism were seen as essential to assuring the citizen's nationalistic attachments. Thus, allegiance became a contradictory interplay between visibility and invisibility. Part of this paradox manifests in those period discourses and practices couching nationalism as an emotional germ or infection contained within the body of the immigrant. For many period advocates, true Americans could diagnose the fidelity of the alien body. Even skilled patriots, however, were offered few clues to guide their examination; instead, they were simply advised to keep a watchful eye on markers of difference. Such framing helped constitute a paradoxical visual relationship: immigrants were pressured to show signs of loyalty, yet public discourses stipulated that this evidence was never quite enough to demonstrate a full commitment to Americanism.

Much like the worry over hyphenated Americans, in many public discussions of nationalism, national ardor was figured as an infection or transmissible disease that, without the watchful eye of true Americans, could spread invisibly. The germ metaphor delimited the potential homeland sympathies of immigrants as a menace, a hidden illness that could persist even after careful attempts at Americanization. Such an alarmist concern insisted that loyalty was not easily verifiable to the populace and evinced an urgent demand for identifying the culprits in need of Americanization.

The history of understanding nationalism as a kind of emotional infection stems from two major theoretical and historical trends. First, in the nineteenth century, amid a multitude of historical and popular investigations of racial lineage, the Teutonic germ theory of origins gained prominence.[13] In this postulation, the Teutonic tribes transported their political and social ideals to Britain and America.[14] This theory connected racial ideology to political ideals and social mores.[15] While this concept was debunked by the 1890s, in later popular discourses the idea of a racial germ took on renewed social significance.[16] In part, these new discussions emerged as a result of European upheavals and the increase in so-called new immigrants from Southern and Eastern Europe to the Americas, whereupon popular consideration of these changes invigorated refiguring Teutonic origins with the more fashionable Anglo-Saxon ancestry.[17] Alongside these machinations, by the late nineteenth century, the dissemination of the scientific notion of germs energized public deliberation about a wide array of topics.[18] For immigrants, especially new immigrants, germs became the guiding warrant for their Americanization. Under this rubric, public health agencies often argued that immigrants must become more sanitary to protect the public welfare.[19] Coupled together, the modern fascination with germs and racial genealogy rhetorically fashioned the visual and material terms through which difference bore the potential for an epidemic of disunity. Ethnic populations became seen as potentially infected by a nationalism beholden to the enemy. Indeed, the paradoxical visual logic of emotional nationalism came to a head through metaphors of germ or infection.

Public commentary often hinged on the visual relationship between external evidence and internal emotions when discussing nationalism as an infection or germ. Prominent instances of this logic emerged from President Wilson, who spoke frequently on the need for Americanization. In his 1916 "Loyalty" speech to a citizenship convention in Washington, Wilson admonished Americanizers to act with the best intentions so as to infect immigrants with the ideals of the democracy. He stated,

> So my interest in this movement is as much an interest in ourselves as in those whom we are trying to Americanize, because if we are genuine Americans they cannot avoid the infection; whereas, if we are not

genuine Americans, there will be nothing to infect them with, and no amount of teaching, no amount of exposition of the Constitution,—which I find very few persons understand,—no amount of dwelling upon the idea of liberty and of justice will accomplish the object we have in view, unless we ourselves illustrate the idea of justice and of liberty.[20]

In this speech, nationalism was an infection contained within genuine Americans and transmitted through Americanization. National spirit spread through contagion, and the right citizens could share patriotic germs. The infection proved irresistible so long as the person attempting to assimilate the immigrant could illustrate justice and liberty. Here, immigrants are figured in relationship to the "spiritual" principles of the nation.[21] They learn these principles by modeling legitimate Americans. Significantly, Wilson suggested that rumination on the ideas of liberty or justice would not accomplish the objectives he sought. Instead, illustration by other Americans was crucial to the process of inoculating new citizens with the right spirit.

The visual paradox at stake between internal emotions and external evidence appeared more plainly in Wilson's 1915 speech to the Daughters of the American Revolution (DAR). Wilson opened the address by observing the ease with which the revolutionary generation's national spirit infected subsequent generations, until newcomers tested this covenant.[22] These strangers, according to Wilson, were not yet part of this national spirit. Instead, they held "too general an impression" and had not "entertained with sufficient intensity and affection the American ideal."[23] Throughout the speech, Wilson refers to Americanism as a "feeling," the "heart" of America, or "the things that America believes in."[24] In these postulations, immigrants either loved the nation or failed to love the nation. Yet, in either instance, nationalism was an emotional "infection" that had been easy to spread until a "time of special stress and test."[25] Wilson described nationalism as an internal emotional commitment that infected certain individuals until the war animated homeland sympathies.

Wilson offered little material evidence to determine the nature of the subject's emotional orientation. In some instances, such as the "Loyalty" speech, the individual's socialist or radical leanings were poisonous. Yet, more often, the president indicated that some Americans were especially able to interpret the nature of the immigrant's nationalistic affections. In his address to the DAR, he advised one possible avenue for diagnosis. While Wilson argued that most immigrants held America in their hearts, he nevertheless opined, "I am in a hurry for an opportunity to have a lineup and let the men who are thinking first of other countries stand on one side and all those that are for America first, last, and all the time on the other side."[26] Wilson continued by inviting his audience to prognosticate on the nationalistic infections of others. He affirmed that women were especially suited to this enterprise and could create "an atmosphere of opinion" that would haze ne'er-do-wells into compliance.[27] Wilson's desire for a lineup, while clearly an attempt to dramatize his formulation, still projected the ideal that spiritual infection, despite the invisibility of the germ, could be publicly diagnosed. His recommendation to his listeners was to form their own prognosis about the symptoms of their neighbors. Women of the DAR ostensibly held unique capacities in this public-health endeavor and were expected to act in fellowship to control the spread of disease. Wilson's public arguments, then, identified a paradoxical visual logic to Americanism. While true Americanism was an internal, spiritual, and emotional principle, Americans themselves (at least the members of the DAR) possessed the tools to diagnose the vigor of that dedication via external markers.

More generally, the infection metaphor animated the need for public policing. This association entrenched the concern that despite widespread Americanization, immigrants' emotional loyalties required public markers given the ambiguity of discerning emotions. For example, in his 1917 report to the secretary of labor, Commissioner of Naturalization Richard K. Campbell proposed that the infection of disloyalty was obvious to the American public. He asserted, "Since this Nation has been plunged into the horrible vortex that has been raging for the last three years all over the seas and with increasing intensity upon the European soil, the necessity for the Americanization, the transformation, the arousing of the spirit of America within the hearts and breasts of the resident alien body has been more and more painfully apparent."[28] Campbell indicated that the disease was patently evident to other Americans. He diagnosed symptoms not as general conditions, but as within the heart and breast of the resident alien. He noted that while "some [immigrants]" have "tangibly and some intangibly, adopted this country," there "are those who are inimical in their hearts to the well-being of this country."[29] For Campbell, emotional ties to the homeland could not be overcome without comprehensive Americanization. His discussion tethered Americanism to public acts—citizens could assess the emotions of immigrants through tangible results.

Given the visual politics of this understanding of nationalism, Americans were induced to act against this potential plague and taught to read ethnic difference as the symptom of potential infection. As Vanessa B. Beasley notes of this period, immigrants were treated as inherently contrary to Americanism.[30] As such, popular authors invited Americans to keep a watchful eye for signs of disloyalty. In a 1922 article for *Scribner's Magazine*, popular literary critic Ernest Boyd described heavy-handed attempts at nationalization as manufacturing a pseudo-Americanism. Boyd contended that "the process of Americanization only too frequently means the infection of the newcomers with this virus, which they pass on from one to another."[31] For this author, Americanization resulted in artifice, individuals cloaking themselves in the veneer of Americanism while failing to embrace the true spirit essential to unity. His discussion insisted that soon after arrival, immigrants lost the characteristics of the old country, but only managed to find a false uniformity rather than true Americanism. Boyd pushed this logic to its extreme, implying that all individuals in the public eye were of questionable loyalty. He asserted that "real Americans" have "receded into the background of public life" to protect themselves from the "immigrant tide," while "ex-Europeans" demean America with "vulgarities and excesses."[32] Yet, he held out hope for "real" Americans to properly direct public life by preserving and maintaining a stalwart Americanism. Boyd's argument identified a paradoxical logic in determining Americanism: external markers of similarity did not prove loyalty.

As a case in point, Boyd averred that immigrants could potentially cover their differences in order to hide their un-Americanism and pass as loyal citizens. Boyd detailed the case of an immigrant who camouflaged himself in the artifice of Americanism. Boyd noted, "Only recently a ludicrous case in point came to my notice in the person of an Alsatian who had done all that popular clothing and a thoroughly native haircut could do to look American, but he preserved an alien mustache! Of this relic of his unregenerate Europeanism he proudly related how a compatriot had refused to go about with him, because 'every one can see by your mustache that we are foreigners'!"[33] Boyd's amusing anecdote illuminates the logics of visibility related to allegiance. The story suggests that despite the invisibility of nationalistic emotions, false loyalty could be discerned through some external markers—even by immigrants themselves. The mustache is the tell that not only exposed the true identity of the protagonist but also revealed the foreignness of his friend. The drive toward uniformity—dressing and acting in ways that connoted Americanism—did not assure loyalty. Instead, for Boyd, Americanism was not so easy to attain.

The infection metaphor delimited publicity as a primary concern of Americanization. True Americans appeared in public as such. Yet, public presentations did not assure internal devotion. As Walter Lippmann noted of Americanization projects in 1922, "Americanization, for example, is superficially at least the substitution of American for European stereotypes . . . the peasant . . . is taught by Americanization to see the landlord and employer according to American standards. This constitutes a change of mind, which is, in effect, when the inoculation succeeds, a change in vision. His eye sees differently."[34] In Lippmann's estimation, the work of Americanization was one of sight: training the eye to look for superficial standards of Americanism. Lippmann decried the artifice involved in such visual perception, in allowing the mind to be governed by stereotypes. The infection metaphor marks this paradoxical association. Immigrants were seen as potentially contaminated bodies that required conspicuous displays of Americanism. These exhibitions did not shore up the status of loyalty. The presumed need for Americanization underscored the ambiguity of patriotic signs. Infection as a significant metaphor for nationalism induced the American people to police the borders of this ambiguity by scrutinizing others. Despite the invisibility of the immigrant's misdirected and treacherous national spirit, something about this infection was supposedly recognizable to the public. The proper American subject could find the means to deliver a diagnosis of the disease. With few absolutes for determining the nature of one's national ties, the true American patrolled the populace by knowing an authentic American when she saw one.

Motivated by the difficulty of determining internal emotions, Americans vigilantly patrolled immigrants to diagnose their potential for perfidy. It is against this backdrop that Americanization experts orchestrated celebratory events that attempted to inculcate patriotic sentiment in attendees and render visible their devotion to the nation.

Americanization Day and Flag Day

The paradoxical logic structuring the relationship between visibility and invisibility induced Americanizers to provide proof of the immigrant's hidden affections through public display. Americanizers labored diligently to locate superior assimilation methods that might easily improve the sympathies of the subject. To confirm that these methods were effective, Americanization experts employed common visual forms to illuminate how these events changed students. Authorities selected a set of particularly nationalistic rituals and pageantry. Public parades and celebrations emphasized hyperpatriotic exhibitions, including immigrants draped in red, white, and blue; appearances by Uncle Sam; parades down main street; the singing of national anthems; and more. In these events, Americanization exercises were not simply focused on extracting the allegiances of pupils, but also on rendering visible the passion of patriotism. These Americanization practices presented a figural relationship between public celebration and the immigrant's rehabilitated spirit: her emotional fidelity became concrete via exhibitions of patriotism. Exemplary case studies in this regard are the 1915 July 4th Americanization Day, the 1916 June 14th Flag Day, and repetitions of these holidays in subsequent years. While today these celebrations are well established, many of the activities performed on these dates were formulized during the early twentieth century. The rhetorical impact of these celebrations did not simply heighten the exhibition of patriotism, but narrowed and codified the evidentiary status of certain patriotic rituals.

The visual work of these parades and celebrations can be productively explored through the trope of metalepsis. Metalepsis is referred to as a trope of resignification wherein a word or trope is re-created into a novel meaning. According to Cummings, Quintilian understood metalepsis to shift a word or meaning to another via remote or distant association.[35] In this instance, Americanization Day and Flag Day attempted to transmute the symbolic associations of patriotic rituals for those who were ostensibly unmarked by Americanism. These holidays demonstrated the success of Americanization in galvanizing the nationalistic emotions of immigrants. Shifting the symbolism of these patriotic celebrations thus was an attempt to affix patriotism as a recognizable quality.

One of the reasons that Flag Day and Americanization Day are important to the visuality of patriotism is the popularity of both these events nationally. The Wilson administration and the NAC worked in tandem to promote these events as significant demonstrations of nationalism and the success of Americanization. Motivated by President Wilson's address in Philadelphia inviting immigrants to become "thorough Americans," Frances Kellor, president of the Committee for Immigrants in America (later the NAC), speedily organized Americanization Day festivities in cities throughout the nation.[36] With the support of mayors, civic groups, churches, and schools, at least 107 cities celebrated Americanization Day in 1915, and many more cities took up the holiday in subsequent years.[37] Wilson worked diligently to support both programs. For instance, he marched at the front of Washington, DC's Americanization Day parade, an image that graced the front page of newspapers across the country.[38] Carrying an American flag, Wilson's boater hat and white pants allowed him to stand apart from his cabinet members, who wore top hats and tails (see figure 4). Dressed more as an onlooker than commander-in-chief, Wilson led the parade as though he was one of the people. Visually, the image and its circulation indicated the president's support for the event and for the American people with whom his dress aligned him. This holiday was to be understood as an important moment for defining the meaning of Americanism for the people. Americanism was delineated by the public exhibition of one's innermost feelings of loyalty.

More pointedly, Americanization Day attempted to concretize those emblems that could demonstrate the patriotism of new citizens. Parades, speeches, choral ensembles, dances, and other patriotic celebrations took place on Americanization Day. Whereas these acts were already nationalistic, they now stood in metaleptically for the patriotism of immigrants. Selected performances and symbols represented nationalism;

President Wilson marching at the front of Washington, DC's Flag Day Parade in 1916. Courtesy of the Library of Congress, Prints and Photographs Division, photograph by Harris and Ewing [LC-DIG-hec-06986].

Independence Day parade in New York City [between 1910 and 1915]. Courtesy of the Library of Congress, Prints and Photographs Division, George Grantham Bain Collection [LC-DIG-ggbain-09531].

they became indicators of the patriotic feelings of immigrants. Though symbols of the homeland appeared at these events, the most prominent emblems emphasized the Americanism of immigrants. Kellor promoted this day as a holiday to honor newly naturalized citizens, distributing thousands of placards and posters with the slogan "Many Peoples, One Nation."[39] In line with Kellor's claim, ethnic groups often deployed tokens of their homeland—flags, dress, and dances—but markers of allegiance to the United States appeared far more frequently. In the Indianapolis Americanization Parade of 1918, immigrants not only donned ethnic costumes and constructed floats referencing their national history but also carried American flags, rode patriotic floats, and those of German and Hungarian ethnicity "wore red, white, and blue sashes in the parade that carried the inscription 'America First.'"[40] Old Glory, Uncle Sam, and other "sacred emblems" of the American nation littered the festivities (see figure 5).[41] As a case in point, a photograph of native Swiss walking in the parade highlights the importance of American traditions. The U.S. flag is the most pronounced symbol of the group. While some marchers wear folk costuming, the lead participant is dressed in a suit with a straw hat while another person wears a boater's hat. Throughout the parade, the veneration of selected American symbols outstripped any nod to a nostalgic vision of the homeland.

Americanism became redefined through these rituals as a superficial mode of representation. Immigrants and the larger public were being taught what signs counted as indicators of patriotism. On a broader scale, the goal was to create a recognizable national culture. Given that Americanism was defined through its emotional qualities, these celebrations formulized how patriotism was manifest in a heterogeneous population. For many progressives, *all* Americans could prove their feelings through allegiant exhibitions. Yet, the demand for such publicity was an outcrop of fears that immigrants might infect the populace with foreign sentiment. Americanization was to fashion a new visual rubric of nationalism, a metaleptic transformation of commonplace symbols into a set of clear, distinguishable markers. For immigrants in particular, the goal was to highlight the ways they might validate their Americanism. Without such demonstrations, commentators maintained that the depths of homeland sympathy would remain invisible.

To wit, many of these events emphasized America's revolutionary history and the coming war as celebratory themes that might prompt immigrants to unhinge themselves from old-world allegiances. Channeling the legacy of the Revolution to new ends marked a tropological shift in the figuration of Americanism. For participants in Americanization Day and Flag Day, the Revolutionary War was not simply a moment of independence, but rather the coming war and the Revolutionary War were tied together by the need for unification. The Great War was not cause for lamentation, even for a heterogeneous nation, but the time to draw together. Just as the Revolution was simultaneously a moment of separation and unification, for immigrants, the Revolution demarcated the need to extract oneself from the old country and unite as a nation.

The visual symbols of these holidays reinforced both the revolutionary history of the United States and the preparedness needed for the Great War. First, organizers and presenters ensured that participants in Americanization Day and Flag Day understood Old Glory as a hallmark of America's rebellious spirit. Wilson's Flag Day address in 1917 used the flag to connect the spirit of the Revolutionary War to the mission in Europe. Commenting on the American Revolution and the need to support yet another overthrow of tyranny, Wilson contended that the flag "shall wear a new luster" and that "once more we shall make good with our lives and fortunes the great faith to which we were born."[42] As with Wilson's statement, the symbol of the flag was re-created into something new—it was transformed by the war. For immigrants at these events, such a statement underscored America's revolutionary origins and couched the symbolism of the flag as imbued with the defiant spirit of democracy. Wilson framed the flag as an emblem of democracy, embodying the will of the people to dismantle the violence of tyranny. Indeed, Flag Day celebrations in 1916 were synonymously named Preparedness Parades. The title accented the nation's readiness for war. Immigrant attendees were invited to see the flag as a battle cry for democracy, a marker of American exceptionalism that encouraged the dissolution of European loyalties. While reaction to such a message likely varied dramatically among audiences, the rhetorical work of these events declared the war as that which demanded loyalty so as to end the tyranny of despots.

More generally, the flag was metaleptically resituated as a symbol that injected immigrants with patriotic sentiment and inaugurated a global change. Metalepsis as a layered figure predicated on distant associations is significant to the rhetorical machinations of the flag. The flag was selected as a symbol that could both infect immigrants and demonstrate their own nationalism. The slippage between cause and effect here is metaleptical insofar as it transgresses the initial logic of infection. Immigrants were not simply carriers of a foreign virus, but could become hosts for a new vision of nationalism. For instance, event organizers distributed miniature flags to immigrant attendees on Americanization Day and Flag Day as tokens of patriotic virtue. In some communities celebrating Americanization Day, small children clad in red, white, and blue fashioned a human star spangled banner as they sang patriotic anthems.[43] P. P. Claxton, the commissioner for education, proposed that the Americanization Day program should include recently naturalized citizens reciting the Pledge of Allegiance as the American flag was unfurled behind them. Scores of articles in newspapers across the country indicate that many celebrations implemented his plan.[44] While the Pledge of Allegiance was not federally legislated until the 1940s, the use of this verse alongside the opening of the flag highlights the metaleptic association between specific visual spectacles and a broader national change. The pageantry of immigrants reciting the Pledge of Allegiance in front of Old Glory was an attempt not simply to continue the project of Americanization, but to advertise the success of its emotional reorientation. The symbols of Americanism were to expand to new bodies and thereby provide the possibility of a more inclusive nation. As Claxton argued, Americanization Day was a "patriotic call to all citizens, American-born and foreign-born alike, adults and children, to rally to American ideals, purposes and common interests of many people united into one nation."[45] To suggest that a holiday in which immigrants were featured as visual lessons for the entire nation, then, underscores the idea that the selection and amplification of certain displays of Americanism could herald the success of Americanization.

Experts attempted to secure the evidentiary and transformative status of selected emblems of Americanism through other elements of celebration. Here, the push to recalibrate markers of patriotism as proof of Americanization metaleptically highlights the slippage between the remote associations of cause and effect. Pointedly, patriotic ritual became situated both as affecting emotions and as demonstrative of internal change. For example, the singing of patriotic songs on both Americanization Day and Flag Day were used to inculcate patriotism while simultaneously displaying immigrants' loyalties to the new nation. Newspaper accounts in major cities throughout the country detailed immigrants singing national anthems on Americanization Day, including "America," "The Star-Spangled Banner," and "The Battle Hymn of the Republic."[46] Patriotic songs were similarly performed on Flag Day. In Washington, DC, the Marine Corps band played a number of nationalistic anthems that inspired singing in nearby marchers.[47] Perhaps the best example of such patriotic clamor came from a "little regiment of Italian boys" in Syracuse who wrote their own hymn for Americanization Day, including the following closing verses:

> America, we sing of thee, Adopted country, great and free. To thee, not to the native fatherlands, We give our lives, our work, our brains, our hands. America, O land of blessed peace, Our love to thee shall never, never cease, And for thy weal—if need there be—With hymns of joy, we'll die for thee.[48]

Through this creative expression, these young men clearly enunciated their own belonging, their loyalty and utter dedication to the United States. The zeal of certain patriotic pageantry both invented and presented the mode of allegiance most desired by Americanization experts: devotion to the ideals of the United States and the rejection of old-world ties. In so doing, these celebrations attempted to present patriotic acts as proof of an emotional transfiguration even as these events were designed to shift emotions in their enactment.

Marching and other forms of ceremony proved yet another method through which immigrants learned Americanism and evinced their allegiance. These exhibitions worked not only to instill American ideals, but also to *display* the immigrant's body as unified—marching in step with the nation. In New York City, one hundred and twenty-five thousand Flag Day marchers crossed under an enormous electric sign emblazoned with the words "Absolute and Unqualified Loyalty to Our Country."[49]

As opposed to some July 4th celebrations renowned for deadly, illegal fireworks, 1915's Americanization Day was publicized as a "safe and sane" celebration filled with patriotic pomp.[50] Through these exercises, immigrants verified their fidelity to the republic. Moreover, concretized visual forms of Americanism formulized signs of emotional nationalism. Once immigrants stepped alongside their American brothers and sisters, their belonging was made visible: swathed in red, white, and blue, parading with other Americans, they could experience the joy of national belonging and simultaneously confirm their devotion.

While these events attempted to sway the affections of attendees and to reveal their sentiments to the public, these holidays simultaneously demarcated how patriotism should be understood by the general populace. Thus, the goal was not simply to reform the spirits of immigrants, but to address the public in such a way that Americanism in immigrants could become recognizable. If Americanization agents could circumscribe the registers of nationalism, they might better demonstrate their efficacy. To be sure, Flag Day and Americanization Day were not the only events designed to reshape the nationalistic attachments of attendees. Americanization experts also developed community-singing programs and public choral ensembles to spark the patriotic feelings of those new to the United States. While choral singing ensembles were used to shift the feelings of immigrants, they also highlight the contradictory rhetorical logic of these events. Namely, immigrants publicly singing patriotic songs did not simply show immigrants as becoming Americans but also underscored the need for Americanization. One of the interesting features of metalepsis is that it often stretches the figural work of transformation such that it is often referred to as a failed figure. Thus, this trope can help explicate the paradox of visuality at stake in the evidentiary status of public Americanization celebrations.

Community Singing and Americanization

A number of Americanization Day and Flag Day activities incorporated public singing and choral ensembles as part of their patriotic pageantry. The inclusion of public singing at these celebrations was no accident.

During the war years and shortly after, preparedness advocates and Americanization experts promoted community singing as a way to meld the disparate populace into a unified whole. These experts extended an older understanding of community singing that began in the 1820s, wherein choral ensembles were a form of civics education particularly important during times of war.[51] For Americanization experts, community singing attempted to extract patriotism from immigrants by drawing on the sensations delivered by the act of vocalization. At the same time, choral ensembles, such as the regiment of Italian boys from Syracuse, offered identifiable proof of immigrants' loyalties. While community singing was thought to translate a love of music into a recognizable form of nationalism, these events marked ethnic populations as potentially un-American. Immigrants who participated in community singing and other Americanization festivities became situated as individuals that needed Americanization, even as their participation attempted to prove their devotion to the United States. In particular, I argue that singing was described as a potentially transformative act that forecast national belonging as an imagined potential future. Immigrants did not become patriots in the moment of utterance. Rather, community singing encouraged immigrants to long for a future in which they would be enfolded into the American nation. At the same time, the act of singing accented the chorus as external to this bright future—as fundamentally not American. In this way, these performances operated as a form of visual metalepsis by breaching the boundary between the fiction of Americanization and the reality of exclusion.

During the early part of the twentieth century, community-singing proponents contended that public choral ensembles promised a disparate nation the solution to fashioning unity. To broaden popular enthusiasm for music and music education, women's clubs advanced music programs in settlement houses, public schools, and at community events.[52] As World War I began to occupy public conversations, community singing was declared a technique that might sustain the fighting spirit of the troops, develop the patriotism of communities, and teach the newly immigrated vital principles for civic investment. The National Committee on Army and Navy Camp Music and the Commission on Training Camp Activities sponsored choral ensembles as a method of teaching English to soldiers and boosting troop morale.⁵³ Community-singing advocates maintained that music seduced the affections of the choralist more than traditional public address, reasoned argument, or instruction. While sparse historical record creates difficulties in accurately assessing the extent to which organized community-singing programs for immigrants actually materialized, Weaver Pangburn, division secretary for War Camp Community Service, argued in 1920 that "Community singing has swept the country from the Atlantic to the Pacific."⁵⁴ Hundreds of newspaper, magazine, and journal articles from this period attest to a plethora of public singing activities provided for immigrants. Americanization jubilees, liberty choirs, public concerts, music appreciation classes, factory singing programs, civic choral ensembles, and Americanization dramas are simply a few of the means through which public singing was employed to acculturate new immigrants. Supporters pledged that community-singing programs would allow immigrants to sing their way to a truer citizenship. For example, Pangburn contended that these performances were central to melting "civic indifference" given that singing was a mode of "Americanization that will teach American ideas, customs, standards of living, democratic traditions, and social life as well as the English language."⁵⁵

Set in opposition to acculturation activities focused on naturalization classes and English literacy, community singing was advertised on the notion that music could uniquely solicit patriotic ardor. For example, Anne Shaw Faulkner wrote in the preface of her widely distributed songbook, *Americanization Songs* (1920), that the war "awakened" the people to the notion that we "loved to sing," and as such we must employ our cherished music "as the strongest link in our great chain of Americanization."⁵⁶ Here, the immigrant's assimilation hinged upon citizenship and national belonging as an intimate emotional investment in the nation—a venture robustly gained through song. Similarly, Woodrow Wilson's daughter Margaret traveled the country organizing patriotic choral ensembles. She heralded singing as soliciting the national affections of those engaged in the enterprise. In an article from the *Dallas Morning News* from 1917, she asserted that music was essential to the nation's unity and war efforts: "When we bring our people together in great groups for mass singing; when we encourage singing among the men who make up the American fighting forces, we are freeing a vital agent for the eventual Americanization of all our people."⁵⁷ Margaret Wilson's statement suggested that singing redirected the immigrant's emotions: the singer learned to act in concert by feeling as one with fellow Americans.

Advocates for this practice articulated the origin of singing's matchless suasory capacity on the universal appeal of music. In an article from 1919 in the *New York Times*, music was described as the "common language of mankind."⁵⁸ This common language would supposedly allow disparate peoples to unite under the language of rhythm and meter—a dialect that ostensibly transcended every possible division. The universal language of music similarly appeared in a Victrola print advertisement from 1919 wherein the spirit of the immigrant was coaxed by music. A record of patriotic music played on a Victrola was described as a "common ground" and the "most natural approach to the foreigner in welding him into the spirit of true Americanism."⁵⁹ Simply by listening to a patriotic tune, the immigrant could develop the strength of her allegiance and potentially become a fully devoted American citizen. As such, this company sought to expand the community-singing movement to provide an "immeasurable good in this wholesome movement of Americanization."⁶⁰ While Victrola's motivations were largely monetary, its promotion of Americanization was not assured to increase profit. Importantly, the advertisement employed a populist appeal, claiming music was the location through which the people might transcend difference.

Americanization authorities attempted to evoke allegiance to the United States through the emotions singing and music inspired. As championed by journalist Charles Rosebault in 1920, "The problem is how best to bring the alien to citizenship and to such interest in the affairs of the country as to assure his irrevocable allegiance."⁶¹ Experts posited singing as soliciting loyalty by virtue of the sympathetic relationships between music, love, and the nation. If the singer could access a deep emotion during the midst of his song, that intensity might be directed toward the United States. Community-singing advocates vowed that accomplished in wide measure, such emotional work could fashion a love of country among all newcomers. As written in the *New York Times* (1919), community singing was the best mechanism for unifying the United States, a harmony "upon which depends our strength as a nation."⁶²

Americanization musicologists hoped they might compel allegiance from newcomers; yet, much of this ambition was merely an optimism mortgaged in the future. Singing as an Americanization activity predicted belonging and unity as a possibility—a projection that promised the immigrant the sensation of comfort once her national ardor was properly managed. Notice the tenor of a 1918 article describing music settlement work with immigrants: "Through the gift of music, the power of the spirit is being translated into forms in which it can be of practical service in the doing of innumerable things that have got to be done if the nation is to survive and triumph; forms of right living as well, which can do what nothing else except music can do. Hate and greed separate, but music inspires and unites hearts."[63] Here, choral ensembles are in the process of building a bright future, of uniting hearts and allowing the nation to triumph. Melody and the promise of "right living" and national unity it offers became a possibility actualized through the fruitful work of music. This tone continued in a passage from *The Outlook*. The author wrote that the growth of community singing "is of good augury for the future" given that "people act less on reasoned convictions than on the spur of emotional or instinctive attitudes."[64] The passage elaborated, "Americans, for example, will act as a Nation less through thinking alike (if this were possible or even desirable) than through feeling in sympathy, feeling themselves one people," a sympathy fashioned "more directly" through "the common making of music."[65] In this passage, music generates the possibilities of a prosperous future and the emotional connections of nationalism. Much like visual education techniques, such rhetorical framing articulated a pregnant time and distance between the immigrant's present status and the future possibility of belonging.

Similar promises appeared in the songs selected for Americanization performances, wherein the immigrant's current anthems pledged future belonging. Common songs used for Americanization festivities included "America," "The Star-Spangled Banner," and "Columbia, Gem of the Ocean." Robert Branham argues in his work on the song "America" that these selections invited immigrants to sing in the first person and translate the emotions aroused from singing into a claim of attachment for the United States. Yet, as this author notes, the claim to possession remained fraught with alienation. The first-person narratives of these anthems often failed to resonate for the newly immigrated.[66] Lines such as "my native country" and "land where my fathers died," and, for some, singing in English, widened the gap between the immigrant's story and national history.[67]

Less frequently, immigrants were invited to sing in their own language or express songs from their homelands in English. All of these tunes, however, were couched as important to melding the immigrant's spirit to the United States. For example, Faulkner wrote in her songbook (1920) that immigrant songs "had already been assimilated by Americans."[68] For those that had not, Faulkner's book arranged them in English to use music as a "universal language" of Americanization.[69] Thus, Americanization authorities assured immigrants that even songs from their homeland would one day feel "natural" as a part of the United States' hymnal. Concomitantly, immigrants might deduce that they could achieve that same natural comfort through the power of song. They were to engage in community singing because it aired a romantic anticipation proclaiming that one day all these songs were rightfully theirs as citizens.

Much of the publicity at stake in these choral performances rested on the same logic as Americanization Day and Flag Day festivities. These aesthetic activities were claimed to be particularly effective for transforming the hearts of immigrants. Yet, publicly performing and demonstrating such effectiveness aimed to convince the American public that Americanization had indeed changed the emotional nationalism of immigrants. Singing the national anthems of the new country worked by simultaneously imbibing and exhibiting the principles of Americanism.

The performances of community singing highlight the metaleptic contradiction at the heart of Americanization. While Branham notes that immigrant choral ensembles enunciated a conflict for the singer, the public was also beholden to an incongruous understanding of the immigrant's faithfulness. In their extended treatise on the song "America," Branham and Hartnett aver that immigrant children's choral ensembles in the 1830s demonstrated the success of cultivating "civic virtue" via music.[70] Yet, for the Americanization movement of the early twentieth century, the demonstrable effectiveness of public singing was strained. Namely, while celebratory modes of Americanization aimed to inspire a love for country that might be publicly identifiable, the presumed need for Americanization undermined the terms of identification. Though the immigrant presented as a committed American, the necessary publicity of these events created a metaleptical substitution that breached the original signification. The immigrant figured as a potential American disrupted the idea she was currently an American.

Analyzing the public pageantry of Americanization through metalepsis indicates the complexity of the project. Scholars have long considered metalepsis a difficult figure to grasp. For Quintilian, metalepsis is a "movement from one trope to another."[71] Later scholars have suggested that metalepsis is a replacement trope or a layering of figures.[72] Importantly, much of the scholarship on metalepsis admits that it is a challenging figure to understand because it often works by stretching rhetorical figures to the "breaking point."[73] Gérard Genette employs this breach when he suggests that in narrative, metalepsis is the rupture of different levels of the story and the interplay between fiction and reality.[74] Here, the visuality of representation stretched the rhetorical scheme to the breaking point. Immigrants could not simply be presented as Americanized, but rather that very publicity underscored un-Americanism. Warranted by the notion that nationalism was a patent emotional infection, the need to display the Americanized newcomer publicly fractured the myth that Americanization could fashion Americanism. Indeed, the simple representation of immigrants as Americans was overlaid with the anxiety that their emotional fidelity to the nation remained suspicious.

More pointedly, the performative contradiction between the hope of belonging and manifest exclusion was made abundantly plain in community-singing activities. That is, immigrants were asked to sing publicly to assure the community that their bodies and souls labored to experience appropriate feelings of patriotism. Yet, singing was not proof that immigrants *were* Americans, but rather that they were in the process of *becoming* Americans—a progression that forecast inclusion as yet to come. Community singing therefore exacerbated the concern that immigrants were not yet assimilated.

A 1918 article in the *New York Times* exemplifies the paradoxical status of singing as evidence of Americanization. The author discussed a congregation of Spanish worshipers at Calvary Episcopal Church in Manhattan and the patriotic songs they sang in Spanish during services, including "America." The author noted,

> The effect both artistically and emotionally is fine—a real show of Americanization and patriotism portrayed in a way that carries meaning to the participants. Here is a body, speaking a foreign language given opportunity to express itself patriotically. Too often social workers make the mistake of believing their communities Americanized, because their people sing the national hymns of the country, when in nine cases out of ten the words are meaningless and the spirit equally so.[75]

This author is one of the few discussing community singing who praised immigrants singing in their own tongue (though significantly, the parishioners' first language was not German). Yet, despite the author's acclaim for the feelings espoused by immigrants singing "America," the writer insisted that more often than not, such expressions of Americanism were inauthentic. In other words, even though singing patriotic songs attempted to demonstrate fidelity, the author averred that most of these performances were meaningless: immigrants had failed to develop a commanding love for the United States. Here, singing could be, and was commonly read as, an empty act that did not reveal a true spirit in the chorus. The paradoxical status of recognizing Americanization in immigrants is thus laid plain in this passage. Immigrants were invited to display their devotion, yet for onlookers, such displays could not ensure their affections (or infections) were properly oriented.

Even for sympathetic community-singing experts, there were a number of pitfalls in the lessons of community singing, all of which circumscribed the possibility of proving Americanization. An associate professor of music at Harvard University, Archibald T. Davison, asserted in a 1923 edition of *The Playground* that community singing was a failed activity that had not yet yielded aesthetic or civic success. Davison was a stalwart proponent of musical education who authored several educational works on reforming musical curricula.[76] For Davison, the American pursuit of community singing was "like the gambler, who, in the face of almost certain loss will risk one more turn of the wheel, or like the hero who, though he attempt the impossible, will give to the limit of his strength notwithstanding."[77] His reasons for such failure were numerous, including the American inability to appreciate the serious study of music, an infatuation with mediated music (e.g., the phonograph, player piano, and radiophone), and the songs selected for performance. Ultimately, Davison insisted that while immigrants came to the United States with a love of song and a "will to sing," the aesthetic work of community-singing programs floundered at "generating good emotions and of stimulating right thinking."[78] Though Davison argued that certain tactical choices might correct such obstacles, his discussion belied the point. He maintained that the songs selected for Americanization were "primarily physical," rather than emotional. He offered no standards to measure the difference, nor mentioned what selections could inculcate correct emotional commitments. Instead, the paradoxical status of recognizing Americanization turned not on false performance but rather on the idea that emotions were challenging to rouse with current instruments. Nevertheless, the enigmatic need to substantiate such emotional change remained. For Americanization experts, proving the emotions of immigrants had been transformed remained a difficult, if not insurmountable, task.

The tensions between the individual singer, the singing ensemble, and the nation as a whole fueled the paradoxical status of evidencing Americanization. In this simplest sense, singing in a chorus was meant to demonstrate one's fidelity to larger national virtues. For Americanization experts, presenting a group of immigrants as Americanized—warranted by their crooning of national anthems—homogenized the individuals of the group such that they seemed unified. Read as a figural substitution for the nationalistic goals of Americanization, the association rendered new citizens as part and parcel of the nation writ large. Yet, the necessary publicity of these demonstrations begs the evidentiary status of such an association. What that performance means cannot be secured so easily. Judith Butler and Gayatri Chakravorty Spivak comment on the ambiguity of a similar, contemporary occasion in *Who Sings the Nation State?* For them, nationalistic singing is a plural act claiming belonging in the nation yet professing that belonging through a performative contradiction: namely, that the immigrant's status as outsider is abundantly plain in a chorus signifying equality.[79] In other words, the plural act of enunciating belonging to a collectivity simultaneously highlights the separation of those reaching toward membership. Music reformers and educators labored to find a form of music that might sway immigrants to sing the national anthem as their own. Yet, as Spivak argues, the national anthem "does not carry within itself a performative promise of this new thinking of rights to come"; it is "in principle untranslatable."[80] The song's public performance by immigrants marks the aporia between belonging and manifest exclusion.

Given this tension, Americanization singing did not tender a veritable path for verifying belonging, but rather operated by asking immigrants to endure in the hazy location of uncertainty. Public discourses encouraged immigrants to embrace the promise of Americanization. That promise was premised on a strategic ambiguity: claims toward nationalization, such as community singing, reified immigrants' necessary exclusion from the nation. Newcomers were entreated to work toward an emotional union with the nation—to feel comfort and love in a new home—and yet the display of emotional commitments simultaneously marked them as not yet American. Immigrants were distinguished as external to the nation and yet asked to reach toward the sentiments of patriotism with loving piety. Americanization, thus, offered citizenship as a form of longing, not as a goal that might someday be attained fully. The terms of actual membership could rarely be realized as the process itself demanded that immigrants and the community publicly recognize a fundamental, emotional difference to proceed with the process of Americanization. In so doing, immigrants lived within the scene of possibility, bargaining for a future of comfort and belonging while recognizing that status remained difficult to attain. In this way, patriotic rituals such as parades and community singing were a visual form of metalepsis: the presentation of successful Americanization was undermined by an inability to prove internal devotion. Nevertheless, in publicly singing the national anthem as a method of Americanization, immigrants were asked to imagine a future of salubrious citizenship and yet remain spellbound in the ambiguous, adoring scene of that desire.

Failure as Productive

In the January 1923 issue of *Recreation*, popular author and speaker Dr. Frank Crane wrote, "'A singing nation is a happy nation,' and surely the first business of a state is to make its people happy."[81] Adapting the "pursuit of happiness" for his own ends, Crane promoted music as an emotional force for democracy, allowing singers to achieve considerable benefits for "unifying the mind of the people, in brightening their lives, and in relieving the whole commonplace of our industrial civilization."[82] Crane contended that singing served these ends by allowing the person to participate in an imaginative and energizing activity. In line with those choral proponents who suggested that national harmony was central to the war effort, Crane framed music as a soothing influence on the nerves of those living in the tumults of modernity. The power of song relayed the emotions of love and joy to modern life. Crane relied on the same paradoxical assumptions as Americanization enthusiasts. As he concluded the piece, he wrote, "A person might attend concerts and grand opera til three-score years and ten and not know much about music or get the soul of music in him. But he could not habitually sing in chorus or perform in an orchestra without absorbing a real knowledge of music and being inoculated with its beneficial results."[83] For Crane, the techniques of music were important to understanding its emotional effect. Some forms of demonstration proved more recognizable than others. Yet, even while Crane delineated the difference between listening and singing, he nevertheless stretched the association between emotion and music, relying on a strategic ambiguity in his assessment—the same failed figural relationship between display and emotion that structured the pursuit of Americanization. Even years after the armistice, the democratic ethos of music remained beholden to the paradox of public appearance.

Americanization Day, Flag Day, and community-singing advocates proclaimed these celebratory activities as evidence of the success of Americanization. These events became situated as innovative Americanization tools because they allowed immigrants to prove the intensity of their patriotism. At the same time, these spectacles publicly presented immigrants as engaging the process of Americanization and reaching toward fidelity to the republic. Up against concerns that loyalty in immigrants was not easily visible—the notion that ethnic populations were infected with a devotion to another country—these festivities aimed to assuage public anxieties. As such, these celebrations were positioned as rhetorical events that could shift the passions of immigrants and redress public concerns about difference. Practices of Americanization worked by identifying visual displays of Americanness that immigrants might perform to render themselves intelligible as loyal citizens. Participants in Americanization rituals learned to show certain emblems and practices of patriotism. All the while, the presumed need for these publicly marked forms of patriotism undercut the terms of belonging.

Nevertheless, the Americanization project proved productive insofar as invitations to special recognition for immigrants iterated the command that one's status as an American was never quite secure, but appropriate modes of display and national sentiment promised the possibility of legitimacy. In this way, those participating in Americanization were entreated to engage in Americanization to demonstrate their commitment to becoming Americans. Specifically, community singing and public pageantry pledged to immigrants that membership, fellowship, and inclusion would come. They would locate a brighter future just around the corner. Yet, both the covenant promised within Americanization discourses and the supposed necessity of patriotic celebration arranged the terms of belonging as a yearning for a future that could rarely be attained. Instead, immigrants were asked to labor in the ambiguous realm of possibility. The visuality of Americanization, particularly as manifest in these patriotic celebrations, reinvigorated the fantasy that the foreign-born might pass as loyal, unhyphenated Americans. Thus, it matters little if the efficacy of the Americanization project completely assimilated immigrants or truly instilled the emotions requisite to citizenship. Rather, the project "worked" if it inspired the desire to become Americanized, to engage in the performance that proved one had cast off her affections for the homeland and embraced the passionate performance of becoming American.

In part, the paradox of visuality rested on the turn to emotional understandings of citizenship. In keeping with the modern reinvention of citizenship in the liberal-democratic tradition, citizenship during the early twentieth century became more ethereal than homogeneous modes of identification. As Hariman and Lucaites write, "Liberal-democratic citizenship is of necessity ambiguously defined, loosely enforced, relatively abstract and, therefore, a questionable basis for collective action."[84] In keeping with this change, Americanization crusaders and progressives sought a more flexible understanding of citizenship, one in which Americanism could be defined through emotional or other abstract principles rather than strict material bases. Nevertheless, the use of visual performances to demonstrate the emotional commitments of immigrants placed a strange burden on the Americanization project. Such moves are not purely liberal-democratic in their ambiguity, but attempt to connect the material foundations of citizenship to more profound modes of belonging. Nevertheless, the vacillation between recognizable, visual proof and the undecidability of internal emotions generated the pursuit of Americanization.

As made plain in parades, festivals, and singing ensembles, the visual proof of Americanization marked a certain kind of productive rhetorical failure. Metalepsis is often called a "failed figure," or that which may be best understood as an attempt at rhetorical ornament gone wrong.[85] In the simplest sense, rituals of Americanism failed to illustrate exactly how Americanization succeeded in transforming immigrants. Yet, here the metaleptical relay between the immigrant as future citizen and the possibilities of the present is not merely a failed rhetorical experiment. Instead, this contradiction or breach generates the need for unified and continual displays of patriotism. In this use, metalepsis is a generative figure that fuels Americanization publicity. These events did not simply fail at their purpose, but provoked the frantic and overwhelming need for public displays of Americanism.

A telling example in this regard appears in an address delivered by Mr. Thomas Woods Stevens, a theater director from the Carnegie Institute of Technology in Pittsburgh who turned his talents to Americanization.[86] At the 1919 Bureau of Education Americanization Conference, Stevens explained to his audience how they might enlist immigrants in theater projects. In particular, he advised avoiding Americanization pageants that only lauded American virtues in favor of honoring symbols and figures of immigrants' homelands. Despite the director's careful exegesis on the effectivity of such sympathetic pageantry, he noted that often Americans themselves did not recognize the virtue of these plays. As one Americanization committee member put it while watching a scene honoring Italian history, "thought that WOP would never quit."[87] Even more revealing is the reaction of an audience member at the Americanization conference. Despite Stevens's admonition against jingoism, one audience member objected:

Our experience with the league of foreign-born citizens has been that the spectacles or productions of the pupils or the members of the classes should be more of an American nature—such chauvinistic spectacles as those are not likely to arouse any strong Americanization feeling. I do not mean to say that nationalistic feelings have to be eradicated, but such pageants are not very productive, and will not tend to bring out those emotions or those feelings that we are striving for and which we would like.[88]

As is apparent in this example, while Americanization proclaimed to instill the feelings of patriotism in immigrants, the crux of this audience member's objection is that the form of "chauvinistic" patriotic display *still* did not produce an Americanism that could assuage the concerns of the broader public. In fact, she was answering the query posed by Stevens, "how best to achieve this getting together [national unity] and the suppression of the idea of a foreign-born group."[89] In short, while visual methods of Americanization attempted to wrench from immigrants a love for their new home, those forms of display did not dispel fears of adulteration. Instead, the vacillation between public displays of Americanism and the ambiguity of their connotation continued to drive the pursuit of Americanization.

In some ways, the public performance of patriotic rituals only amplified the disparities between immigrant and supposed native. Holiday and choral-ensemble organizers insisted on a certain set of patriotic displays as both successful pedagogies and veritable methods of diagnosis. The presumption of infection conscripted immigrants to capitulate to these performances. It is the paradox of this visual logic that aids in understanding the zealot-like crusade for Americanization. If nothing else, Americanization projects were dramatically successful in demarcating those rituals of Americanism that were recognizable to the public, even if the meaning of those forms remained in dispute. Importantly, though, Americanization did not fail in its ambitions simply because programs did not produce naturalization or assimilation in large numbers. Instead, Americanization succeeded by creating the conditions through which Americans were recognizable as such. It is the work of recognizability that defines how Americanization changed public culture writ large.

CHAPTER FIVE

Recognizing Americans through Scouting

———•◆•———

In her 1918 handbook on the management of girls' clubs, Helen Ferris suggested methods for forming clubs among immigrant girls. She directed readers, presumably club leaders and members, to find a "foreign girl" with whom you may "get acquainted with most easily."[1] Ferris continued: "Ask her to introduce you to other foreign girls who she thinks would like to make the summer useful by learning more about America, by learning how to do something, and by having good times."[2] For Ferris, girls' clubs aided the acculturation of the "foreign girl" to the American way of life. Ferris was not alone in this belief, as many period pedagogues contended that children's clubs proved a tremendous force in the Americanization of immigrant youth.[3] The Americanization work of girls' clubs, including two popular clubs during this period, the Girl Scouts and Camp Fire Girls—the primary case studies upon which I draw—encouraged immigrant children to learn English as well as American traditions and customs. To do so, both organizations employed visual and performative rhetorical pedagogies. These lessons invited immigrant members to act as Americans through patriotic rituals such as reciting the Pledge of Allegiance, learning the history and care of the American flag, and the application of domestic skills such as understanding proper nutrition for children and infants, and maintaining high standards of household cleanliness. Americanism was translated to these young women as an embodied, and thus privately and publicly identifiable, performance of national rituals and proficient domesticity.

Importantly, the Americanization work of the Girl Scouts and the Camp Fire Girls did not simply endeavor to assimilate second-generation immigrant members, but also reflected the Americanism of the larger organization. Both scouting organizations were fledgling startups at the dawn of World War I. Plagued by a series of challenges, these groups used the war as an opportunity to prove their own merit. The daunting task of demonstrating their worth indicates the significance of scout Americanization work. Scouting organizations not only trained immigrant girls in the practices of American womanhood, but also visually positioned successfully Americanized members as evidence of the groups' virtues. In this way, the Americanization work of the Camp Fire Girls and Girl Scouts is best explained through the trope of prosopopoeia. In English, the term itself means "making a mask," and classical scholars such as Quintilian often used the label to differentiate between a theatrical speaker and the role he played.[4] Later scholars have maintained that prosopopoeia is a kind of speaking through others.[5] Extending this modern definition, I contend that scouting organizations were able to speak through others to recruit immigrant daughters while they simultaneously used the visual and public display of Americanized members to speak on behalf of their own patriotism. These organizations both taught immigrants how to act as Americans and reified those public performances of nationalism that could ostensibly verify the patriotism of all citizens. In a larger sense, the Americanization work of scouting organizations is an exemplar for understanding how the rhetorical pedagogies of Americanization reshaped public culture. Americanization not only was an attempt to change immigrants, but reshaped the public registers of nationalism.

In many ways, scouting organizations responded to a set of public discourses, largely from social reformers and sociologists, that gendered the immigrant crisis through the rhetorical construction of a "girl problem." Girls' clubs, specifically the Camp Fire Girls and Girl Scouts, combated the "girl problem" through Americanization. In their Americanization work, the Girl Scouts and Camp Fire Girls operated similarly, including their recruitment tactics, how both groups narrated their histories through what Bonnie Honig calls the figure of the foreign-founder, as well as the ways both organizations employed patriotic regimens and lessons in domestic skills to teach immigrant daughters those talents said to be central to American womanhood. Ultimately, the public display of Americanized members worked as a form of redress against some of the challenges faced by scouting clubs in the early part of the twentieth century. Scouting organizations thus illustrate how speaking through others reflected on the Americanization movement and the nation as a whole.

Delinquency and the Girl Problem

As part of the more general concern with immigration, social reformers and social workers bemoaned the cultural rift between parents and their American-born offspring—a division that supposedly led to juvenile delinquency. While many advocates insisted that children in public schools would quickly assimilate to the American way, they often lamented the resentment fostered between the first and second generations.[6] For instance, in his 1907 book *Races and Immigrants in America*, John Rogers Commons, professor of economics, wrote that the "amazing criminality of the children of immigrants" was the result of a generational division.[7] Given this condition, many authorities presumed that children would lash out at their un-American parents and engage in all manner of scandalous activity. Often, commentary on delinquent children would gender the circumstances such that the immoral habits of girls and boys were of varying levels of importance. Public discussions of child delinquency described the problems of young girls as detrimental to the future of the nation. Against this backdrop, Americanization pedagogies ostensibly fortified the mothers of the coming republic.

A number of period investigations identified child delinquency as a condition created by the surge in new immigrants from Southern and

Eastern Europe. The Dillingham Commission report dedicated an entire section to the nature of juvenile delinquents in relationship to "foreign parentage."[8] The report laid the bulk of child crime at the feet of parents, asserting that "the most important thing to be known regarding juvenile delinquents" was that a large number of criminals were "the children of immigrants."[9] Similarly, in their extensive study of juvenile delinquency in Cook County, Illinois, Sophonisba Preston Breckinridge and Edith Abbott analyzed the records of all "delinquent cases" brought before the county court from July 1, 1899, to June 30, 1909.[10] As they illuminated the results of their investigation, the authors averred that one of the prime reasons for child delinquency was the impossibility of "proper discipline of the American born children" by guardians.[11] According to these studies, the dislocation engendered between immigrant parents and their American children presented significant challenges.

Often, conversations on juvenile crime focused on boys and adolescent men. To be sure, in the early years of the twentieth century, boys outnumbered girls dramatically in delinquency court cases.[12] The conditions of the home were typically blamed for wayward boys. In her groundbreaking 1907 study, sociologist Mabel Carter Rhoades argued that contrary to the belief that children inherited criminal tendencies, the juvenile delinquency of boys could be wholly attributed to a mismanaged home life.[13] Likewise, Commons suggested that the gulf between immigrant parents and their American-born children changed boys irrevocably. As he wrote, "The boys, especially, at an early age lose respect for their parents, who cannot talk the language of the community, and who are ignorant and helpless in the whirl of the struggle for existence, and are shut up during the daytime in shops and factories."[14] In effect, "the children evade parental discipline, and for them the home is practically non-existent."[15] Repeatedly, as is evident in these assessments, boys are positioned as scamps who roam the streets and fall easily into a life of crime. Boys turned to crime because their parents reportedly lacked the resources to properly care for them. In part, many of these reformers maintained that misguided boys could be redirected through transforming the household. These types of claims often displaced the fear of all youth crime onto young women and their future roles as mothers.

For young immigrant females, juvenile delinquency was uniquely inflected as a part of the immigrant "girl problem."[16] Specifically, as sociologist June Purcell-Guild argued in 1909, working girls, overwhelmingly from immigrant families, acted out against the "tragic inharmony" between themselves and their "foreign-born parents."[17] According to experts such as Purcell-Guild, daughters rebelled against the strict, old world rules of their parents, seeking American entertainments that often led to petty theft, premarital sex, and prostitution. As a rhetorical construction, the girl problem identified the ways in which Americanization should proceed: girls should learn wholesome American ways before wages from employment perverted their appetites.

Caseworkers and social reformers contended that the girl problem developed from several aspects of the daughter's upbringing. First, new immigrants stirred significant controversy by sending their children to parochial rather than public schools. Amid the fear of Catholicism as a religion that prevented Americanization, popular writers and sociologists argued that public schools socialized and educated immigrant children in American life, while parochial institutions precluded their assimilation.[18] For example, Abbott and Breckinridge contended that parochial education perpetuated old world allegiances, leaving children unlearned in the English language and American customs.[19] Parochial schooling ostensibly marked the failures of immigrant parents who deprived their children of American public schools, leaving them illiterate in English and ignorant.

For reform advocates, this ignorance became a significant problem for immigrant daughters once parents forced early employment. Employment obliged girls to travel alone in the downtown, thereby falling prey to the dangers of city streets. As Jane Addams explained in *The Spirit of Youth and the City Streets*, work in the "modern city" left young girls unguarded, particularly the daughters of immigrants.[20] Breckinridge and Abbott maintained that immigrant girls, forced into "early employment" (typically at fourteen years of age) to support their families, must frequent the "down town" for their job.[21] Simply by walking to and from work "unprotected" in the city, these girls "fell into" "wrongdoing" and "delinquency," ultimately working in a "house of prostitution" with their "health ruined."[22] For these authors, immigrant status stood in for a certain ignorance found in both the parent and the child—the parent for forcing early employment outside the protective family home, the child for lacking street smarts.

Of course, even if she overcame such naiveté, the immigrant girl still proved problematic insofar as social reformers and social workers claimed that once she earned wages, she would not heed the strict, old world rules of her parents. These authors argued that the girl's employment and paycheck afforded her freedoms that spurred rebellion: she supposedly used her hard-won wages to frequent illicit establishments that led to delinquency. In a 1913 volume based on evidence from two thousand social workers, Robert Archey Woods and Albert J. Kennedy asserted that the "pay envelope" was a "potent instrument of newly gained power"—a shift that created an impatience with "narrow conditions."[23] Martha P. Falconer, superintendent of a reformatory for delinquent girls, wrote that "Girls are incorrigible because of foreign-born parents—the girl is restless under their iron rule."[24] Used as a discursive construction, employment drove a wedge between foreign-born parents and their daughters, generating delinquent behavior.

One such place for offending behavior was the dance hall, a seedy establishment that purportedly compounded the immigrant girl's gullibility and freedom. H. W. Lytle and John Dillon, in the 1912 anti-prostitution treatise *From Dance Hall to White Slavery*, noted the "tragedy" of an "immigrant girl" who frequented a dance hall.[25] Stefania Zradska, an immigrant from Poland, worked diligently in a tailor's shop for three years. After that third year, Stefa (as she was called by friends) felt "sufficiently prosperous" to "take from the city the pleasures that are the inalienable rights of its citizens" and attended her first public dance.[26] In this passage, the phrase "inalienable rights" pits the new world against the old, the constitutional provisions of the United States against the rules of the familial home. Of course, the story takes a dramatic turn when Stefa falls for a young man whom she meets at that first dance. Less than one week later, readers surmise that Stefa had sex with the young man, as in two months time, she informs a midwife of "her situation" and ultimately takes her own life.[27] Readers are left with the impression that the trusting "foreign girl" is "hopelessly at [the] mercy" of the "hunters of the innocent."[28]

In a certain sense, the girl problem gendered more general concerns about immigration by translating the problems of acculturation onto the offenses of the daughter. With unassimilated parents and parochial schooling, daughters allegedly remained too callow to successfully negotiate the dangers of modern America. Once the girl reached the age of employment, she was said to rebel against the strict, old world rules of her parents and crave illicit American entertainments. The girl's amusement supposedly led to delinquency as the dance hall and other downtown amusements perverted her appetites, precipitating the fall into immorality. In short, the daughter was trapped between the old world and the new, a position that, experts claimed, prompted licentious behavior.

But the girl's problems were not simply her own. Reformers and social workers insisted that the problems of the child hindered the assimilation of her parents and progeny. First, the cultural rift between parent and child reportedly prevented the girl from bringing her Americanization lessons home for her parents. Americanization advocates redressed this fear by working to narrow the supposed division between parent and child. For example, in her 1914 study of the girl problem, Harriet McDoual Daniels maintained that social workers should resolve the "gulf between parent and daughter" as a solution to the "girl problem."[29] Once daughters reconnected to family life, they were better able to guide their mothers toward the acquisition of American customs. As mother and daughter began to understand one another, the girl "reconciled to her parents' home" and prepared for her "future home."[30] Immigrant daughters Americanized their parents by teaching proper care for children and the household. Against the fear of new immigrants as filthy and slovenly—a condition that purportedly increased infant mortality and the spread of communicable illnesses—immigrant daughters learned methods of cooking, cleaning, and childcare promoted by health and Americanization agencies.[31] Once the girl became Americanized, she was encouraged to become a teacher for her mother.

Second, immigrant daughters who were properly Americanized promised that their own children would grow up as Americans. For example, in 1913, writer Olivia Howard Dunbar explained the importance of home visitation in her discussion of the North American Civic League (NACL). The NACL taught the daughters of immigrants domestic science and proper hygiene "in order to be well loved and have happy homes later on."[32] Education in English, domestic science, and hygiene was said to compensate for the failures of immigrants and to ensure Americanized parents, children, and grandchildren. As Dunbar wrote discussing the benefits of domestic science education, "the [settlement] workers find that all the instruction given the girls is carried directly home to the mothers and then applied by both."[33] The work of the NACL was vigilant in terms of training women for Americanized motherhood.[34] In another 1913 article on the work of the NACL, an advocate for the organization contended that the most important "educational experiment" was domestic education for girls.[35] With domestic education in "American standards of living," including ventilation, sanitation, infant care, and hygiene, the "rising generation" would bring forth a stronger generation than the present, a third generation of children assimilated to American culture.[36]

Of those organizations managing immigrant daughters, girls' clubs reigned supreme. That is, period pedagogues and social reformers touted the girls' club as one of the finest resources for adolescent immigrant females. Woods and Kennedy claimed that clubs dedicated to "folk-dancing, nature study, literary interests of any kind, handicraft, and a considerable amount of purely recreational activities" lured adolescent girls away from the illicit dance hall and back to "sympathy with the more conservative interests of home and family."[37] In a similar vein, Helen Ferris suggested that the club disciplined the child when her parents could not. She wrote, "The parents frequently do not realize the problems the girl is meeting on the streets. . . . Every good [club] Leader should help her girls by . . . giving them necessary discipline."[38] Such discipline ensured a "high standard of conduct."[39] Luther Gulick, a noted expert on play and the founder of Camp Fire Girls, contended that clubs provided a "new and better" activity to divert the girl's attention from the "bad dance-hall."[40] Up against the rhetorical construction of the "girl problem," these clubs proved useful in recruiting and managing immigrant girls.

Girls' Clubs and Americanization

The Camp Fire Girls and Girl Scouts, arguably the two most popular girls' clubs of the period, participated significantly in the Americanization campaign, focusing their time and resources on leading immigrants and their children into American traditions.[41] An article in the May 1915 *Wohelo*, the magazine of the Camp Fire Girls, encouraged members to plan a "celebration which will bring the whole community together in patriotic ardor," particularly the "community made up of many foreign elements."[42] Likewise, the Girl Scouts organized community service under the banner of Americanization. As Juliette Low wrote in a 1919 *Bulletin* article, "Girl Scouts found a very special patriotic service in teaching through Girl Scout troop work the ideals of American citizenship to the children of foreign parents."[43] In tandem with these local Americanization efforts, both groups took part in a national Americanization campaign, "America First." In *The Rally*, the magazine of the Girl Scouts, a letter from the assistant to the executive chairman of the "America First" campaign asked Girl Scouts to "make the foreign people about you hear 'America First'—see 'America First' every day! All this is service of which you will be proud and glad to give the foreigners who have come to our shores,—for the sake of this country we all love."[44] Similarly, as written in *Wohelo*, "They [immigrants] need to be patiently led into our ways and into our traditions, that they may understand our country and our Government."[45] As part of the more general campaign for Americanization, and as is clear in the passages above, both groups invited the knowledgeable scout to reach out to immigrants. Like many other organizations involved in the Americanization campaign, members of the Camp Fire Girls and Girl Scouts worked diligently under the banner of Americanization at the dawn of the war and decreased their efforts in the early 1920s.[46]

While many contemporary scholars briefly mention the Americanization work of the Girl Scouts and Camp Fire Girls, very few engage in sustained analysis.[47] Laureen Tedesco thoroughly examines the Americanization work of the Girl Scouts, noting that the Girl Scouts assisted "conformist Americanizers" in the "drive for 100 percent Americanism."[48] While attending to the broad values the Girl Scouts may have imparted to immigrants, Tedesco centers her analysis on how white, middle-class girls of privilege implemented Americanization measures to embody those "'womanly' values" heralded by Progressive Era social reformers.[49] Indeed, conventionally, those studying the Girl Scouts and Camp Fire Girls demonstrate how these groups constructed ideal white, middle-class womanhood.[50] I conduct my analysis of these organizations, on the other hand, by focusing on how the Girl Scouts and Camp Fire Girls Americanized the daughters of immigrants and thereby mirrored their own Americanism.

The rhetorical significance of scout Americanization campaigns is that they demonstrate how these lessons created broader changes in recognizing Americanism. Both the Girl Scouts and the Camp Fire Girls used Americanization to demonstrate their own worth and to dispel public animosity toward girl scouting. Significantly, both organizations spoke through the figure of the immigrant to recruit members and to demarcate their own patriotism. The trope of prosopopoeia helps to explain the narrative and visual logic of their efforts. For Paul de Man, prosopopoeia assigns a voice or a name to that which is absent.[51] It is an attempt to represent the ineffable. For the Girl Scouts and the Camp Fire Girls, the use of foreign-founders as recruitment devices and the public presentation of Americanized members expressed the qualities of scouts as true patriots representing the best of American girlhood and womanhood. In this way, Girl Scouts and Camp Fire Girls managed their public image while simultaneously giving form to the emotional or abstract qualities of patriotism. As an exemplar, scouting organizations illustrate how selected performances of patriotism became key to recognizing patriotism in all Americans. Scouts, then, represent the broader changes to public culture during this period: they contributed to the amplification of patriotic symbols and performances as rubrics for judging the Americanism of all residents.

Both Girl Scouts and Camp Fire Girls courted daughters of immigrants to join their organization, and upon joining, worked to acculturate these members. Little historical evidence remains to document the number of Girl Scouts or Camp Fire Girls who participated in Americanization campaigns, the count of immigrant peoples these groups tutored, or the total of immigrant members who joined these organizations. Yet, the existence of settlement house troops, articles on Americanization from the magazines of both groups, and internal documentation on Americanization from the national organizations all point to the Girl Scouts' and Camp Fire Girls' substantive involvement in the broad Americanization movement as well as the recruitment and acculturation of immigrant members. Significantly, while leaders from both of these groups considered the organizations ideologically distinct—differences that prevented their assimilation into a single club—both used similar strategies in the Americanization of immigrant members.[52] Each recruited the child by inviting her to dissociate from her former ethnic identity. Both groups narrated their organizational histories through foreign-founders—figures that allowed the daughter of immigrants to understand herself as an American so long as she revered the virtues of national loyalty, unity, and service these figures were made to represent. Finally, both clubs employed visual and aesthetic pedagogies, including patriotic regimens and domestic lessons, to concretize the practices of American womanhood. These groups taught the girl how to recognize herself as an American and publicized the patriotism of the group by displaying her Americanization to the public.

In their recruitment efforts, the Girl Scouts and Camp Fire Girls leveraged the "tragic inharmony" between youth and their foreign-born parents to invite the immigrant member to dissociate from her old world ethnicity. Camp Fire leaders directed members to enlist immigrant girls using tactics that preyed upon the division between the new world girl and her old world family. Rowe Wright, in the February 1919 *Wohelo*, challenged members to recruit immigrant girls: "Think of the hundreds of girls in your own town who have in them a great longing to become real Americans, but have no way to learn the intimate, homey, American traditions."[53] Wright's invitation pitted the immigrant girl's ethnicity, a marker of her un-Americanism, against her yearning for national belonging. Such tactics divided the girl's sense of self from her ethnicity—she was not merely an old world immigrant. The Girl Scouts used similar measures. In a January 1918 issue of *The Rally*, readers learned about the "Black Eyed Susan Troop" comprised of Italian girls, whose membership in the Scouts distanced members from the "severe restraint" of parents, allowing them "a larger measure of wholesome, happy freedom than they have ever before enjoyed."[54] Moreover, the girl's membership provided her parents "a new understanding of American life."[55] In sum, the discourses of the organization depicted the girl as unique from the old world of her parents—she need not identify solely as an immigrant, but could become an American girl.

Once the girl joined these clubs, the discourses of the groups rendered her dissociation complete—she was no longer Italian, Russian, or

Slovak, but simply a Girl Scout or Camp Fire Girl. In a July 1918 issue of *The Rally*, Caroline E. Lewis told readers that at her summer Girl Scout camp, various ethnicities all combined as scouts: "Representing fourteen different nationalities at one time, with traditions and ideas as varied as the trees around them, they met on common ground, because they were scouts, in a spirit that was truly wonderful."[56] Membership in the Girl Scouts offered girls of various nationalities a substantive base for identification, allowing members to see themselves simply as scouts.[57] The Camp Fire Girls echoed this comment a few months later. A photograph in the February 1919 issue of *Wohelo* shows twenty girls sitting on a hillside. The caption announces, "There are seven different nationalities represented, but as you can see Camp Fire has made them all into typical American girls."[58] Membership in the Girl Scouts or Camp Fire Girls supposedly divorced the girl from her ethnicity; she need not identify as any particularity, but as a part of a troop or Camp Fire (the name for a group of Camp Fire Girls).

As the groups worked to divorce the immigrant daughter from her own ethnic heritage, they simultaneously prompted her to reimagine herself as an American girl. Specifically, both groups narrated their organizational histories through legends of foreign-founders. Bonnie Honig describes a foreign-founder as a figure who establishes, restores, or refounds a particular order by domesticating alien qualities as virtuous supplements to the prevailing regime.[59] The figure also serves a prosopopoeic function: it articulates a purportedly lost history to make present the girl's place in the nation. Camp Fire Girls used "Indian" legends in its handbooks to constitute the emotional virtues members should embody—unity, devotion, and altruism. Likewise, throughout its guidebooks, the Girl Scouts referenced foreign-founders, adventurous young women from the past, as pioneers who created the principles and laws of scouting by which young girls should abide—once again, focused on allegiance, dedication, and helpfulness. While for middle- to upper-class white members these rhetorical figures appropriated the romance of the other, for the immigrant girl, narratives touting the pioneering and adventurous spirit of historical "Girl Scouts" or "Camp Fire Girls" made it possible for her to see herself as an American. These heroines were prosopopoeic rhetorical figures narrating an immigrant made into a virtuous citizen. For the immigrant girl, this figuration allowed for the logic of substitution: she could imagine herself as an ideal citizen precisely because she was a pioneer in a strange land. Once the girl identified with the Girl Scout or Camp Fire Girl legend, she embraced the emotional and moral obligations these figures mapped onto her membership.

The Camp Fire Girls spoke through the figure of a foreign-founder via myriad references to "Indian legend."[60] Specifically, the Camp Fire Girls adopted "Indian symbolism," "names," and "design," prompting members to outwardly symbolize their own service and "practical citizenship."[61] While obviously steeped in the racist imagery of the noble savage, for the leadership, this symbolism referenced the origins of the Camp Fire spirit. For the member, this imagery identified "Indian" motifs as highlighting the girl's service to others, and thus, her duty to the community and nation. Significantly, the 1922 handbook described this symbolism as different from the "practical lives of most American homes."[62] Contrasting modern America with the romance of the other constructs this imagery as a foreign additive, a form of symbolism unknown in modernity, used to display the achievements and community service of contemporary Camp Fire members. As a number of scholars have noted, the appropriation of indigenous figures and symbolism can render American Indians[63] as foreign while simultaneously appropriating and authenticating stereotypical qualities as constitutive of American identity.[64] Camp Fire Girls commodified the mythos of indigenous peoples to serve their own purposes. By becoming a scout, the girl evinced her own Americanism.

The idealized foreign-founder deployed the trope of prosopopoeia to speak through an imagined history and crystallize the benefits of membership. For example, the Camp Fire Girls adopted emblems and names from "Indian lore, because it is suggestive of the spirit of out-of-doors, of the ingenious use of the materials at hand, and is so distinctively American."[65] Sentiments such as this marked domesticated foreigners, American Indians, as those who possessed "out-of-door" virtues making for "health and vigor" helping "girls and women serve the community."[66] The immigrant child, herself displaced among a people and a time—old world vs. new world—not entirely her own, could identify with this legend and simultaneously adopt the virtue of service. In addition, this naming and embellishment allowed the girl to recognize and display her loyalty and devotion to the group, community, and nation. As girls read in the 1913 guidebook, Camp Fire Girls appropriated names from "Indian legends" and symbolism that was "a living, speaking part of herself."[67] She could become part of the Camp Fire legend and in so doing dedicate herself to her club and "nation."[68] The girl could identify or speak through this modernized legend to mark the qualities that she, as an immigrant, offered to the country.

In a more elaborate fashion than the Camp Fire Girls, the Girl Scouts referenced foreign-founders to historicize their organization. Here, the Girl Scouts used prosopopoeic fictional characters to dramatize the benefits of scouting. Immigrant members were asked to identify with these heroines as part of the process of Americanization. In Girl Scout manuals, brief stories depicted legendary foreign women, émigrés to North America, as those who inaugurated the spirit of girl scouting in the American nation by embodying scouting principles. Like the Camp Fire Girls' "Indian" symbolism, these figures taught immigrant members that national service, loyalty, and unity were key American virtues. The 1913 R. F. Hoxie manual highlighted Mary Brent, a colonist whose intelligence allowed her to serve Maryland and the nation, and who marked the "character" of American women.[69] In the 1600s, Brent studied law and became a "trusted adviser of the governor and founder of the colony."[70] Denoted as a woman transplanted in an American province, Brent helped to shape the "wise policy that so successfully carried Maryland through the many vicissitudes of its early history."[71] Scouts should "be proud of our country when we find among its founders women such as she."[72] This foreign-founder was a legend to which girls should aspire, a woman who shaped the nation by providing dutiful service to the governor and state. The immigrant girl could invent herself as a continuation of this history—she too was an alien in a new land building leadership through scouting.

By the 1920 manual, the Girl Scouts established its organizational history through another foreign-founder, "Magdelaine de Verchères," named as the "first girl scout in the New World."[73] Repeating the legend of Marie-Madeleine Jarret de Verchères, the Scouts declared this young woman as a founder of "Scout Laws," who courageously overcame tremendous obstacles to maintain loyalty to her new home.[74] The Girl Scouts adopted the Canadian Verchères to prove that loyalty was an American (in this case, North American) and scout virtue. The story began: "It is a great piece of luck for us American Scouts that we can claim the very first Girl Scout for our own great continent, if not quite for our own United States."[75] The manual explained that Verchères was a colonist in Quebec, a foreign "French girl" who held the fort against Iroquois attacks for eight days.[76] While Verchères was displaced from her old home in France, she still defended her new home, inspiring "a message of loyalty, of courage and of devotion."[77] She was an ideal new citizen whose allegiance inspired national loyalty for the daughters of immigrants. By enacting loyalty, courage, and devotion, Verchères became the embodiment of nationalistic emotions and actions. For immigrant daughters, this figure personified the possibility of virtuous citizenship in the new world.

In the same 1920 manual, the Girl Scouts nominated Sacajawea as an "honorary" Girl Scout, as "this sixteen-year-old girl" emphasized the qualities that "women of the nation" must possess.[78] Sacajawea, though a "plucky Indian girl," founded the American nation and the "spirit" of women in the nation: she acted as guide to Lewis and Clark, leading them to open up the "Great Northwest."[79] Scouts continued this "Great spirit" though the "principle[s] of Scouting."[80] Contrary to the danger presented by the Iroquois in the Verchères story, Sacajawea is the helpful "interpreter" between Lewis and Clark and "the various Indian tribes they had to encounter."[81] Of course, the story omits much of the real history of this Lemhi Shoshone woman, including her abduction, her matrimonial slavery under Charbonneau, and the incredible role she played in the expedition, certainly beyond that of interpreter. Instead, the guidebook simply depicts Sacajawea as a foreigner who contributed "great virtues of daring and endurance" to "the race," and especially "women of the nation."[82] Through this language, she became both foreign, insofar as she performed as native interpreter, and national, insofar as she was a great woman of the United States. For the immigrant daughter, the Sacajawea story allowed her to establish herself as part of the American project, as an adventurer in a strange land, scouting her way toward becoming American. In addition, as in the Verchères story, Sacajawea emphasized the emotional qualities of patriotism. References to her "great spirit" and pluck were not arbitrary, but indexed the abstract or emotional qualities of patriotism. They codified the ways women of the nation should feel about their roles.

Within the manuals and stories of the scouts, these narratives used prosopopoeia to speak through an other and created the possibility of identification. Here, prosopopoeia operates in a traditional sense: it is a narratological trope inviting the audience to identify with the Americanism of scouts. Each foreign-founder offered the child of immigrants the figural ground to establish herself as a Camp Fire Girl or Girl Scout and as an American. She, too, was a true American insofar as she adopted the symbolism of such lore. She, too, was an outsider whose service might guide the nation's future. She, too, was a loyal citizen who would protect her new home. She, too, was a devoted young American scouting her way through a strange land. Once the girl identified as an American Girl Scout or Camp Fire Girl, she embraced unity, loyalty, and service as moral obligations. Yet, the Americanization work of the scouts did not simply address an immigrant audience. Instead, the scouts used their Americanization efforts to substantiate their own patriotism.

Prosopopoeic Americanism and Scouting

While the narratives of the groups invited the immigrant member to understand herself as an American, the patriotic regimens and domestic lessons of the group worked to exhibit the Americanism of new members and the group writ large. Specifically, the clubs trained immigrant girls in the practices of patriotism and the skills of the American housewife. These lessons were an attempt not simply to concretize American virtues in immigrant members, but to demonstrate both to the club and the public that their lessons were successful: all members could perform specific qualities of American womanhood. In so doing, these performative and visual lessons highlighted the prosopopoeic visual logic of scout Americanization projects. Namely, that the Americanized immigrant member refracted the patriotism and dedication of the larger organization.

Gavin Alexander writes that in its theatrical usage, prosopopoeia is most persuasive when the performer can move the audience by "moving himself."[83] In this way, prosopopoeia is to present a role while performatively becoming or identifying with that role. As it relates to Americanization, the visual and performative presentation of patriotic members contended that the Girl Scouts and Camp Fire Girls were all-American organizations capable of transforming the populace. This rhetorical exhibition suggested a kinship between scouts and the nation: not only were these young women capable of assimilating newcomers, but they were also undoubtedly wholesome and patriotic. Up against a number of challenges faced by these groups, the visual symbols and public performances of members sought to publicly demonstrate their national worth.

The years surrounding the First World War were a period of dramatic growth for both the Camp Fire Girls and Girl Scouts. By joining war preparedness campaigns and positioning themselves as distinctively nationalistic, both groups' membership rolls flourished.[84] The Girl Scouts blossomed during the war, counting over eight thousand members by 1918.[85] By 1920, the Girl Scouts exponentially increased membership, assembling fifty thousand girls.[86] The Camp Fire Girls boasted substantially more members than the Girl Scouts until 1930.[87] In the founding year of the organization, 1912, the Camp Fire Girls estimated sixty thousand members.[88] Both organizations participated heavily in civilian war initiatives, efforts that enabled the growth of membership and a change in public perceptions of the organizations.

Each organization stressed preparedness and the important role of women on the home front.[89] Even before the outbreak of war, both groups situated themselves as all-American by teaching the ideals of citizenship. The earliest Girl Scout manuals were titled *How Girls Can Help Their Country*.[90] As Tedesco writes, the Girl Scouts and Camp Fire Girls "touted their new programs as nonsectarian, transmitting an 'American' ideal that transcended denominational and cultural barriers."[91] These nationalistic practices ramped up during the war. The Girl Scouts sold over nine million dollars in war bonds, a feat rewarded by the U.S. Treasury "minting a Girl Scout Liberty medal."[92] Similarly, the Camp Fire Girls instituted a "Minute Girl Program" as part of the larger preparedness campaign.[93] The program taught principles of health as well as "food and resource conservation."[94] The war provided the organizations with opportunities for publicity events demonstrating their commitment to the United States.

In part, the Girl Scouts' and Camp Fire Girls' extensive investment in the war was an attempt to redress apprehensions about the gender dynamics at stake in their programs. As Kathryn R. Kent makes clear, in the early years, "fears ran high that the Girl Scouts were trying to turn girls into men."[95] The anxiety surrounding this issue was so steep that the leader of the Boy Scouts, Robert Baden-Powell, suggested that the Girl Scouts merge with the more demure Camp Fire Girls.[96] In addition, it was recommended that the organization change its name from Girl Scouts to Girl Guides, the latter downplaying apprehensions about the adventurousness that scouting implied.[97] As Baden-Powell argued, the term "guide" referenced the girl's roles as mother and wife while the term "scout" mimicked the Boy Scouts.[98] The Camp Fire Girls emphasized domesticity in many ways to lessen the concern that they were "imitation Boy Scouts."[99] Thus, the dedication of the Girl Scouts and Camp Fire Girls to the war effort stressed traditional femininity to counter arguments on the presumed masculinity of scouting.

As part of their war work, the Americanization practices of scouts ostensibly managed these anxieties by presenting their members as all-American girls. The exhibition of Americanized members spoke prosopopoeically on behalf of the larger organizations. Both organizations taught members American customs and habits via visual and performative pedagogies. Through the regimens of the group, the member did not simply identify as an American girl, but publicly demonstrated those practices necessary to acculturation. Girl Scout manuals and Camp Fire books awarded honors for demonstrating knowledge about American history and the performance of American rituals. For example, in the 1913 *Book of the Camp Fire Girls*, members could earn "red, white and blue honors" for telling "the history and meaning of the National flag and of the flag of the country from which your ancestors came."[100] While this directive honored the girl's heritage, American history and rituals were held supreme as the singing of "The Star Spangled Banner" was part of the girl's membership requirements. The Girl Scouts took this a step further. In its 1917 manual, readers learned about the origin of the American flag, the care and display of the flag, the principles of democracy, and the lyrics to patriotic songs, including "America" and others.[101] This history proved required reading for Scouts to become a Tenderfoot—the first grade of

Girl Scout in 1917.[102] These regimes habituated members to enact Americanism, to perform as patriots adept at the nation's customs.

In addition to these explicitly patriotic performances, members learned practical skills requisite to running a proper, sanitary American household. In so doing, the girl learned to exhibit her Americanization both in the home and in public sites. Against the fear of slovenly old world immigrants, members were disciplined in the domestic function of women's citizenship, embodying hygienic household skills central to American womanhood. Merit badges in each of the Girl Scout handbooks from 1913 to 1920 included recognition for childcare, housekeeping, and cooking.[103] The guidelines for these awards focused on healthfulness through systematic cleaning and sanitary cooking procedures. Skills included ridding the bedroom of dust to avoid lung contamination and knowing the conditions under which germs thrive.[104] The group provided opportunities for the member to prove such talents. The October 1917 *Rally* references a camp at Bear Mountain for 178 girls from New York City as a "significant example" of democracy and Americanization.[105] Girls from fifteen different nationalities participated in a "careful program of play, study, and work," learning a "well-studied" regimen of "housekeeping" focused on "principles of dietetics and food conservation."[106] The Camp Fire Girls championed similar talents, inviting members to execute domestic skills to move up the ranks. To become a Fire-Maker, the second of three rankings, members were to "help prepare and serve" two meals for the Camp Fire, mend assorted articles of clothing, learn the "chief causes of infant mortality in summer," and know what "civil department" to notify if they smelled something "bad" in the neighborhood.[107] By completing domestic labor, the immigrant member exemplified the modern, hygienic, American housewife.

In a larger sense, these modes of public display and performance attempted to represent the emotions and abstract virtues of scouts. While guidebook narratives touted loyalty, unity, and service as quintessential qualities of scouts, the public remained reportedly unconvinced of their respectability. These domestic lessons and patriotic practices, then, dramatized the virtues and emotions scouts proclaimed. It was insufficient to simply suggest that scouts felt patriotism or love of country. As with the larger Americanization movement, emotions and character were to be

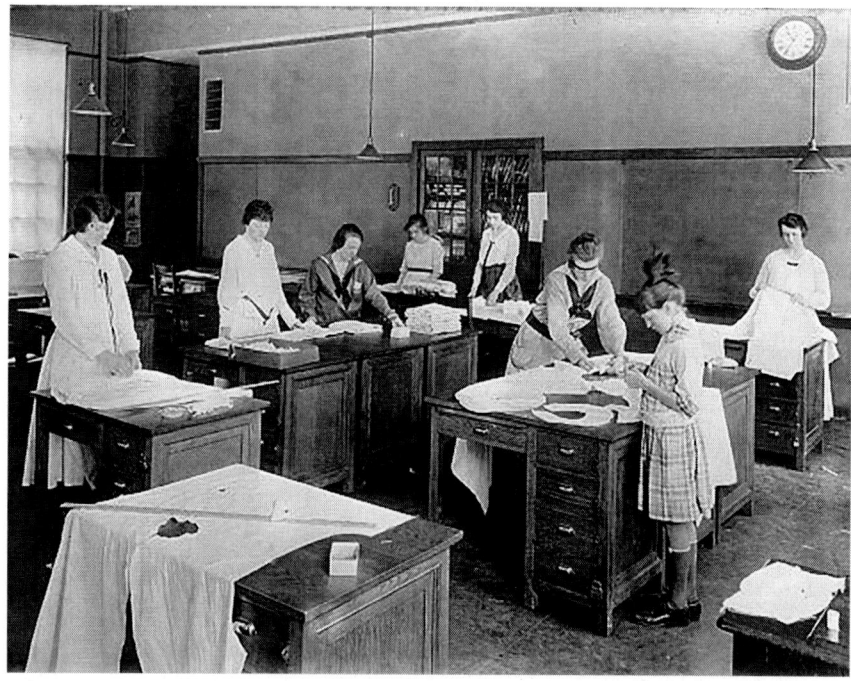

Girl Scouts sewing for the Red Cross, 1917. Courtesy of the Library of Congress, Prints and Photographs Division, photograph by Harris and Ewing [LC-DIG-hec-09627].

made public. Many group initiatives thus presented public demonstrations of scouting as distinctively nationalistic.

The Girl Scouts provided specific publicity opportunities for members to show their prowess as American girls. In exercises photographed for public consumption (see figures 6 and 7), the Girl Scouts touted their stalwart Americanism. Girls are shown sewing for the war effort and caring for young children. As Tammy Proctor makes clear, Girl Scouts used every publicity opportunity available to them to popularize the group.[108] For the broader organization, these press photographs advertised their dedication to the war effort. Yet, given that the group was understood to be contributing to the Americanization campaign, these photographs also spoke to the patriotism of all members. They advertised the uniformity of the club despite a somewhat heterogeneous membership.[109] Girl Scouts were all-American girls who could transform new members into the same.

Girl Scouts caring for children, 1920. Courtesy of the Library of Congress, Prints and Photographs Division, National Photo Company Collection [LC-DIG-npcc-02709].

The Camp Fire Girls and Girl Scouts also deployed embodied rhetorics of display to unify and exhibit their members as dutiful patriots. Much like the use of parades and public singing in the Americanization movement, such pageantry readily presented members as dedicated patriots. Specifically, the dress of both groups worked to erase ethnic difference and mold the troop or Camp Fire as a singularity—a union of patriotic American girls.[110] In the Girl Scouts, the standardized uniform prompted members to become one body. While uniforms were not required, the leadership suggested that it was "advisable" for girls to wear uniforms because it "puts every girl on the same footing."[111] In head-to-toe khaki, Girl Scouts' ensembles composed the troop as a unified whole. Likewise, Camp Fire Girls strongly recommended uniforms, arguing that standardized dress fashioned girls into a singular patriotic entity serving their nation.[112] As the leaders wrote, the uniform "dramatized just as the army is dramatized before our eyes so as to enable our souls to realize the essence of the spirit and the entity which is that of service.""[113] Uniforms, then, were not simply to costume immigrant girls as Americans, but to visually arrange the entire troop as one patriotic union.

The militarism of both the Camp Fire Girls' and Girl Scouts' uniforms not only demonstrated unity, but also displayed members as regimented patriots. Erin McMurray notes that during World War I, the Camp Fire Girls designed a new uniform for the "Minute Girls."[114] Comprised of a "red tie, white blouse, blue skirt, and white navy cap," the uniform draped the girl in the colors of the flag.[115] The founder of the Camp Fire Girls, Luther Gulick, suggested to President Wilson that all girls and young women wear the outfit and donate the money saved on clothing to the American Red Cross.[116] While Gulick's recommendation was not adopted, his advocacy nevertheless contended that the Camp Fire Girls were wholly dedicated to the war effort. In 1914, the Girl Scouts included a khaki middy blouse as part of their uniform. The middy blouse echoed shirts worn by U.S. sailors during the Spanish-American War and the Philippine-American War.[117] The use of khaki material was important to the Girl Scouts as it imitated the uniforms of U.S. soldiers—so much so that the national organization issued a statement in 1917 proclaiming that the uniforms were a tribute to the armed forces, not usurpation.[118] In these ways, the groups used uniforms not simply to homogenize members, but to amply illustrate their nationalism. The uniforms enabled all members to speak through the role of scout as young women dedicated to their country.

The prosopopoeic function of uniforms also redressed anxieties about the femininity of scouts—an argument made plain by the discourses surrounding the ceremonial ensemble of Camp Fire Girls. During monthly meetings, initiation ceremonies, and exhibitions, members wore a ceremonial gown, fashioned by their own hands to look like an "Indian squaw's" dress (see figure 8).[119] For the Camp Fire organization, the ceremonial gown, "founded on the Indian symbolism," represented a distinctively American style.[120] For the larger organization, the ceremonial gown displayed members' feminine virtues. This dress became the feminine corollary to the noble savage stereotype that, according to S. Elizabeth Bird, indexed Americanism and native nobility.[121] By speaking

Charlotte Gulick and Camp Fire Girls in their ceremonial gowns [between 1910 and 1915]. Courtesy of the Library of Congress, Prints and Photographs Division, George Grantham Bain Collection [LC-DIG-ggbain-19166].

Girl Scouts marching in a 1917 Preparedness Parade. Courtesy of the Library of Congress, Prints and Photographs Division, photograph by Harris and Ewing [LC-DIG-hec-06783].

through the mythos of the so-called Indian, the gown attempted to present all members as uniquely American women. As Philip Deloria illuminates, the "Indian activities" of the Camp Fire Girls emphasized "middle-class notions of gender" by valuing the purported beauty and naturalism of work in the home.[122] Deloria writes, "As signifiers of the universal, Indians evoked the primal secrets of adolescence and womanly domestic virtue."[123] Here, the costume did not simply recruit immigrant members to join, but highlighted the femininity of all members. The myth of naturalism bestowed upon the American Indian projected the domesticity of members.

Both Girl Scout troops and Camp Fires planned or contributed to public pageants and parades for the war effort and for Americanization to demonstrate their own commitment to the nation (see figure 9). For example, the magazine of the Girl Scouts encouraged troops to organize a patriotic rally to show the public what Girl Scouts are "doing for the girls" of the nation.[124] Rallies, including semaphore signaling, marching, and drilling, were "an interesting way of getting Girl Scout work before people, and of showing them how girls can be trained out of school for individual usefulness and intelligent citizenship."[125] With no less grandeur, Camp Fire Girls arranged parades and pageants. An article from the May 1915 *Wohelo* invited Camp Fires to help plan a parade or pageant for Independence Day. Such events not only dramatized the "ideals" of the Camp Fire but also celebrated "the oppressed races of many lands who have come to our country, seeking Liberty."[126] Rallies and parades, particularly in settlement houses or ethnic neighborhoods, highlighted the Americanism of the troop or Camp Fire as well as the group's ability to Americanize others. Take, for instance, the photograph of Girl Scouts marching in a 1917 Preparedness Parade. The use of uniforms, numerous American flags, and white gowns marked the patriotism of members. Indeed, the white dresses signified purity while the militaristic uniforms and flags connoted nationalism. As an image, it summarized the war work and Americanization projects of scouts: they were true American girls who could teach others how to be the same.

In all of these exhibitions, the public was invited to see the Girl Scout or Camp Fire Girl as an exemplary citizen. Public pageantry advertised members as dutiful patriots, while Americanization meetings and events assured the public that these groups would acculturate immigrants. Scouts ensured the reproduction of Americanism in both the immigrant girl and her family, redressing those anxieties articulated to the girl problem. More generally, the Americanization work of the Girl Scouts and Camp Fire Girls operated through the figure of prosopopoeia. By speaking through Americanized immigrants, the groups rhetorically demonstrated their own patriotism. In so doing, public performances of Americanism addressed concerns about national unity while simultaneously responding to criticisms of girls' camping groups. In a broader sense, these visual performances promised that national unity could be attained, even by adolescent girls.

Americanizing America

The visual and performative pedagogies used by scouting organizations rhetorically delimited those forms of patriotism that might identify members as Americans. Militaristic uniforms, patriotic rituals, housekeeping and childcare training, and publicity events all situated scouts as devoted citizens. They rendered the abstract and emotional qualities of patriotism into identifiable actions and performances. The visual logic of scout Americanization projects thus attempted to manage public apprehensions about femininity and patriotism by teaching the public to recognize what actions demonstrated internal commitments.

Taken as an exemplar of the Americanization movement, scouting organizations indicate how patriotism changed during this period. It was not simply that nationalistic performances were heightened. Rather, the strategic deployment of selected performances of patriotism and the presentation of Americanized members codified what counted as Americanism. In this way, scouts used visual and performative rhetorical pedagogies to create the conditions in which Americanism could become recognizable in those whose patriotism remained unverifiable. By situating Americanism as a collection of signs that could be publicly performed, these organizations participated in broader cultural changes. The culture shifted such that particularized acts—for women, immigrants, etc.—were positioned as emblematic of national dedication.

Of course, the prosopopoeic visual logic of scouts also animated the wider strategies of the Americanization movement during this period. As this book has suggested, visual methods of Americanization aimed to ease acclimation and to clarify how Americans perform as such. The exhibitions of nationalism chosen by the Girl Scouts and Camp Fire Girls echoed those forms highlighted in other Americanization endeavors. Adoration for American historical figures, participating in the customs of American home life, and nationalistic pageantry were all visual forms that aimed to create a recognizable patriotism. For educators and Americanization experts, these visual and performative lessons were to transform the immigrant into an American. Yet, they also had the larger effect of rhetorically recalibrating the Americanism of the broader citizenry. As a rhetorical pedagogy, Americanization shifted what came to be understood as a demonstration of patriotism.

Indeed, the rhetorical work of prosopopoeia in this case study points to Americanization as a movement that changed the nation's patriotic practices. Americanization was needed for more than immigrants. Rather, the nation's capacity to Americanize immigrants refracted the patriotism of the populace. As is clear with the Girl Scouts and Camp Fire Girls, the organizations used tutelage in Americanization to demonstrate their own worth as all-American girls. To wit, the phrase "Americanizing America" took on particular importance during this period.[127] Consider for a moment the discussion of "Americanisms" offered in a seventh-grade composition textbook for the schools of Toledo, Ohio. The writing prompt began with the following: "What does it mean to 'Americanize America'? It means just this, that we want all the people of this country to be not only good citizens but good Americans."[128] The prompt continued by asking pupils to name the specific tasks and behaviors of good Americans and to consider what brought immigrants to this nation. Given this posturing, the rhetorical work of "Americanizing America" is prosopopoeic—the point is to identify how all citizens can embody Americanism by delineating for newcomers what counts.

The notion that Americanization *refracted* the patriotism of the populace is significant to understanding the visual logic of the period. Americanization not only reflected how patriotic the populace was, but also these endeavors redirected and transformed what Americans saw as important. As literary critic Karen Strassler writes of the term "refracted": it "illuminates the processes of transformation that occur as ways of seeing, modes of interpretation, and habits of practice attached to one photographic genre or representational form refract within another."[129] Here, the figural work of Americanization also refracts the patriotism of the nation. That is, the attempt to present immigrants through visual rhetorical relationships intelligible to others also illuminates the way Americanism was understood by the public. In the physical world, refraction identifies how light bends as it moves through a medium. Similarly, the Americanization of the immigrant is not a perfect reflection of the glorious patriotism of the nation. Instead, the refraction, what is represented, changes based on the circumstances. In the visual practices of Americanization, how the nation speaks and what is said varies based on the figure doing the work.

The discourses and practices of Americanization often focused on the visuality of difference and attempted to reconfigure Americanism as a set of discernible practices everyone might perform. For Americanization experts, defining nationalism in such abstract terms was preferable to a nationalism predicated on bloodlines or other immutable qualities. Yet, Americanization as a larger movement nevertheless remained at least partially beholden to a rather particularistic set of standards: a politics that demanded visual or demonstrable proof of patriotic emotions. In these ways, the driving goal of Americanization was to demarcate those patriotic practices that illuminated one's national devotion and belonging. This lofty goal was plagued by the fact that such performances also underscored the persistence of difference—rendering the successful transformation of immigrants nearly impossible.

By design, the very visual performances and rituals encouraged by Americanization were predicated on a remarkably white, privileged understanding of Americanism. As with the Girl Scouts and Camp Fire Girls, invitations into patriotic pageantry were situated within what Sherrie Inness calls "bourgeois" notions of American womanhood.[130] Considering that the Camp Fire Girls appropriated American Indian figures and stories to substantiate their worth, the extension of Inness's argument is that these practices simultaneously identified a particular racial and ethnic hierarchy. Supposedly lower racial groups were encouraged to aspire to the customs of white, privileged classes. In these ways, Americanization reified a palpable caste system. Yet, such a pecking order did little to diminish the drive for Americanization as a pursuit for all. A number of historians have already demonstrated the racial hierarchy at stake in Americanization that specifically excluded Asian Americans, Mexican Americans, black Americans, and others from the possibility of belonging.[131] Such arguments mark the very ambiguity at stake in the relentless pursuit of national unity. These reforms were invested in the visual display of Americanism to shore up anxieties about difference, not simply to improve immigrants. Nevertheless, overinvestment in such visual displays could not lessen concerns about that which remained invisible: the disaffection and disloyalty in the hearts of those whose difference was seen as intrinsic. Indeed, the racial and ethnic hierarchy at work in Americanization programs sustained that disaffection by insisting on an immanent alterity.

The persistence of difference and the impossibility of representing the interiority of patriotism is emphasized by the trope of prosopopoeia—a figure that underscores the paradox animating Americanization. Though Americanization was an attempt to represent the emotional qualities of patriotism and include new members in the nation, such representational efforts remained constrained by the impossibility of representing the invisible. For de Man, prosopopoeia is hallucinatory in that to make the "invisible visible is uncanny."[132] Speaking through an other is precisely this kind of unsettling figuration. Prosopopoeia is a rather important figure in that it highlights the ambiguity and slipperiness of all tropological representation. De Man asserts that prosopopoeia "undoes the distinction between reference and signification"—the very basis of semiotic order.[133] The perverse work of prosopopoeia is its impossibility—a function made plain in the visual paradox of Americanization. Broader attempts to codify representations of emotional nationalism remained fraught and thereby animated public anxieties regarding patriotism. Thus, while prosopopoeia is an important figure, its tropological work is inherent to the ambiguity of all visual or performative signification. Representing that which remains invisible—emotions, assimilation, etc.—cannot resolve broader concerns about difference. Yet, rather than deflate the ambitions of Americanization enthusiasts, it is this ambiguity that fuels its robust pursuit. The palpable work of this problematic paradox can be explored productively in the debates surrounding Americanization's efficacy and immigration restriction.

CHAPTER SIX

The Paradox of Americanization

A fter the armistice, a number of legislative and other endeavors increased Americanization initiatives. In New York, Governor Al Smith composed a Reconstruction Commission to shepherd the state through the postwar period. One of the proposals included in reconstruction enlarged funding and opportunities for Americanization. Proponents, progressive state legislators Abram Elkus and Felix Adler, sought to Americanize the least educated residents of the state. Their Americanization plans remained in keeping with the emotional nationalism of wartime programs. As they wrote in 1919,

> Americanization has an intellectual aspect, an emotional aspect, and a volitional aspect. The aim should be to educate the mind, the feelings and the will in a certain way. To be genuinely Americanized is to think as an American, to feel as an American, to act as an American, to understand the spirit of America.[1]

For these men, "learning by doing" could teach immigrants how to "think in the American way, feel in the American way, but also to act as an American."[2] Through Americanization pedagogy, the intellectual and emotional aspects of citizenship would manifest in the actions and behaviors of all Americans. As with many other proposals, Elkus and Adler's understanding of Americanism was beholden to a visual logic, a defined set of normative precepts for determining the dedication of others. It is precisely this visual logic that animated the contradictions of Americanization.

Indeed, the paradox of Americanization was predicated on the rhetorical connections between the emotions of Americanism and public display. Living as an American, parading in patriotic festivities, singing the national anthem, or dressing as an American were all modes of representation that attempted to affirm the patriot's commitment. Yet, for immigrants, Americanization remained an onerous endeavor. Demonstrating that one felt in kinship with fellow patriots was incredibly difficult to prove given how patriotism became marked. That is, despite attempts to codify those actions, symbols, and performances that could ostensibly warrant the changed disposition of immigrants, the need for demonstrable proof could not satiate larger concerns surrounding the disaffection of difference. In this way, Americanization created a paradoxical visual logic in which patriotic markers could not confirm nationalism, but residents, especially immigrants, were pressed to continually exhibit patriotism. Ultimately, then, the vicissitudes of proof generated the drive toward Americanization and public proclamations of its deficiencies.

Despite the brief postwar increase in Americanization, persistent questions remained regarding the efficacy of its programs. The visual paradox at stake in this pedagogy helps explain the simultaneous failure and success of Americanization apparent in the extant literature on the period. For some scholars, Americanization fundamentally changed the meaning of Americanism.[3] For others, Americanization was a largely unsuccessful movement that did not increase naturalization or successfully oppose the claims of immigration restrictionists.[4] The contradictory visual logic of Americanization explicates the mechanisms through which Americanization could both change the larger culture yet fail in other outcomes. Namely, it was precisely the inability to definitively demonstrate the internal commitment of immigrants that both doomed the

Americanization project and sustained the anxiety demanding visual and performative markers of patriotism.

Tropes, as devices that leverage structures of representation, are useful methodological tools to understand the tensions or paradox at stake in Americanization—including its simultaneous failure and success. Tropes are modes of representation enabled by the contingency of signs. These forms exploit the gap between figure and referent to illuminate a quality not always seen by audiences. In the visual lessons of Americanization, tropes explain the visual logic of the movement—how Americanism could be rendered apparent in immigrants and indeed all Americans. Yet, tropes also help to explain the paradox that animated Americanization. The contingency of tropes suggests that acts of representation are enabled and constrained by the catachrestic potential of signs. The slippage between figure and referent both undermined and animated the pursuit of Americanization. Given that contingency is not a quality of a singular form but of all figures and tropes, this chapter does not emphasize any particular trope, but rather suggests that the form of tropes as a promiscuous coupling illuminates the fraught foundation of Americanization. To wit, the paradoxical visual logic of Americanism played into anxieties about racial and ethnic difference and prompted an obsessive concern with demonstrating patriotism.

Proof Is Never Enough

For a number of historians, the war years and Red Scare animated a panic surrounding disloyalty—particularly for German immigrants and German Americans. In many historical accounts, the terms paranoia or hysteria best characterize this zealot-like atmosphere. Scholars explain that patriotic salutations were driven to extremes through propaganda, fears of espionage or Bolshevism, governmental surveillance, and jingoism.[5] A number of examples of mob violence warrant this view. In Jefferson City, Missouri, a crowd beat a man of German ancestry when he drunkenly praised German victory.[6] A Kansas posse demanded that Mennonite Walter Cooprider buy war bonds or be tarred and feathered.[7] Ohio vigilantes terrorized German neighborhood residents who failed to remove their hats for John Philip Sousa's "Stars and Stripes Forever."[8] German Americans were also painted yellow and asked to kiss the American flag.[9] And in 1918, residents of Collinsville, Illinois, lynched Robert Prager, a socialist German miner, after parading him through town draped in the American flag. The mob murdered Prager for his presumed disloyalty, despite the fact that he had registered for the draft and was in all other ways loyal.[10] As was often the case with those who lynched black Americans, the attackers were acquitted.[11] According to many historians, a panicked climate resulted in a number of punitive actions against immigrants, particularly those of German lineage.

Yet, given the broader visual logic of the period, judgment of the immigrant's status often focused on her exhibition of Americanism. As the previous examples indicate, a heightened concern with patriotism did not simply stem from propaganda, government surveillance, or hysteria itself, but was overwhelmingly concerned with specific public acts of disloyalty or loyalty: praise for Germany, buying war bonds, singing nationalistic songs, or showing love for the flag of the United States. Thus, while scholars have rightly acknowledged that wartime suspicion of espionage, postwar bombings, and the wanton use of propaganda contributed to this panicked environment, there is little recognition of the way the rhetoric of Americanization contributed to the conditions in which specific markers of Americanism became both a cure and a cudgel. Put simply, the tenuous connection between sign and referent—patriot and act—did not just undermine the presumed loyalty of immigrants, but animated public demonstrations of Americanization while corroding the efficacy of that proof. In this way, explicating the tensions at stake in signifying Americanism adds much to the understanding of the paranoia of these years.

One of the most intriguing case studies in this paradoxical visual logic appears in Americanization registration cards created by the Committee on Public Information (CPI). The CPI was an extraordinarily important governmental tool during this period given that it was charged with stoking the fires of patriotism to promote United States involvement in the war.[12] Significantly, a few of the CPI's initiatives focused on Americanization. In particular, the CPI engaged in a number of enterprises that taught immigrants the meaning of Americanism and combated supposedly radical influences among immigrant laborers. One of these endeavors included the collection of Americanization registration cards. In March and April of 1918, the director of the CPI, George Creel, invited public librarians throughout the country to circulate Americanization registration cards to the heads of immigrant societies and stakeholders in the Americanization movement.[13] While there is virtually no academic research on these cards, ostensibly they were an attempt to catalog Americanization work done among immigrant societies—possibly to aid in the distribution of CPI propaganda. For my purposes, these cards are compelling historical evidence in that responses emphasized the need for public demonstrations of patriotism while they expressed trepidation in appeasing the CPI. Both are related to one another and indicate the paradox at stake in proving Americanism.

Registration cards informed readers of the meaning of Americanization and invited respondents to log their membership numbers, report on their activities, and communicate how they promoted Americanization. In part, the cards detailed specific markers of patriotism and thereby identified a particularly narrow vision of Americanization. The cards began by defining Americanization for the reader:

Americanization means
- The use of a common language for the entire nation.
- The desire of all peoples in America to unite in a common citizenship under one flag.
- The combatting of anti-American propaganda, activities and schemes, and the stamping out of sedition and disloyalty wherever found.
- The elimination of causes of disorder and unrest, which make fruitful soil for the propaganda of enemies of America.
- The abolition of racial prejudices, barriers, and discriminations, and of immigrant colonies and sections, which keep peoples in America apart.
- The maintenance of an American standard of living through the proper use of American foods, care of children, and new world homes.
- The discontinuance of discriminations in the housing, care, protection, and treatment of aliens.
- The creation of an understanding of and love for America, and of the

desire of immigrants to remain in America, to have a home here and to support American institutions and laws.[14]

These statements align with the vision of Americanization described in this volume as emotional ideals manifest in public exhibitions. The CPI outlined Americanization as the desire to become an American, and simultaneously the embodiment of the American lifestyle—patriotism was an internal devotion with publicly accountable traits. However, even in this simple registration card, the tension between invisibility and visibility generated the terms through which Americanism became seen as a paramount, yet virtually insurmountable goal. Americanization was a complete overhaul of one's affections, actions, and lifestyle—a laundry list of requirements that proved difficult, if not impossible, to fulfill. The CPI adopted this overwrought vision of Americanism, delineating patriotism as a formidable demand.

Those individuals submitting registration cards responded to this tension, often couching their replies in ways that aimed to verify their loyalty.[15] For instance, Reverend Henry G. Stott of the First Evangelical Reform Church in Milwaukee did not simply write on the half-page registration card, but instead submitted a letter extolling how his congregants displayed American qualities. While Rev. Stott acknowledged that no work was "needed on americinasation [sic] for this congregation, because the overwhelming number has been born in America and speaks the English language," he nevertheless seemed obliged to recount the church's Americanization activities.[16] After detailing when English and German were spoken in worship services and church activities, Rev. Stott elaborated on a six-week daily vacation Bible school the church provided for public school children. He explained that each session began with a flag drill, then the "children first sing one verse of 'America' and then repeat in concert the following pledge, raising their right hand at the forehead in a salute to the flag, 'I pledge allegiance to my Flag, And to the Republic for which it stands, One Nation indivisible [sic], With liberty and justice for all.'"[17] After their pledge, the children sang another verse of "America" and saluted a flag representing the Christian church. Notice that Stott did not simply remark that his church was involved in teaching Americanism to "many children of different nationalities," but indicated to the CPI exactly those ritualistic practices that could inculcate, as Stott wrote, "the strong influence" of Americanism.[18] His discussion thus seemed to acknowledge the proof needed to verify the internal feelings of Americanism. Elizabeth B. Suchman, head of the Bertha Fensterwald Social Centre in Nashville, noted that the settlement center's work in Americanization included "Instruction in English, Urging and assisting in naturalization, clubs and classes in civics, Teaching of American cookery in domestic scienc [sic] classes. Patriotic meetings. Encouraging the adoption of American customs, life, and manners."[19] As is clear in these brief examples, representatives of these groups quickly surmised that abstract appeals to patriotism must be justified through concrete practices.

Registration cards signaled a strong impulse to authenticate the Americanism of immigrant groups. As is clear in the responses from Stott and Suchman, the tropological sleight of hand between proof and ornamentation sustained the anxieties surrounding Americanization. The need to visually or performatively establish immigrant patriotism became a contradiction: immigrants were invited to demonstrate loyalty while such a demand thwarted the possibility of success. Indeed, the CPI's insistence that patriotism was an internal affection, an "understanding of and love for America," with demonstrable qualities such as a "common language" and the maintenance of American standards, highlights the contradiction. The connection between external evidence and internal affection is a figuration sustaining the contingency of proof. The need to affirm one's emotional nationalism or love of country via specific acts—and most importantly, the command that public acts were essential—created the conditions through which patriotism was both a panacea and a punishment. Exhibiting patriotism was necessary to proving one's faithfulness, but a nearly impossible requirement to satisfy completely. The assumption that the true affections of immigrants remained hidden, that they fomented "disorder and unrest" or harbored disloyalty, undermined the impact of patriotic expression.

Thus, some responses substantiated the strength of their Americanism while acknowledging the tenuous nature of such validation. Pastor George Gona of the Slovak Lutheran Holy Cross Church in Pennsylvania noted his own behavior as a model for his congregation: "Whenever and wherever I see an opportunity I preach true Americanism and *always live up* to my preachings. When I urge my people to help the government, buy Liberty Bonds etc. I always see to it that I have done first so I could point them to follow my example. You know that example is the best teacher."[20] Pastor Gona's emphasis on example accents how these performances became seen as a requirement that remained insufficient to combat doubt. Despite his own exemplary behavior, Gona cautioned against overzealous Americanization, noting that "the true, genuine American spirit is in the hearts of immigrants," and its "inherent properties" would result in "American language and habits."[21] Although his claim attempted to note the invisibility of emotional nationalism, Gona's admonition nevertheless fell in line with the visual logic of the period insisting that Americanism was a spiritual quality that created acts of patriotism. The mutability of evidence sustained the need for Gona to show his patriotism even as he admitted that true patriotism remained in the hearts of immigrants.

Replies also seemed to mark a fear of government monitoring and the need to demonstrate loyalty in ways that might mitigate the presumption that immigrant societies fomented sedition. The paradoxical visual logic of Americanization entrenched the possibility of punitive repercussions. Nick Nistor of the Roumanian Beneficent Society in Pennsylvania appeared to respond specifically to the campaign for "100% Americanism," offering that "Our members, while they come from Austria recognize Roumania as our Fatherland and are 100% loyal to the United States and American institutions."[22] E. J. Avey of Elma, Washington, wrote that members of his organization were "100% loyal . . . and we will do work of *any kind* calculated to aid the government or whip the Prussian gang."[23] These responses trafficked in hyperbolic patriotism and overemphasized the extent to which group members were devoted to the United States. A telling moment emerges in George Gona's letter, which begins with the following statement: "I have no idea who sent you my name."[24] Seemingly alarmed by the watchful eye of the government, Gona concludes, "As a loyal citizen and a Lutheran christian [sic] I consider it my sacred duty to help the government in any and every way. . . . if I can be of any service to you I will gladly and with pleasure 'do my bit.'"[25]

Given that the CPI monitored foreign-language newspapers for anti-American sentiment, and censored media content that could incite radicalism, the fears recorded in these cards were not entirely misplaced.[26] Naturally, some respondents directly addressed the potential for sedition. Manuel Alaniz, president of Laredo's Sociedad Mutualista Hijos de Juarez, boasted, "I am duly authorized by the Society to adopt all the necessary measures to prevent any propaganda against our government, and I in particular, will do all in my power to help the U.S. as an American citizen loyal to his country."[27] George Polinka, president of a society in Friendship, Wisconsin, was more explicit: "Our people all is nice we have no pro germans or agents [sic]."[28] The consternation apparent in the words of Alaniz and Polinka firmly suggests that first- and even second-generation immigrants felt compelled to confirm that they were wholly patriotic, all the while acknowledging the futility of such proof.

In these ways, the CPI's registration cards underscore the force of the paradoxical visual logic of Americanization. The link between external sign and internal referent did not simply fail to warrant the success of Americanization, but the slipperiness of the tropological relay reified the frantic pursuit of proof while it simultaneously ensured that such efforts could never shore up public anxieties about difference. The registration cards were the CPI's efforts to document work that was beyond the scope of federal and state-based Americanization programs. In light of the CPI's efforts to surveil and censure the foreign-language press, it doesn't seem farfetched to imagine that Creel and his compatriots used these cards to penetrate those societies that seemed closed to outsiders and bore the potential to agitate dissent. In much the same way as sympathy and disloyalty were rhetorically described as invisible to the public, the practices of these groups were commonly shielded from public view. Responses on these registration cards acceded to this visual logic, carefully marking both the abstract qualities of Americanism and the visible practices of patriotism members embodied. The demand for visible signs of assimilation, then, generated the need for registration cards to uncover the sentiment of those societies concealed from the watchful eye of government. The paradoxical visual logic of Americanization compelled immigrants to capitulate to the Americanization project, while nevertheless such participation could never overcome arguments about the fundamental differences of immigrants. It is no wonder, then, that Americanization faced significant objections as the nation entered the 1920s. The incessant demands for patriotism could hardly persist without resentment or an acknowledgment that the terms of success were unachievable.

Immigrant Indigestion and the Foreclosure of Americanization

By the early twenties, and as evidenced by the dissolution of funding for various Americanization programs, public figures often contended that Americanization was a failed experiment.[29] In many instances, arguments about the flaccid work of Americanization often focused on the inability of immigrants to prove their Americanism. This premise was one of the major arguments used to forward permanent immigration restriction. Following the Emergency Quota Act of 1912 and the Immigration Act of 1917, Congress passed the Johnson-Reed Act, also known as the Immigration Act of 1924. The bill institutionalized a stiffly limited quota system for immigration and barred Asian immigration. The Immigration Act of 1924 was not the first act of immigration restriction, but as historian Mae Ngai writes, this legislation was the "first *comprehensive* restriction law," a law that codified a "*global* racial and national hierarchy."[30] For most historians, immigration restriction proves the triumph of eugenics, a pseudo-science in which claims of racial hierarchy purportedly validated the inferiority of certain races.[31] Yet, the success of immigration restriction was not solely attributable to eugenic ideology given that an overwhelming majority of progressive and conservative legislators—with a whole host of viewpoints—supported restriction.[32] Instead, these deliberations emphasize how the typologies of eugenics mingled with the visual logic of Americanization practices such that the possibility of assimilation hinged on the discord of racial difference. Restriction advocates often contended that even if immigrants cloaked themselves in the façade of Americanism, their devotion to the nation could never be guaranteed given the pollution of racial and ethnic characteristics. In effect, no outward protestation could defeat the belief that certain races and peoples remained divorced from the sentiments of patriotism.

The paradoxical function of Americanization's visual logic is salient to understanding why restrictionists were successful in legislative debates, even as the opposition highlighted the patriotic acts of immigrants. Kenneth Burke suggested in *A Rhetoric of Motives* (1950) that the drive to unite with one another, to feel oneself as part of a community, is facilitated by our relationship to the feel and texture of rhetorical form.[33] The nature of this relationship is explained in his 1925 discussion of rhetorical form, in which he articulates the connection between psychology and form such that "form is the creation of an appetite in the mind of the auditor, and the adequate satisfying of that appetite."[34] Americanization rituals attempted to create an appetite that might wrench the desire for American belonging from newcomers and ensure national unity. Given the paradox between visible proof and invisible difference, though, Americanization authorities could never satisfy those appetites. Performances of Americanism were often seen as a farce that failed to adequately demonstrate immigrants' true affections. As Paul de Man writes, the seduction of the form or trope is not simply that it creates pleasure, but that it "creates the illusion of meaning."[35] What seems nominal is in fact predicated on the impossibility of determination. Taken more generally, all tropes and figures (indeed, all signification) work to impose meaning even as such a task remains elusive. The constitutive function of this paradoxical endeavor is featured in congressional debates on immigration restriction. In these discussions, the visual logic of patriotism mingled with race theories to warrant legislative change. To wit, Americanization was both a failure and a success in that performances of Americanism did not resolve broader concerns, while simultaneously legislators suggested that a true nationalism would be obvious.

Historians have amply demonstrated how theories of eugenics motivated those legislators seeking restriction, and the popular public support afforded the curtailment of immigration.[36] Of course, eugenic principles had become part of the cultural landscape by the early 1920s. Importantly, eugenic scientists strategically involved themselves in the legislative adjudications on immigration. Jonathan Spiro's richly documented *Defending the Master Race* illustrates how eugenicist Madison Grant aggressively lobbied for immigration restriction. Grant's 1916 best-selling eugenicist manifesto, *The Passing of the Great Race*, claimed that the white race was being adulterated by inferior bloodlines and must be preserved through staunch measures including forced sterilization and immigration restriction.[37] To achieve the latter in the United States, Grant courted the chairman of the House Committee on Immigration and Naturalization, Albert Johnson (R-WA), to push immigration restriction.[38] Grant surrounded Johnson with fellow eugenic scientists who were then called to testify before Congress. Grant's efforts facilitated the Emergency Quota Act of 1921—the bill that set in motion the strategy restrictionists pursued in the debates of 1924.[39]

During congressional debate on the Johnson-Reed Act, legislators espoused eugenicist race ideology in their fearmongering. Nativists insisted that the Nordic race lay at risk, and without severe curtailment of immigration, the American nation would face imminent decline. In his comments on the bill, Senator Ellison DuRant Smith (D-SC) invited his fellow legislators to read Madison Grant's work. Drawing on Grant's argument, Smith stated,

> Thank God we have in America perhaps the largest percentage of any country in the world of the pure, unadulterated Anglo-Saxon stock; certainly the greatest of any nation in the Nordic breed. It is for the preservation of that splendid stock that has characterized us that I would make this not an asylum for the oppressed of all countries, but a country to assimilate and perfect that splendid type of manhood that has made America the foremost Nation in her progress and in her power, and yet the youngest of all the nations. I myself believe that the preservation of her institutions depends upon us now taking counsel with our condition and our experience during the last World War.[40]

Here, Smith justified restriction on the basis of America's strength—the United States prospers when the Anglo-Saxon race remains pure and strong. The terms "Anglo-Saxon," "Nordic," "stock," and the phrase "type of manhood" are all beholden to racial hierarchies evident in Grant's and others' publications. The "experience" of the war implied that new immigrants had failed to aspire to the ideals of "Anglo-Saxons." Racial-typology arguments and the failure of Americanization during the war thus became used as concrete evidence of immigrant unassimilability.

Eugenicist understandings of race so permeated the culture that even those representatives opposed to severe restriction often drew upon arguments of racial hierarchy. Nathan Perlman (R-NY), himself an immigrant, evoked racial typologies in his claims. To counter the follies of exclusion, he argued that no "racial stock has a greater share in America than any other racial stock."[41] While his argument suggested that all immigrants took part in building the nation, his use of the phrase "racial stock" played into the arguments of eugenics. Likewise, one of the most vocal opponents of the bill, Rep. Emanuel Celler (D-NY), cited statistics that purportedly proved that Southern and Eastern European immigrants applied for citizenship more quickly than their Nordic counterparts.[42] Jeanne D. Petit proclaims the argument of James A. Gallivan (D-MA) as emblematic of the eugenicist logic of the period. For her, Gallivan averred that new blood invigorated the racial stock of the United States. As he stated, "The race has been ever on the move. . . . In my judgment, that constant addition of new energy and new blood to the Republic is as necessary for the health and refreshment, the expansion and continuance of civilization and all it means today."[43] Gallivan's claim insisted that new racial stock strengthens the nation. His argument relied on racial metaphors that did not successfully deny the eugenic principles of Johnson's supporters.[44] While opponents also argued the bill would damage the United States in other ways—most notably in labor supply and foreign relations—eugenicist arguments nevertheless emerged as the litmus test for the possibility of assimilation. Ultimately, opponents of the bill failed to mobilize resistance, and the Johnson-Reed Act not only became law, but set the tone for immigration policy for decades to come.

Proponents posited the 1924 act as the apotheosis of eugenicist policy and imagined that the legislation could help fortify the native Anglo-Saxon stock of the United States.[45] Thus, restriction legislation enabled a new era of xenophobia while simultaneously codifying a national hierarchy of race. For Ngai, the quota system enacted by the Emergency Quota Act and the Johnson-Reed Act constituted a regime through which all Europeans became designated as white and therefore eligible for immigration, while all "'colored races' (black, mulatto, Chinese, Japanese, Indian)" became seen as ineligible or undesirable for naturalized citizenship.[46] Alongside the segregation and deportation of Mexican immigrants, Ngai suggests that these legislative acts reified a palpable, albeit convoluted, racial hierarchy. Matthew Frye Jacobson arrives at a similar conclusion:

"The Johnson Act did not invent the hierarchy of white races, but merely formulized a refined understanding of whiteness that had steadily gained currency."[47] As these scholars demonstrate, these laws did not simply respond to popular understandings of race, but actualized a legally binding understanding of racial difference. In this new taxonomy, the descendants of Northern and Western Europe retained their supremacy over Eastern and Southern nationalities while nearly all others became seen as unassimilable. The force of immigration-restriction legislation ultimately concretized race in such a way as to render racial characteristics immutable. Restriction laws created the standards against which immigrants were judged, and simultaneously marked all nonwhite bodies as harbingers of un-Americanism.

Importantly, deliberation on the importance of restriction often focused on the visual markers identifying Americanism in relationship to racial typologies. Specifically, in congressional debates, restriction was justified on the idea that Americans ought to be recognizable as such. These claims often played into the racial categories of eugenics. Consider DuRant Smith's questions to his fellow legislators during the April 1924 deliberation on the Johnson Act:

> I think we now have sufficient population in our country for us to shut the door and to breed up a pure, unadulterated American citizenship. I recognize that there is a dangerous lack of distinction between people of a certain nationality and the breed of the dog. Who is an American? Is he an immigrant from Italy? Is he an immigrant from Germany? If you were to go abroad and some one were to meet you and say, "I met a typical American," what would flash into your mind as a typical American, the typical representative of that new Nation? Would it be the son of an Italian immigrant, the son of a German immigrant, the son of any of the breeds from the Orient, the son of the denizens of Africa?[48]

DuRant Smith invited senators to consider what image they conjured up when asked to identify a "typical American." Uneasy with pure-bloodlines typologies, as he noted in his "breed of a dog" comment, he nevertheless maintained that racial markers of Americans ought to conform to a Nordic standard. The whiteness of an American should serve as the cardinal feature of the nation's race. In this statement, the visual aspects of eugenic ideology dovetailed with the visual and performative elements of recognizing Americanism. DuRant Smith suggested that Americans patently appear in the mind's eye through Nordic characteristics. For this legislator, such imagery could be forever modified through the muddling of America's racial stock.

The public display of Americanism also played into arguments about identifying true patriots among racial types. In these claims, the visual logic of Americanization was brought to bear on the race-based arguments of restriction. For many legislators, the failure of Americanization to cultivate the sympathies of new residents warranted the need for restriction. Representative Grant Hudson (R-MI) lamented the myths of assimilation:

> All we needed to do was to let them see the flag, put their children in the public school, teach them to speak English, and the miracle was performed. We have become sadly disillusioned. The "melting pot" has proven to be a myth. We are slowly awakening to the consciousness that education and environment do not fundamentally alter racial values.[49]

Notably, Hudson highlighted the presumption that seeing American symbols and experiencing the American way of life would create new Americans. For him, racial differences proved the falsity of melting-pot ideology. He continued by lambasting even those immigrants who naturalized as a "great menace to all law," in that such individuals veiled themselves in the "veneer of 'Americanization'" without the "spiritual community" of the nation.[50] For Hudson, Americanism could not be cultivated in certain racial types—neither long-term residence nor naturalization secured the kind of commitment desired. His arguments leveraged the ambiguity of visual signs of Americanization against the staunch racial hierarchy of eugenics. If the patriotic acts of immigrants were a mere veneer that occluded their true spiritual orientation, then restriction was the best course of action.

The ambiguity of the visual logic of Americanism held a significant place in structuring congressional debates. On the one hand, Americanism was manifest in particular qualities—seeing the flag, speaking English, attending public schools, etc. On the other hand, these same symbols and actions could simply cloak un-Americanism. Once again, the ambiguity of the sign undermined the definitive meaning of these visual and performative acts. The illusion of meaning was exposed by the invisibility of immigrant sympathies. The force of this interplay did not simply doom Americanization enthusiasts or progressives while bolstering the claims of immigration restriction. Instead, the rhetorical work of this visual logic was to tether Americanism to visual acts even as those acts were insufficient forms of proof. Put simply, the failure of resignification was constitutive of the ways the restriction debate unfolded. Thus, it is too easy to blame legislators for their simplistic arguments rather than tease out the visual logic framing the debate. Studying the visual paradox that animated these discussions enriches period history by emphasizing the extent to which visual and performative acts of patriotism organized how Americanism became recognizable and thereby impacted public policy.

To be sure, patriotism as visually and performatively enacted structured how legislators recognized Americanism. Opponents cited the public acts of immigrants to substantiate their worthiness for citizenship, against presumed racial deficiencies.[51] Congressman Adolph Sabath (D-IL) launched an impressive array of arguments against this bill. While Sabath nevertheless favored some form of restriction (as did most legislators of the period), he alleged that the racial basis of the quota system did not fully account for the ways some races had already assimilated. Much of his evidence rallied observable data from his district. For instance, deploying the notion that second-generation immigrants were fully Americanized, Sabath noted, "Their children, whether they were born in this country or arrived here at an early age, have been trained in our public schools and can rarely be distinguished from native Americans of older generations."[52] Sabath's use of the word "distinguished" stresses visual markers of Americanism. The importance of not being able to tell that someone is foreign in sympathy or otherwise is crucial to Sabath's appeal. Representative Jeremiah O'Connell (D-RI) employed a similar strategy, noting that while immigrants may appear dissimilar, their participation in industry proved their Americanization. As he contended, "The spirit of America is strong and unmistakable. The wheels of industry turn with wonderous speed, the hum and throb of loom and shuttle keep time to the heartbeats of a people attuned to a spirit of love for the country of their adoption. America has first place in their hearts."[53] For O'Connell, laborers imbibed the spirit of Americanism, and their industriousness exposed their spiritual dedication—it was *unmistakable*. O'Connell provided a series of examples of loyal patriots who worked diligently, participated in civic affairs, and furthered the ambitions of the nation. Decidedly, these legislators attempted to confirm that some races were desirable and capable of demonstrating their American commitment. For both Sabath and O'Connell, Americanism was not only within the hearts of immigrants, but publicly verifiable.

Yet, despite the evidence provided by Sabath, O'Connell, and others, most legislators persisted in their condemnation of immigrants as spiritually disloyal—even those immigrants who naturalized. These claims deployed the paradox of visuality surrounding Americanization. While legislators insisted that immigrants ought to speak English, pledge the oath of allegiance, and mingle among true Americans, these performances could never dispel the distress surrounding the disaffecting nature of difference. For instance, John D. McSwain (D-SC) summarized the failure of naturalization or Americanization to curtail sympathy for the homeland:

> When the war broke out in Europe in 1914, it became manifest that we had not really assimilated these alien additions to our population in any appreciable degree. Though millions had been naturalized and had renounced legal relations with their native kings and countries, yet this formal court proceeding had not cut the ties of affection that gathered round their hearts. Their native home countries were still dear to them.[54]

For McSwain, despite outward presentations of Americanism, affections for the homeland still squelched American sentiments. The formidable standards for demonstrating allegiance are perhaps best described by Representative Scott Leavitt (R-MT), "'As a man thinketh in his heart, so is he,' and he has not become an American, regardless of his citizenship, as long as he views American problems in his inner thinking, first and instinctively, from the angle of his foreign birth or parentage. This is after all the real test—the inner thinking rather than the outer protestations."[55]

For Leavitt, visible forms of patriotism were insincere against a nevertheless undocumentable inner orientation. Thus, the vicissitudes of proving emotions undercut claims of allegiance and lent credence to the idea that some immigrants could not assimilate.

Congress members accentuated the paradoxical status of visual proof to insist that even patent forms of Americanism could prove the opposite. For most legislators, patriotism ought to be demonstrable in concrete terms. Representative Stanley Kunz (D-IL) asserted: "Look at the statistics. You have 5,000,000 aliens in America who are not loyal to the flag, who are not loyal to the Stars and Stripes. If they were, they would take the oath of allegiance. They would prove to the people of this country that they are loyal Americans, but they are not; and yet you open the gates to the very same class that you are to-day objecting to, and you permit them to come in here in the future."[56] For Kunz, loyalty required verifiable proof in the form of the oath of citizenship. He further criticized the conspicuous fact that only "300,000" of the total "400,000" foreign-born soldiers "took the oath of allegiance" when offered the opportunity.[57] Even a 75 percent naturalization rate proved negligible for this legislator. Despite Kunz's claim that immigrants could validate their allegiance through citizenship or military service, other commentators questioned such modes of proof. Elton Watkins (D-OR) expanded on Kunz's statement, noting that even soldiers were not necessarily defending the United States but were also "protecting their mother country, whose cause was ours, and they were fighting for their native land."[58] Watkins stressed the contradictions undergirding the possibility of assimilation. For him, fighting in the armed forces was not an act of loyalty, but homage to the homeland. The ambiguity of reading these signs as proof of loyalty was thus exercised in these discussions as counterevidence.

The visual logic of patriotism espoused in larger public discourses became transmuted in these debates from an affection contained within all immigrant bodies to a devotion only available to certain races. Many legislators contended that the nation suffered from "racial indigestion," a condition created by the hard lump of immigrants unable to Americanize. Representative James Byrnes (D-SC) deplored the fact that millions of immigrants remained unnaturalized and unlearned in English. He asserted that these circumstances "indicate that the United States is suffering from indigestion of aliens, and the remedy is the passage of this bill."⁵⁹ For him, racial indigestion stemmed from the unknowing attachments of foreign interests. As he noted, "Many aliens unconsciously . . . are influenced by what they believe to be the best interests of other governments instead of this Government."⁶⁰ Congressman Ira Hersey (R-ME) bolstered his support of the Asian Exclusion Act through the notion of indigestion: "Asia and southern Europe, the Malay, the Mongolian, the oriental with their strange and pagan rites, their babble of tongues—a people that we can not digest, that bear no similarity to our people, that never can become true Americans, that add nothing to civilization, but are a menace to our form of government."⁶¹ For Hersey, these "strange" peoples could not become Americans given their essential differences. Likewise, Benjamin Rosenbloom (R-WV) employed germ-theory metaphors to describe the taint of unassimilable bodies: "The body politic, however, is not unlike the human body. We are taught that germs of all diseases lie in the human system, and we are dependent upon the power of the system to generate enough combative force to destroy those germs."⁶² Taken together, these legislators declared that some immigrants were culturally and racially conditioned in such a way that Americanism remained an impossible ambition.

Members of the 68th Congress insisted that communism, Bolshevism, and radicalism resulted from immigrants' national disaffections. Of course, against the recent fears associated with the Red Scare, these arguments are not surprising. What is noteworthy is the idea that many legislators conjectured that certain races and nations bred radicalism by virtue of their sentiments. House member John Robsion (R-KY) asserted that "the people coming from eastern and southern Europe until recently were under the despotic governments of Russia, Bulgaria, Turkey, Austria, Hungary, and so forth."⁶³ For him, these individuals "nursed hate from their mother's breast and were taught to despise their oppressors and governments at their mother's knee. . . . Out of this condition naturally grew anarchism, bolshevism, communism, syndicalism, and other monstrous conceptions of law and government."⁶⁴ Ultimately, Robsion supported restriction, given that these immigrants "transfer their hate for government and those in authority from Europe to America."⁶⁵ While Representative Rosenbloom's symbolism highlighted foreign bodies as a menace, his description of the breeding grounds for their antipathy moved away from racial typologies to affirm that the "aftermath of the war" bred a "bitterness of heart."[66] Representative McReynolds (D-TN) approvingly cited President Calvin Coolidge, noting that American citizens must be familiar with principles of "self-government," and the United States could not "absorb" those who had lived under another type of government.[67] Meanwhile, Representative Robert Allen (D-WV) claimed that "radicalism is said to be provoked by the situation resulting from admitting masses of indigestible foreigners" who have proven "their dangerous character."[68] In these statements, the differences created by national cultures and racial ideology fashioned an emotional state that did not simply preclude assimilation but actually propagated radicalism.

As is clear from this analysis, congressional debates on immigration restriction did not merely rely on eugenicist arguments to forward restriction. Instead, eugenic arguments and visual typologies juxtaposed with the visual logic of Americanization to undermine the presumed possibility of assimilation for certain groups. The visual contradictions at stake in Americanization structured the terms through which patriotism could be understood and recognized by both legislators and the larger public. Americanization initiatives encouraged pupils to assimilate in ways that could readily identify their Americanization, yet such displays could never mitigate the apprehension surrounding their mismanaged affections. In much the same way as wartime discussions insisted that the invisible sympathies of immigrants jeopardized American loyalty, postwar discussions of race extended this argument to the conclusion that some racial stocks could not become true Americans. Immigration restriction, then, became warranted on the presupposition that some races and nations cultivated emotional dispositions incompatible with American patriotism. Such claims were particularly acute when leveled against certain groups. As house member John F. Miller (R-WA) stated of Japanese immigrants, "Their national sentiment is fixed, their faith is pledged."[69]

Up against the demand to prove loyalty—a stipulation that could not be entirely satisfied through either naturalization or military service—the status of the immigrant remained suspect. The Johnson-Reed Act was not simply the triumph of one party over another, but rather a bill that illustrates how the ambiguity of demonstrating Americanism impacted the contours of immigration policy. If Americanization countered fears of invisible disloyalty and racial difference, then assimilation could never be proven fully. Against the threat of radical agitators, this difference appeared as the cauldron of revolution. The risk calculus of immigration restriction insisted that true Americans must be preserved, not created.

The Success and Failure of Americanization

By 1919, even the ever-vigilant Frances Kellor lamented that Americanization had floundered.[70] She joined a whole host of popular discourses proclaiming that the movement had failed to assimilate immigrants.[71] Historians have robustly argued for and against Americanization's success. For a number of scholars, Americanization was a farce that used progressive ideals to colonize immigrants.[72] For other historians, the movement fundamentally transformed American culture, even if it bred resentment and resistance.[73] The analysis presented here suggests that both arguments are true: Americanization was simultaneously a resounding success and an abysmal failure. Americanization succeeded in delimiting those forms of patriotism that could indicate the patriotism of all citizens while it failed to create the conditions through which such proof was sacrosanct. Rather than reading this outcome as simply disastrous, I argue that the paradox of this visual logic animated public understandings of who could become an American.

The slipperiness of trope, the possibility that meaning could be otherwise, is significant to grasping the impact of this visual logic on immigration policy. It is not merely that Americanization discourses and practices created new symbolic endeavors that fixed or adjusted the meaning of Americanism. Rather, the ambiguity of all tropes became constitutive of the anxiety motivating the need for demonstrating patriotism while undercutting the strength of such proof. In this way, using tropes to dissect the Americanization movement accents the constitutive work of this slippage, the paradoxical understanding of evidence it animated. Congressional debates offer robust consideration of how visual and performative acts of patriotism did or did not merit inclusion. Indeed, the ambiguity of proof structured debate proceedings.[74] Without an understanding of the vicissitudes of representation, the historical record on Americanization is incomplete. Analyzing the Americanization movement and immigration restriction through the lens of rhetoric offers a more informative account of this period. Americanization was not only a failure or a success, but rather the tropological structure of representation it inaugurated constituted the parameters of recognizing and misrecognizing Americanism.

Using a rhetorical method to analyze the Americanization movement demonstrates that the movement was uniquely important to period understandings of nationalism. Indeed, a rhetorical lens insists that the tensions and paradoxes of meaning-making shifted the contours of public culture in important ways. As Hariman and Lucaites write, studying "public culture requires seeing more than an evacuated signifier and less than a single rhetoric of the image that reinscribes a national mythology. As one examines the use people make of the image, it becomes clear that its connotative power is modulated . . . to negotiate relationships regarding the state, history, political conflicts, social conflicts, generational changes, culture wars, the culture of consumption, and more."[75] In this way, studying the visual logic of Americanization as constitutive of recognizing Americanism is not to suggest that it stabilized the meaning of Americanism. But rather, a rhetorical take on this history argues that the *attempt* to fix meaning negotiated a series of conflicts. By constituting markers of Americanism as cardinal to patriotism, Americanization set the terms of recognition. The framework of nationalism generated by Americanization became a guiding politics situating Americanism as a recognizable public good, albeit one that could not be embodied fully by certain populations.

Taken together, the discourses and practices of Americanization rendered the qualities of Americanism as rather shallow protestations. Despite continued insistence that emotional nationalism bound a heterogeneous population together, evaluations of who could become an American rested largely on visual inspections. CPI registration cards and congressional adjudications employed and reified these metrics. Here, the modern foundations of nationalism came to fruition. Whereas emotional nationalism dated to the colonial era, this new vision of emotional nationalism centered on display such that publicity orchestrated the contours of belonging. Americanism became a recognizable quality through the work of interconnected and relatively organized missions. In much the same way that the birth of public relations during this period shifted how the media impacted public opinion, Americanization on a broader scale managed the public's understanding of nationalism. Who an American was and what America could mean was relegated to superficial, visceral assessments of patriotism and loyalty.

The tensions and paradoxes of Americanization's visual logic crucially illuminate the legacy of Americanization and its impacts on public policy and mores. Americanization aspired to an ambitious national agenda: a sweeping emotional transformation that allowed immigrants to become Americans and encouraged the public to recognize Americanism as a demonstrable quality. At the same time, the ambiguity of signification sustained the idea that immigrants and others remained disaffected by difference—their public acts of patriotism did not necessarily mean what Americanization experts portended. Ultimately, immigration restriction and the demise of Americanization programs are the logical outcomes of this ambiguous relationship. Given broader, racist formations and the machinations of government, Americanization could not merit its own continued work. Often, proof is never enough.

Conclusion

In his 1915 Flag Day speech, President Wilson argued that the flag was an emblem of the nation's possibilities. That token reminded citizens that "national life" was created not by abstract ideals, but by the "actual daily endeavors of a great people to do the tasks of the day and live up to the ideals of honesty and righteousness and just conduct."[1] His words tied behavior to national ideals—an association that heralded the actions of "sober, quiet" citizens, not "swashbuckler[s]."[2] His goal was to honor the quotidian nature of citizenship, those who did not attract attention to their patriotism and yet continued with the everyday habits of nation-building. In the peroration, Wilson reflected on the place of the flag as a symbol trumpeted only on special occasions. "I am sorry that you do not wear a little flag of the Union every day instead of some days," he stated. "I can only ask you, if you lose the physical emblem, to be sure that you wear it in your heart, and the heart of America shall interpret the heart of the world."[3] The necessity of wearing one's patriotism in this

1915 speech is enunciated somewhat differently than in subsequent Flag Day celebrations. While the president acknowledged the importance of emotional nationalism, outward demonstration of one's dedication was not a fundamental imperative. If someone lost her lapel pin, patriotism could be worn in the heart.

By 1924, federal celebrations of Flag Day under President Coolidge were informed by the patriotic rituals of the intervening years. The ceremony began and ended with prayer and included a hefty amount of community singing. Singers who crooned "The Star-Spangled Banner," "Flag of the Free," and "Columbia, the Gem of the Ocean" accentuated those markers of patriotism deemed worthy of the occasion.[4] Even Secretary of War John W. Weeks, who provided the address, suggested that awardees for the corresponding national essay contest had "proved themselves to be real patriots" by penning the papers.[5] To be sure, the contrast between 1915 and 1924 is not dramatic insofar as both are steeped in the heightened patriotism of the period and reference the emotional foundations of nationalism. Yet, by 1924, the rituals of patriotism had become formulized such that community singing, prayer, and flag-wearing were essential to exhibiting Americanism. Regular, outward displays of patriotism became cardinal to public recognition of allegiance. Those who wore their patriotism with bravado had replaced sober, quiet residents.

Taken more generally, Americanization lessons, including Flag Day festivities, engendered a significant shift in public culture. Patriotism became an emotion displayed on the bodies of patriots. Emblems and performances of loyalty were used to visualize Americanism. Thus, the use of community singing in 1924 Flag Day exercises was not simply a nationalistic ritual but an attempt to warrant the patriotism of attendees. For immigrants living during these years, the work of Americanization transformed the conditions through which they might be seen as Americans. These discourses and practices articulated the worth of citizenship. Valued citizens made visible their devotion to the nation and rejected difference in favor of national unity. Waving the flag, singing national anthems, or participating in the American lifestyle all announced the Americanism of the individual.

Americanization thus constituted a visual logic of Americanism—a set of specific standards for measuring the patriotism of all citizens. By publicly exhibiting a select set of emblems and performances, residents capitulated to, and reified, the metrics evaluating patriotism. What proves remarkable about the Americanization movement is not that it spawned a zealous patriotism. Rather, the significance of Americanization is the movement's focus on visuality and display. Visual lessons were thought to perform a kind of nationalistic miracle: they birthed a robust love of country that might overwhelm homeland commitments. Yet, as Americanization enthusiasts redefined patriotism in abstract, emotional terms, they simultaneously attempted to prove the efficacy of Americanization through demonstration. Over time, the repetition of Americanization lessons and related pedagogies across public culture fashioned the rubrics through which patriotism became a feeling patently manifest in all Americans. By coding particular performances of patriotism as evidence of internal devotion, these discourses and practices constituted the visual logic through which Americanism became recognizable. Appearance framed the conditions of seeing Americanization and Americanism more broadly. In other words, Americanization was predicated on rhetorically creating a set of standards for visually marking and identifying Americanism as a public good.

As a rhetorical pedagogy, the lessons of Americanization progressed inductively from individual to the nation writ large. The stimulation of the visual supposedly arrested the pupil and opened the pathway toward a deeply felt patriotism. Housing reform and community celebrations might deliver students to a positive emotional outlook: contentment and happiness facilitated the bonds of patriotism. Later lessons were to demonstrate to the public that Americanization was an effective pedagogy—it could create Americans capable of being identified as such. The goal, then, was not merely to change immigrants, but to manufacture a set of pedagogical lessons that could both teach immigrants to see themselves as Americans and to transform the ways the public apprehended Americanism. Although emotional nationalism had long been significant to the republic, Americanization's emphasis on public display shifted period understandings of nationalism. Patriotism was not simply a ritual or a feeling; it was manifest in one's actions and significations. Americanization shaped the desires of the larger public by creating "the American" as a recognizable subject. In this way, its discourses and practices also created a longing to secure that subject as an actuality. Americanization impacted public culture by insisting on the possibility that Americanism was both recognizable and decipherable in oneself and in others.

Yet, the terms of identifying Americanism in immigrants and others remained fraught. Thus, while Americanization attempted to secure a set of markers for determining patriotism, the invisibility of loyalty undermined that goal. This failure was productive as it motivated the pursuit of vigorous acts of patriotism. That is, this pedagogy sought to create citizens for the republic: those who might understand the performances of immigrants and others as legitimate forms of national service. While legislators and others remained unconvinced that immigrants could ever embody that status, Americanization as a pedagogy nevertheless succeeded in creating a goal. Members of the public pursued that goal even while acknowledging its impossibility. Indeed, it was the very ambiguity of becoming an American that motivated Americanization as a broad educational campaign.

The visual logic at stake engendered an obsessive appeal for proof that could not be sated. Given concerns about the mutability of the immigrant's affections, the question of identifying one's national allegiances became a guiding visual politics. The antagonism between enemy and patriot turned on the invisibility of emotions. As this book has illustrated, this rift emerged from hundreds of popular claims that negotiated the contours of a diverse country by figuring the ways in which similarity and difference enhanced or malformed the nation. Despite the movement's focus on an internal and invisible spirit, the rhetorical obsession with invisibility turned on this logic, ultimately encouraging a public search for visible proof of internal affection. To try and meet this hyper-demand, Americanization experts rhetorically arranged the public acts of immigrants to prove their dedication. Immigrants were invited to participate in numerous (and perhaps continuous) displays of Americanism—from enrolling in Americanization classes and living in American residences to parading in national celebrations and encouraging daughters to become scouts. Ultimately, all Americans, and particularly immigrant populations, were pressed into these nationalistic performances.

Americanization thus promised a bright democratic future that proved difficult to materialize. Americanization's focus on spirit and sympathy advanced Americanism as a demonstrable attitude, an affection that should be felt even by those excluded from rights and opportunities. In defining Americanism as a sentimental attachment, educators and experts disengaged from dealing with those structural changes that fostered discontent. Anxieties about the alienated populace functioned as the discursive terrain upon which the nation reconfigured difference as a threat to national unity. Set against the backdrop of the Great War, the fundamental diversity of the American population became the warrant for inculcating conspicuous performances of patriotism. The trauma of war "over here" engendered a demand for consensus on the home front. The need for demonstrable patriotism was commonly distanced from mere naturalization. Instead, patriotism and allegiance became tethered to a certain set of actions and performances that rarely begat rights or structural opportunities. The goal was to create national harmony through patriotic education, a campaign in which difference was managed by transforming the appearances of residents and little else.

In some sense, then, Americanization's paradoxical logic undercut the broader changes it aimed to foster. Cecilia E. O'Leary argues that the "paradox of patriotism" revolves around the "recognition that American identity and loyalty are historically steeped in contradictory patterns and ambivalent relationships."[6] For her, these "unresolved tensions" create a "sense of betrayal" for the subjugated and "have driven wedges into the body politic."[7] By identifying the problems of modern democratic praxis, O'Leary rightly contends that the promise of inclusion overwhelms the oppressive reality many experience. In some ways, this book has demonstrated how the ideals of Americanization corroded the very possibilities of advancement. We cannot forget that thousands experienced the very betrayal and violence O'Leary notes. Forced detention, government surveillance, vigilantism, and persecution are all rendered even more violent by the very contradictions entailed in the democratic ambitions of the nation. To be promised rights and belonging while experiencing abject alienation is an incredibly palpable treason.

Yet, the paradoxes of Americanization need not be understood solely as betrayal; rather, rhetorical analysis shows that the paradox of patriotism engendered the conditions of the Americanization project, including its possibilities and foreclosures. By moving away from pure ethnic or nativist definitions of nationalism, civic nationalists sought to create a new set of standards for defining national identity. Progressives responded to ethnic nationalism by suggesting that true Americans could be fashioned from an increasingly heterogeneous population. The work of visuality in these efforts highlights how the slipperiness of meaning proved essential to the Americanization movement. The very ambiguity of determining Americanism supplied the possibility of resignifying who could become an American. The battle between ethnic nationalism and civic nationalism should not be understood as a moment when the progressives lost and thereby doomed immigrants and others to the pronouncements of reactionaries. Instead, it is the potentiality of resignification, the rhetorical operations of reenvisioning nationalism and national identity that structured the terms of this exchange.

Thus, Americanization cannot be studied as simply a failure or as a success. Instead, Americanization both succeeded and failed in relationship to the productive ambiguity at its core. In other words, the work of redefining American qualities was essential to the project's motivation and subsequent admonitions on the project's failure. The question at the heart of the project—how do you know an American when you see one?—supplied the framework for how Americanization proceeded. The question itself did not need a resolute answer to provide a foundational set of principles for assessing patriotism. The strong connection between internal emotions and external markers remained despite legislative and other pronouncements on the demise of the Americanization movement. Visual assessments continued to animate larger public discussions on the patriot even as many acknowledged the uncertainty of such evidence. In this way, the relay between visual proof and internal feelings founded larger changes in national identity.

Americanization changed public culture by creating a broad set of rubrics for recognizing fellow Americans, even as individual performances could never satisfy completely such standards. The role of Americanization was constitutive, a rhetorical endeavor that oriented how patriotism and Americanism could be pursued. Jennifer Mercieca argues that American political discourse is "a rhetorical fiction that appears faithfully to describe political reality while it is also used to create political realities."[8] Political narratives are used as founding fictions, stories that serve a persuasive function in managing the public. With Americanization, the foundational mythos of nationalism was not fully narratological. Instead, visual markers of patriotism constituted the paradoxical relationship between fiction and reality—a generative failure that shaped the pursuit of Americanism as a recognizable public good even though few could live up to that ideal.

To be sure, the ambiguity at stake in the Americanization project did not impact all residents equally. The tension between external proof and internal affection remained burdened by larger understandings of racial difference. The racial hierarchy evident in Americanization underscores how visuality became both an access point to acceptance and a brutal measuring stick used to punish those who appeared different. Desmond King contends that the discourses of Americanization and assimilation reinforced prejudices against already existing groups.[9] He maintains that while Americanization and similar discourses evoked melting-pot liberalism, that myth clashed with groups for whom race, ethnicity, and nationalism bore material significance.[10] For King, nationhood was managed via the tensions among group identity, individualism, and national unity. The concept of nationalism during this period relied on a clear "hierarchy of groups at its core."[11] The visual logic of Americanization was beholden to this hierarchy of nationalism, the set of exclusions defining broad categorizations of groups and peoples. As a case in point, the intimate correspondence between visual proof of patriotism and eugenic typologies played a significant role in congressional debate on immigration restriction. For those who could perform in publicly acceptable terms, the opportunities for draping oneself in patriotism seemed easier. For others, that possibility remained a distant option. Nevertheless, the paradoxical relationship between external signs and internal disaffection supplied the terms of recognition.

An exemplar of this disparity is clear in those Americanization programs designed for minority citizens at the time, including mountaineers, black Americans, American Indians, and others.[12] Like those lessons catering to immigrants, programs designed by the Department of the Interior, university scholars, and others often focused on those minority citizens who ostensibly lacked patriotic enthusiasm.[13] In these efforts, racial, regional, and ethnic groups were deemed unlike most Americans because they did not *feel* the same way about the United States and therefore did not *show* a robust love of country or attempt to assimilate. As with the focus on happiness and tranquility in housing reform, Americanism became predicated on embracing positive emotions over disaffection. Yet, despite such antipathy, the solution was not to remedy the circumstances fostering the wrong feelings, but rather to transform sentiments through Americanization. Americanization enthusiasts focused on the feelings caused by unequal conditions, rather than the structural and material changes that might inspire national devotion. Here, the underlying assumptions driving Americanization stressed reforms that bolstered patriotic action to embolden the spirit of the disenfranchised. Given that Americanization reduced the possibilities of inclusion to shallow and superficial markers, these changes protected, rather than removed, the very system of exclusion breeding disaffection.

Black public intellectuals certainly did not ignore the enmity cultivated by such haphazard schemes. Commentary on the privileges afforded immigrants over minorities and the contradictions of attempts to Americanize current citizens, particularly black Americans, emerged in a number of outlets.[14] In *The Crisis*, W.E.B. Du Bois regularly commented upon and, in his editorial role, included stories and pieces of interest on the perception of un-Americanism in black citizens. For instance, in 1922, Du Bois quoted a representative from Yale University who told a "colored graduate" that "We do not want Jews or Negroes or Chinamen at Yale, we want *Americans*."[15] Against this ideology, Du Bois presciently argued that Americanization was not an attempt to make "this country one great homogenous whole working for the same ideals, defending the integrity, preserving its hard found liberty."[16] Instead, Americanization was "the determination to make the English New England stock dominant in the United States, and to make it dominate not only in its fine language and democratic ideals and freedom of thought, but in any modern narrowing and contradiction and denial of these older ideals which newer and lesser men may bring."[17] The end result, for Du Bois, of Americanization was "the disenfranchisement of Negro, Jew, Irishman, Italian, Hungarian, Asiatic and South Sea islander."[18] Du Bois thus railed against the Americanization system as affording more rights to preferred groups while circumscribing opportunities for unwanted groups. Ultimately, Du Bois's critique described Americanization as a movement touting an ideal, unified democracy while disavowing the exclusions at stake in its methods.

The hierarchy of race, ethnicity, and nationalism evident during this period is imbricated within the paradoxical visual logic of Americanization. The entire mission of Americanization was an attempt to overcome the limitations of nativist commitments, to suggest that an American could become something other than previously imagined. As a progressive, even liberal doctrine, it managed the concept of nationalism by redefining the rubrics of inclusion. Yet, as Michael Kaplan argues, "Liberalism is not only one among several possible solutions to the 'democratic paradox'; rather, it is *nothing other than the discursive production of this paradox as an organizing political trope*."[19] To negotiate individual autonomy and collective rule, the people must opt into such a paradoxical condition. That is, the people must presume that their individual autonomy is protected by a democratic system based in majoritarian decision-making. In this way, paradox is a constituent feature of national public life during the modern era. Americanization discourses and practices sought to overcome nativism by proving the emotional dedication of immigrants. Thus, while scholars have amply demonstrated how Americanization focused on creating particularized subjects—white, Anglo-Saxon, Protestants—understanding its visual logic suggests that the fantasy of transcending difference nevertheless animated the entire project.[20] Negotiating the balance between national unity and group difference was foundational to the logic of Americanization. Put simply, scholars can neither treat Americanization as simply the imposition of normative standards from an elite population, nor view it as a progressive attempt at inclusion. Instead, the visual logic animating the project constituted and reinforced both of these ends.

Rhetorical criticism is especially useful in understanding the paradoxical relations that gave rise to and influenced the outcomes of the Americanization movement. In particular, a tropological analysis indicates how the slipperiness of the sign enabled resignification while circumscribing the possibilities of inclusion. Tropes are methodological tools that help critics decipher the structure and simultaneous ambiguity of meaning. While a number of scholars have suggested that Americanization changed the symbols of national identity or that patriotism became a narrow concept during this period, a tropological analysis affords more nuanced conclusions. That is, Americanization certainly *attempted* to redefine patriotism as a fixed entity, but the indeterminacy of securing meaning haunted the project and motivated its work. If scholars were to only employ the symbol as a mechanism of analysis, they might miss this productive ambiguity. A tropological analysis bears scholarly fruit by considering the relationship between the seen and unseen as a significant rhetorical enterprise.

The visuality of tropes is an especially salient feature of Americanization discourses and practices. In the simplest sense, Americanization lessons aimed to dazzle students with images. Other tutelage used public performance and display to render immigrants' affections recognizable to the public. These exhibitions presented immigrants through rhetorical forms that strove to meaningfully appease proclamations of disloyalty. Visual aids and performative rituals supplied ostensibly effective pedagogy and demonstrable forms of proof. Tropes thus access the structure of representation at stake in these rhetorical lessons. The visual logic of Americanization constituted the means through which the public could recognize new populations as capable of patriotism.

Visual tropes and figures of representation often operate differently than language-based tropes or even narratological schemes. Americanization as a tropological endeavor ventured to change the visual contours of Americanism, to create a set of signs indicating emotional fidelity. These schemes of representation visualized Americanism, a rhetorical enterprise that modified the visual and performative lenses through which patriotism could be recognized. Throughout these endeavors, figures were not ornaments of language, but rather styles of visual presentation. The sights of the country and the immigrant body were fashioned through rhetorical schemes that conveyed their place in the larger order. These tropological relations were premised on sight or recognition—visual modes of sense-making. The reality of who could become an American was situated within and against visual and performative rubrics of interpretation. Larger shifts in public culture, then, were generated by the visual matrices of nationalism.

One of the most interesting features of tropes is the oft-theorized relationship between linguistic signification and public imagination. For many authors, tropes and figures are language-based, yet when tropes index the image, the poetic function of signification comes to the fore. Scholars who attend to the imaginative potential of language identify the world-making potential of tropes and figures to "set before the eyes," as Aristotle wrote.[21] Tropes and figures are not simply language or ornamentation; they craft the worlds in which humans see and respond to one another. In these accounts, there is a harmonious and inspirational relationship between language and the human imagination: tropes give rise to the images that shape how we see the world and other human beings in it.[22] Yet, in these accounts, the image remains useful only inasmuch as it helps to visualize language. Tropes and figures are beholden to a linguistic understanding of human interaction and its poetic possibilities.

As a case in point, Paul Ricoeur argues that the relationship between language and images is symbiotic, enabling an imaginative potential in the relay. Ricoeur assumes reciprocity between the poetic work of tropological meaning-making and the verbal. As he argues, to "teach the genus, to grasp the relatedness of terms that are far apart, is to set before the eyes."[23] Tropes turn "imagination into the place where the figurative meaning emerges in the interplay of identity and difference."[24] Here, the tensions between the verbal dimension and visual dimension "confront each other" in the figure, in the possibilities of figuring reality.[25] The field of tropological relations generates its rhetorical work in the juxtaposition between image and word. But more importantly, relations of identity and difference are not condensed or collapsed in this economy. Instead, the tension between these two is maintained: they confront each other. Such a confrontation enables the possibility of figuration.

If critics attend to tropes as something more than or unique from linguistic devices, the paradoxical work of imagistic figuration becomes useful as a methodological optic. Just as linguistic tropes are predicated on a potentially productive ambiguity, the image can serve in a similar capacity. W.J.T. Mitchell makes use of Roland Barthes to suggest that the image often evokes a productive paradox. A photograph is paradoxical because it "both is and is not a language."[26] The contradictions of photography are predicated on a message evolving from the illusion of a neutral, non-coded image. What a photograph does culturally or rhetorically is obvoluted in the tensions of signification—the ambiguity undercutting the attempt to fix what something means or is. The contrast between the image and other sign systems, including the linguistic, enables the cultural work of the photograph. The juxtaposition between referent and sign twists and turns to enable the rhetorical work of the image.

Reading the visual logic of Americanization suggests that the paradoxical work of trope pushes on the symbiotic or reciprocal relationship theorized by Ricoeur and others. The confrontation between identity and difference did not shore up the meaning of Americanism or allow radical reconfigurations of national belonging. Instead, the considerable ambiguity of reading patriotic signs persisted. Americanization sought to resignify Americanism through a select set of visual markers and rituals. However, visual typologies did little to combat the perception that difference remained inherent such that a related disaffection could endure. Visual typologies thus reified the differences of immigrants and others to hinder the possibilities of being read as Americans. Identity and difference did not simply confront one another; identity and difference became the grounds of Americanization's doing and undoing. Indeed, this ambiguity was put on public display such that identity and difference were points of ample disputation. Tensions between identity and difference structured the possibilities and foreclosures of Americanization. These tensions were not purely linguistic, but primarily engendered and sustained by the visuality of the Americanization project.

Ultimately, the generative ground for the Americanization project did eventually erode. Immigration restriction and other anti-immigrant arguments succeeded in closing the borders and insisting that true Americans could not be created. The political work of paradox is noteworthy here. For a number of scholars, the figure of paradox enables a "political quietism" or "mystification."[27] The ambivalence of meaning is difficult to mobilize into effective forms of change or resistance, particularly in the realm of politics. In the end, the paradox must be negotiated, often in ways that diminish or disavow any productive prospects.[28] In the United States, the mystical politics of Americanization concluded with immigration restriction and ongoing lamentations on the inherent differences of immigrants and minorities. This end point, however, cannot simply become a retroactive lens through which to view the entirety of Americanization. Instead, it is the predictable outcome of the visual logic of the project. The project was motivated by the ambiguity of the sign while that same ambiguity undermined the possibility of definitive proof. The generative paradox that fueled robust enthusiasm for the Americanization project is the same condition that ultimately foreclosed the possibilities of Americanization.

Yet, the legacy of the Americanization project is not merely jettisoned into the dustbin of history. Traces of its visual logic appear throughout the twentieth and twenty-first centuries. Consider the flag pin controversy of the 2012 election. During presidential debates, commentators began to take interest in whether or not President Barack Obama was wearing a flag pin on his lapel.[29] These queries referenced Obama's claim from 2007 in which he declared that he decided at some point after September 11, 2001, to no longer wear a flag pin, as he believed wearing the pin contributed to false patriotism. Then-Senator Obama stated, "You know, the truth is that right after 9/11, I had a pin. Shortly after 9/11 . . . that became a substitute for, I think, true patriotism, which is speaking out on issues that are of importance to our national security, I decided I won't wear that pin on my chest; instead, I'm gonna try to tell the American people what I believe will make this country great, and hopefully that will be a testimony to my patriotism."[30] After much public criticism, Obama changed his accessorizing practices rather quickly and he began wearing the pin again. Conservative publications were quick to use this history and denounce his return to false patriotism during the 2012 debates against Mitt Romney. Charles Kesler of the *National Review* used Obama as an exemplar for all "liberals" who "have been sensitive about the dimensions of their patriotism."[31] Kesler noted that Obama had been "outmaneuvered" by Mitt Romney in presidential debates as Romney's flag pin was "much larger than Obama's flag pin."[32] The joke enabled Kesler to highlight Obama's "disdain for, or at least impatience with, ordinary American patriotism."[33] Kesler distinguished Obama's high-minded ideals from demonstrative, "ordinary" patriotism.

Concern for the flag-honoring habits of the president and other politicians has not subsided since 2012. Snopes.com, a fact-checking website, has over a dozen entries debunking myths about flag lapel pins, flying the U.S. flag, and other aspects of venerating Old Glory. It seems that in some ways, contemporary measurements of patriotism are very much based on simple assessments. As Gilbert Cruz of *Time* magazine asserted,

"Are you currently wearing a flag pin? Yes? Then you love America. No? Hmm. That's gonna be a problem."[34] According to Cruz, politicians wearing a flag pin or other small symbols of American patriotism is a modern invention—a sartorial practice bequeathed by the conflicts of World War II and the cultural crises kicked off in the 1960s. This simple gesture has become a quick method for determining the patriotism of the wearer. As Stanley Renshon of Politico.com advised, unless patriotic acts are accompanied by other "emotional anchors," they remain suspect.[35]

Contemporary citizens, then, are beholden to a similar paradoxical visual logic to that of the early twentieth century, one in which patriotism is unbelievable without external signs. More tellingly, as with Renshon, those external signs are problematic absent clear "emotional anchors."[36] In part, then, the visual work of displaying patriotism is much older than mid-twentieth-century culture wars. Americanization and the legacy of the Progressive Era can be traced through present-day discussions of patriotic exhibition. Determining the patriotism of oneself and others is often an interrogation of emotional commitments via acts and emblems of loyalty. While investment in media spectacles, consumer understandings of citizenship, and other factors play a large part in measuring contemporary patriotism, the rubrics at stake seem indebted to the paradoxical visual logic of the Americanization movement.

Of course, Obama's sartorial practices are given far more scrutiny than others, and it is here that the disaffection of difference comes to the fore. A number of scholars have shown how Obama's Americanness is questioned via his flag pin practices.[37] As these authors suggest, concerns pertaining to his flag pin or nation of origin (the demand for visual evidence of a long-form birth certificate) are more likely a cipher for racism. Emotional nationalism and racial nationalism intertwine such that Americanness becomes an ideal broadcast in the visual practices of presidential candidates and presidents just as that ideal is undercut by racial ideology. The persistence of differences becomes imbricated in the very quotidian, yet political performances of patriotism. Gestures toward more inclusive models of patriotism are interwoven within racialized understandings of Americanism.

As during the early twentieth century, the fantasy of transcending difference animates political debate just as those same debates are constrained and enabled by broader understandings of the emotional, sometimes affective, foundations of nationalism. In no small way, Americans today are expected to aspire to idealized or normative models of citizenship that categorize appropriate demonstrations of national feelings. As Lauren Berlant writes, "The only way Americans can claim both rights and mass sympathy is to demonstrate, not panic, anger, demand, and desire, but ethical serenity, hyperpatriotism, and proper deference. Political emotions like anxiety, rage, and aggression turn out to be feelings only privileged people are justified in having."[38] For Berlant, there is a "cruelty of sympathy, the costs it extracts in fixing abject suffering as the only condition of social membership, [that] is measured in the vast expanse between the scene of feeling and the effects that policies exert."[39] Thus, while conservatives and liberals alike now assert that national belonging can be attained by anyone, the terms of membership are predicated on adopting certain visual practices and participating in a community of feeling that expects some populations to accept the joy of suffering. In a robust set of contemporary scholarly works, including Berlant, the relationships between public culture, national emotions, and visibility have demonstrated the ways our modern national life is very much predicated on shared feelings that orient nationalism in particular ways.[40]

Contemporary displays of emotional nationalism continue to be paradoxical, even confounding. They are productive failures, perpetuating a self-sustaining cycle. Today the visual display of resentment, rage, and anger impact public discourse and policy, particularly when these feelings are expressed by privileged populations. Antoine J. Banks argues that racialized anger is used to sway white voters on a whole host of policies, including ostensibly non-racialized issues such as the Affordable Care Act.[41] Seen through a rhetorical lens, anger is a suasory performance directing constituents to national policy options. Much as during the early twentieth century, the paradox of displaying emotion and verifying national dedication animates political groups. Anger is a tool for galvanizing voters and a means through which they determine who is invested legitimately in their nationalistic feelings. Importantly, and as Jeremy Engels argues, the politics of rage and resentment perpetuate these public feelings.[42] The relationship between emotion and display sustains the ambiguity undergirding nationalism. Just as in the early twentieth century, the stakes of this ambiguity are not experienced evenly. Anger becomes a political weapon that entrenches oppression, reifies unequal access, and justifies violence. Public displays of rage are a paradoxical and self-sustaining form of public discourse. Current nationalistic emotions, then, resonate with the exhibitionist patriotism of the Progressive Era.

In the early twentieth century, happiness and loyalty were the quintessential emotions of Americanism, while today's emotional nationalism seems centered on fear and anger. This outcome is not surprising. As a popular aphorism cautions, "history doesn't repeat itself but it often rhymes."[43] Given that paradoxes are fueled by a kind of dialectical aporia, the underbelly of positive hyperpatriotism in the early twentieth century was a discontent that demanded redress. In attempting to diminish these negative sentiments, Americanization helped birth modern nationalism—Americanism was defined in resolutely positive, material terms. This endeavor overemphasized superficial markers of belonging, and suppressed dissent and disaffection by enforcing uniformity. In some instances, markers of anti-patriotism were punished by vigilante action. An intense focus on the appearance of patriotism, then, can help fuel anger and fear given the ambiguity of reading signs. Tellingly, the structural inequalities of the present day have exacerbated the conditions in which heightened displays of emotion, especially anger, affect the populace. Yet, the tensions between visibility and invisibility play into the efficacy of anger as a political wedge. Anger becomes a visual form that verifies the legitimacy of one's political position just as it sustains that selfsame antipathy.

As such, rhetorically analyzing the Americanization movement of the early twentieth century supplements how scholars might understand emotional nationalism. The rhetorical relationship between emotional fidelity and the concomitant need for disavowing the particularities of difference is formulized in the visual logic of Americanization. Americanization as articulated broadly across public culture reified larger understandings of nationalism such that membership required citizens to reject their disaffection and embrace regular displays of patriotism. Given that the focus on emotional nationalism did little to combat the bases of animus, immigrants and others were asked to live in the hazy scene of possibility, to reach toward a future in which they might find reconciliation. Today, the politics of anger alongside the need for outward displays of belonging (e.g., flag pins) participate in a similar foreclosure. Much as in the Americanization movement, a paradoxical relationship between display and feeling ensures a continued cacophony of cliquish political arguments with little focus on rectifying the reasons for enmity. The exhibition of anger by privileged populations affirms their entitlements while that same rage dismisses any grievances from minority groups. Nationalistic displays of enmity are predicated on perceived personal losses and therefore dismiss broad efforts toward reconciliation with the disenfranchised. The pageantry of rage dismantles the bonds of community. Examining the visual logic of nationalism in the Americanization movement clarifies the problematic foundations of emotional nationalism. By analyzing the visual contours of citizenship in the early twentieth century, scholars can gain a more robust understanding of the tensions of modern nationalism.

The rhetorical work of Americanization was not to simply define nationalism, but to create the markers through which Americanism could be recognizable. The politics of recognition, of being afforded the benefit of being seen as a possible American, was engendered by the visual logic of Americanization. Before one could be treated as a citizen, bargain for inclusion, or dispute the oppressive practices of the period, one had to grapple with those assessments that constrained who could engage in national politics. The rhetoric of Americanization constituted a set of public norms for being seen as a potential American, and circumscribed those who were able to work within those matrices. Rhetoric, then, created the ground upon which nationalism was framed.

Yet, the impact of Americanization on public culture also informs how scholars can learn from the possibilities of resignification. While this rhetorical history teaches us the damning consequences of particularistic demands, hope remains that historical work can redefine our present understanding of nationalism. Indeed, it is precisely the gap between the figure and the concept that enables the reconfiguration of rhetorical forms and insists that rhetoric can always do something differently. Put simply, what is communicated through rhetorical forms can always be rearticulated. While during the years surrounding the First World War, Americans were largely beholden to hyperpatriotic standards that could not be met fully, the visual logic of nationalism could have engendered other outcomes.

Contemplate, for a moment, the discussion of choral singing ensembles presented earlier in this volume. There, I argued that immigrants singing patriotic songs projected to the public a desire for belonging that could not reassure the public of their allegiance. While the performance might operate as a performative contradiction precluding present belonging, that contradiction need not be understood as a moment of impasse. Rather, much can be made of the paradox of visuality. In my historical analysis, what is "made" is the translation of a performative contradiction into a space of ambiguity. That is, the claim to citizenship enunciated in singing patriotic songs did not ensure national belonging, but rather accentuated the need for Americanization. Yet, despite this rather deflating conclusion, the singing itself expressed the struggle many endured to be heard, seen, and recognized as members of the people, the *demos*. Thus, even if immigrants were asked to live in the scene of possibility, to yield their voice to the unity of the nation, we need not see their efforts as merely palliative. Rather, the very performative contradictions at stake here—belonging/exclusion, citizen/alien, aesthetics/politics—is the very hope offered within democracy as a site of struggle. In these hopeful moments, democratic expression is not a moment of nation-building, or the machinations of government, but an ongoing project within which the people come to claim the potential of a nation of, by, and for the people.[44] As such, this historical case study reminds us that the business of "we the people" is messy, rife with contradiction, and often unfolds in terms that are less than ideal. These paradoxes are not antithetical to democracy; they are the very aporias upon which democracy is founded and that which citizens must nevertheless navigate to reinvent the nation.

To study the rhetorical movements of history reminds us, then, that there is always possibility. While rhetoric can create modes of sense-making that circumscribe opportunity and agency, it is the very contingency of rhetorical arrangements that insist on new horizons and possibilities.[45] This volume has demonstrated how the visual logic of the period not only explains the impossible terms demanded by Americanization authorities, but also illuminates the prospects entailed in those Americanization endeavors able to rearrange broader understandings of nationalism. Americanization was not destined to fail simply by virtue of the fanatical atmosphere of the war years. Instead, an interrogation of the visual logics of Americanization suggests that the promise of Americanization lay in opening up the senses, in allowing for a broader field of recognition than was previously imagined.

By using a tropological lens to grasp the contours of Americanization, scholars not only glean a better understanding of history, but also enable new trajectories for discerning the moments of potential within our own epoch. During the years surrounding World War I, the terms of citizenship were predicated on restricted opportunities. Understanding the limitations of this logic is not simply important to our national history, but also encourages us to interrogate those visual logics of nationalism that overburden our current understandings of patriotism. Informed by studying the period in which many of our sacred national rituals came to be, we must remember that the promise of rhetoric is that much can be changed through effective persuasion. How we see one another matters. Our ability to recognize one another transfigures our relationships. We can learn to see anew, to change how we relate to one another when those forms of kinship become toxic. This is not to suggest that such a task is easy. To study rhetoric is to understand that successful persuasion requires continual accommodation to ever-changing, and often radically contingent, circumstances and worldviews. A reflexive understanding of the terms through which individuals are recognized as patriots, citizens, or even rights-bearing subjects can transform our expectations and the basis of our human ties.

Notes

Introduction

1. Robert Justin Goldstein, *Political Repression in Modern America from 1870 to 1976* (Champaign-Urbana: University of Illinois Press, 2001), 100.
2. Woodrow Wilson, "Proclamation 1335—Flag Day," The Presidency Project, May 30, 1916, http://www.presidency.ucsb.edu/ws/?pid=62991.
3. John F. McClymer, "Gender and the 'American Way of Life': Women in the Americanization Movement," *Journal of American Ethnic History* 10 (1991): 3.
4. Wilson, "Proclamation 1335—Flag Day."
5. See, for example, Paul McBride, "Peter Roberts and the YMCA Americanization Program 1907–World War I," *Pennsylvania History* 44 (1977): 147, 156; McClymer, "Gender and the 'American Way of Life,'" 12; Jeffrey E. Mirel, *Patriotic Pluralism: Americanization Education and European Immigrants* (Cambridge, MA: Harvard University Press, 2010), 56, 78; Michael R. Olneck, "Americanization and the Education of Immigrants, 1900–1925: An Analysis of Symbolic Action," *American Journal of Education* 97 (1989): 412–14.

6. Edward George Hartmann, *The Movement to Americanize the Immigrant* (New York: Columbia University Press, 1948), 58, 112–20, 128–32, 152, 167, 192, 237.
7. Stephen Meyer, "Adapting the Immigrant to the Line: Americanization in the Ford Factory, 1914–1921," *Journal of Social History* 14 (1980): 77.
8. Many historians simply note that Ford used spectacular events. See James R. Barrett, "Americanization from the Bottom Up: Immigration and the Remaking of the Working Class in the United States, 1880–1930," *Journal of American History* 79 (1992): 996; Anne Brophy, "'The Committee . . . Has Stood Out against Coercion': The Reinvention of Detroit Americanization, 1915–1931," *Michigan Historical Review* 29 (2003): 1. Other scholars situate the pageant as indicative of Ford's assimilationist position. See Gayle Gullett, "Women Progressives and the Politics of Americanization in California, 1915–1920," *Pacific Historical Review* 64 (1995): 77; Mirel, *Patriotic Pluralism*, 181.
9. Terry Lindvall, *Sanctuary Cinema: Origins of the Christian Film Industry* (New York: New York University Press, 2007), 86.
10. Mary E. Stuckey, *Defining Americans: The Presidency and National Identity* (Lawrence: University Press of Kansas, 2004), 9.
11. Robert Hariman and John Louis Lucaites, *No Caption Needed: Iconic Photographs, Public Culture, and Liberal Democracy* (Chicago: University of Chicago Press, 2007), 26.
12. Hariman and Lucaites, *No Caption Needed*, 26.
13. On the creation of a deliberative public culture during the Progressive Era, see J. Michael Hogan, "Introduction: Rhetoric and Reform in the Progressive Era," in *Rhetoric and Reform in the Progressive Era*, ed. J. Michael Hogan (East Lansing: Michigan State University Press, 2003), xiv–xv.
14. Terry Papillion, "Isocrates' Techne and Rhetorical Pedagogy," *Rhetoric Society Quarterly* 25 (1995): 152.
15. Ronald Walter Greene, "Rhetorical Pedagogy as Postal System: Circulating Subjects through Michael Warner's 'Publics and Counterpublics,'" *Quarterly Journal of Speech* 88 (2002): 441.
16. Greene, "Rhetorical Pedagogy," 441.
17. Greene, "Rhetorical Pedagogy," 441.
18. Angela Ray, *The Lyceum and Public Culture in the Nineteenth-Century United States* (East Lansing: Michigan State University Press, 2005), 7.
19. Ray, *Lyceum and Public Culture*, 7.
20. David Glassberg, *American Historical Pageantry: The Uses of Tradition in the*

Early Twentieth Century (Chapel Hill: University of North Carolina Press, 1990); Cecilia Elizabeth O'Leary, *To Die For: The Paradox of American Patriotism* (Princeton, NJ: Princeton University Press, 1999).

21. Mary Lou Nemanic, *One Day for Democracy: Independence Day and the Americanization of Iron Range Immigrants* (Athens: Ohio University Press, 2007), 34.
22. Raymond W. Smilor, "Creating a National Festival: The Campaign for a Safe and Sane Fourth, 1903–1916," *Journal of American Culture* 2 (1980): 611–22; John E. Bodnar, *Remaking America: Public Memory, Commemoration, and Patriotism in the Twentieth Century* (Princeton, NJ: Princeton University Press, 1980), 32–33, 80.
23. Nemanic, *One Day for Democracy*, 35.
24. Smilor, "Creating a National Festival," 611; S. W. Pope, *Patriotic Games: Sporting Traditions in the American Imagination, 1876–1926* (New York: Oxford University Press, 1997), 109.
25. Glassberg, *American Historical Pageantry*, 55.
26. Glassberg, *American Historical Pageantry*, 55.
27. Glassberg, *American Historical Pageantry*, 62.
28. Marc Leepson, *Flag: An American Biography* (New York: St. Martin's, 2007), 66.
29. Leepson, *Flag*, 66.
30. Leepson, *Flag*, 66–67.
31. O'Leary, *To Die For*, 230. See also Richard J. Ellis, *To the Flag: The Unlikely History of the Pledge of Allegiance* (Lawrence: University Press of Kansas, 2005), 78–80.
32. O'Leary, *To Die For*, 231.
33. O'Leary, *To Die For*, 231.
34. Glassberg, *American Historical Pageantry*, 25.
35. O'Leary, *To Die For*, 227–30.
36. See, for example, Cara Finnegan, "The Naturalistic Enthymeme and Visual Argument: Photographic Representation in the 'Skull Controversy,'" *Argumentation & Advocacy* 37 (2001): 133–49; Hariman and Lucaites, *No Caption Needed*, 9–10.
37. See, for example, Fahnestock's discussion of Quintilian's notion of metaphor: Jeanne Fahnestock, *Rhetorical Style: The Uses of Language in Persuasion* (New York: Oxford University Press, 2011), 105. Or, Johannesen, Strickland, and Eubanks's reading of Richard Weaver: Richard L. Johannesen, Rennard Strickland, and Ralph T. Eubanks, "Richard M. Weaver on the Nature of Rhetoric: An Interpretation," in *The Vision of Richard Weaver*, ed. Joseph Scotchie

(New Brunswick, NJ: Transaction Publishers, 1995), 93–110. Likewise, John S. Nelson's discussion of tropes as corralling and inventing the political landscape is noteworthy here: John S. Nelson, *Tropes of Politics: Science, Theory, Rhetoric, Action* (Madison: University of Wisconsin Press, 1998).

38. Bradford Vivian, "Neoliberal Epideictic: Rhetorical Form and Commemorative Politics on September 11, 2002," *Quarterly Journal of Speech* 92 (2006): 7. See also Bradford Vivian, *Public Forgetting: The Rhetoric and Politics of Beginning Again* (University Park: Penn State University Press, 2010), 71.

39. Robert Hariman and John Louis Lucaites, "Visual Tropes and Late-Modern Emotion in U.S. Public Culture," *Poroi* 5 (2008): 48.

40. See, for example, Robert Carlson, *The Quest for Conformity: Americanization through Education* (New York: Wiley, 1975), 458; McClymer, "Gender and the 'American Way of Life,'" 7; Stephen Meyer, "Adapting the Immigrant to the Line: Americanization in the Ford Factory, 1914–1921," *Journal of Social History* 14 (1980): 78; Olneck, "Americanization and the Education of Immigrants," 398.

41. Mirel, *Patriotic Pluralism*, 11.

42. See, for example, John J. Bukowczyk, "The Transformation of Working-Class Ethnicity: Corporate Control, Americanization, and the Polish Immigrant Middle Class in Bayonne, New Jersey, 1915–1925," *Labor History* 25 (1984): 53–82; Mirel, *Patriotic Pluralism*, 89–92.

43. See, for example, Anne Teresa Demo and Bradford Vivian, eds., *Rhetoric, Remembrance, and Visual Form: Sighting Memory* (New York: Routledge, 2012); Janis L. Edwards and Carol K. Winkler, "Representative Form and the Visual Ideograph: The Iwo Jima Image in Editorial Cartoons," *Quarterly Journal of Speech* 83 (1997): 289–310; Martin J. Medhurst and Michael A. DeSousa, "Political Cartoons as Rhetorical Form: A Taxonomy of Graphic Discourse," *Communication Monographs* 48 (1981): 197–236; Catherine Palczewski, "The Male Madonna and the Feminine Uncle Sam: Visual Argument, Icons, and Ideographs in 1909 Anti–Woman Suffrage Postcards," *Quarterly Journal of Speech* 91 (2005): 365–94.

44. See, for example, John Higham, *Strangers in the Land: Patterns of American Nativism, 1860–1925* (New Brunswick, NJ: Rutgers University Press, 2002), 300–330; Desmond King, *Making Americans: Immigration, Race, and the Origins of the Diverse Democracy* (Cambridge, MA: Harvard University Press, 2002); James R. Barrett and David Roediger, "Inbetween Peoples: Race, Nationality and the 'New Immigrant' Working Class," *Journal of American Ethnic History* 16 (1997):

32–34.
45. Mirel, *Patriotic Pluralism*, 11.
46. Mirel, *Patriotic Pluralism*. Certainly, Americanization classes were available in other major metropolitan areas (New York City, St. Louis, etc.) and even rural sites, but Chicago, Detroit, and Cleveland hosted a majority of programs and therefore produced a large number of pedagogical materials.
47. See, for example, Noriko Asato, "Mandating Americanization: Japanese Language Schools and the Federal Survey of Education in Hawai'i, 1916–1920," *History of Education Quarterly* 43 (2003): 10–38; Mario T. Garcia, "Americanization and the Mexican Immigrant, 1880–1930," *Journal of Ethnic Studies* 6 (1978): 19–34; Gullett, "Women Progressives," 71–94.
48. Higham, *Strangers in the Land*; King, *Making Americans*; Olneck, "Americanization and the Education of Immigrants"; David R. Roediger, *Working toward Whiteness: How America's Immigrants Became White* (Cambridge, MA: Perseus Books, 2005).
49. See, for example, Gary Gerstle, "Liberty, Coercion, and the Making of Americans," *Journal of American History* 84 (1997): 524–58; Seth Korelitz, "'A Magnificent Piece of Work': The Americanization Work of the National Council of Jewish Women," *American Jewish History* 83 (1995): 201; McClymer, "Gender and the 'American Way of Life,'" 7.
50. Title 36—*Patriotic and National Observances, Ceremonies, and Organizations, U.S. Code* 2006, §110.
51. "The National Flag Day Foundation," http://www.nationalflagday.com.

Chapter One. Public Culture
and the Americanization of Immigrants

1. Jeffrey E. Mirel, *Patriotic Pluralism: Americanization Education and European Immigrants* (Cambridge, MA: Harvard University Press, 2010), 13.
2. Leonard Dinnerstein and David M. Reimers, *Ethnic Americans: A History of Immigration and Assimilation* (New York: Dodd, Mead & Co., 1975), 39–40.
3. John Durham Peters and Peter Simonson, eds., *Mass Communication and American Social Thought: Key Texts, 1919–1968* (Lanham, MD: Rowman & Littlefield, 2004), 22.
4. John Higham, *Strangers in the Land: Patterns of American Nativism, 1860–1925* (New Brunswick, NJ: Rutgers University Press, 2002), 87.
5. Higham, *Strangers in the Land*, 87.

6. Andrew Gyory, *Closing the Gate: Race, Politics, and the Chinese Exclusion Act* (Chapel Hill: University of North Carolina Press, 1998).
7. Higham, *Strangers in the Land*.
8. Daniel J. Tichenor, *Dividing Lines: The Politics of Immigration Control in America* (Princeton, NJ: Princeton University Press, 2002), 128–29; Eric Arneson, ed., *Encyclopedia of U.S. Labor and Working Class History* (New York: Routledge, 2007), 1:365–66.
9. U.S. Immigration Commission, *Reports of the Immigration Commission*, 61st Cong., 2nd Sess. (Washington, DC: U.S. Government Printing Office, 1911), 1:ii.
10. Tichenor, *Dividing Lines*, 129.
11. Arneson, *Encyclopedia of U.S. Labor*, 1:366; Tichenor, *Dividing Lines*, 129–30; Christina Ziegler McPherson, "Dillingham Commission," in *Anti-Immigration in the United States, A-R*, ed. Kathleen Arnold (Santa Barbara, CA: ABC-CLIO, 2011), 160.
12. U.S. Immigration Commission, *Reports of the Immigration Commission, Dictionary of Races or Peoples*, 61st Cong., 2nd Sess. (Washington, DC: U.S. Government Printing Office, 1911), 5:2.
13. Tichenor, *Dividing Lines*, 130.
14. Immigration Commission, *Brief Statement of the Conclusions and Recommendations of the Immigration Commission, with Views of the Minority* (Washington, DC: U.S. Government Printing Office, 1910), 26.
15. U.S. Immigration Commission, *Reports of the Immigration Commission: Immigration and Crime*, 61st Cong., 3rd Sess. (Washington, DC: U.S. Government Printing Office, 1911), 188.
16. Tichenor, *Dividing Lines*, 131–35.
17. Sean Dennis Cashman, *America Ascendant: From Theodore Roosevelt to FDR in the Century of American Power, 1901–1945* (New York: New York University Press, 1998), 222.
18. Jerome Karabel, *The Chosen: The Hidden History of Admission and Exclusion at Harvard, Yale, and Princeton* (New York: Houghton Mifflin Harcourt, 2005), 80.
19. Madison Grant, *The Passing of the Great Race: Or, the Racial Basis of European History* (1916; New York: Charles Scribner's Sons, 1918), 82, 224.
20. Grant, *Passing of the Great Race*, 89–90.
21. Grant, *Passing of the Great Race*, 90. That Grant's conception of Native Americans excluded indigenous peoples was an irony likely lost on him.
22. Desmond King, *Making Americans: Immigration, Race, and the Origins of the*

Diverse Democracy (Cambridge, MA: Harvard University Press, 2002), 50–84.

23. Ramiro Martinez Jr., "Coming to America: The Impact of New Immigration on Crime," in *Immigration and Crime: Race, Ethnicity, and Violence*, ed. Ramiro Martinez Jr. and Abel Valenzuela (New York: New York University Press, 2006), 7–8.

24. Mirel, *Patriotic Pluralism*, 15.

25. Though David Roediger has demonstrated the in-betweenness of race as a fixed category for Southern and Eastern European immigrants, it nevertheless structured the "social and intellectual" placement of new immigrants. See David R. Roediger, *Working toward Whiteness: How America's Immigrants Became White* (New York: Perseus Books, 2005), 8.

26. Diana Selig, *Americans All: The Cultural Gifts Movement* (Cambridge, MA: Harvard University Press, 2008), 6.

27. Hans P. Vought, *The Bully Pulpit and the Melting Pot: American Presidents and the Immigrant, 1897–1933* (Macon, GA: Mercer University Press, 2004), 67.

28. King, *Making Americans*, 63.

29. Jeanne D. Petit, *The Men and Women We Want: Gender, Race, and the Progressive Era Literacy Test Debate* (Rochester, NY: University of Rochester Press, 2010), 31–32.

30. Vought, *Bully Pulpit*, 86.

31. M. M. Silver, *Louis Marshall and the Rise of Jewish Ethnicity in America* (Syracuse, NY: Syracuse University Press, 2013), 144.

32. Gerald L. Gutek, *An Historical Introduction to American Education* (Long Grove, IL: Waveland Press, 2013), 351–52; John L. Rury, *Education and Social Change: Contours in the History of American Schooling* (New York: Routledge, 2013), 98–101.

33. John Rogers Commons, *Races and Immigrants in America* (New York: Macmillan, 1920). On Commons's view of assimilation, see Robert Carlson, "Americanization as an Early Twentieth-Century Adult Education Movement," *History of Education Quarterly* 10 (1970): 447.

34. Carlson, "Americanization," 445. On acculturation, see James R. Barrett, "Americanization from the Bottom Up: Immigration and the Remaking of the Working Class in the United States, 1880–1930," *Journal of American History* 79 (1992): 996–1020.

35. Mirel, *Patriotic Pluralism*, 15.

36. Selig, *Americans All*, 8; Mirel, *Patriotic Pluralism*, 15; Gary Gerstle, *American*

Crucible: Race and Nation in the Twentieth Century (Princeton, NJ: Princeton University Press, 2001).

37. Gerstle, *American Crucible*, 46; Leroy Dorsey, *We Are All Americans, Pure and Simple: Theodore Roosevelt and the Myth of Americanism* (Tuscaloosa: University of Alabama Press, 2007), 17.
38. Gerstle, *American Crucible*, 46.
39. Mirel, *Patriotic Pluralism*, 15.
40. Christopher Capozzola, *Uncle Sam Wants You: World War I and the Making of the Modern American Citizen* (New York: Oxford University Press, 2010), 8.
41. Carlson, "Americanization," 56.
42. Stewart Halsey Ross, *Propaganda for the War: How the United States Was Conditioned to Fight the Great War of 1914–1918* (Jefferson, NC: McFarland & Co., 1996), 215–16.
43. David Kennedy, *Over Here: The First World War and American Society* (New York: Oxford University Press, 2004), 47.
44. J. Michael Sproule, *Propaganda and Democracy: The American Experience of Media and Mass Persuasion* (New York: Cambridge University Press, 1997), 16.
45. Nancy Gentile Ford, *The Great War and America: Civil-Military Relations during World War I* (Westport, CT: Praeger, 2008), 3.
46. Stephen Vaughn, *Holding Fast the Inner Lines: Democracy, Nationalism, and the Committee on Public Information* (Chapel Hill: University of North Carolina Press, 1980), 105.
47. Vaughn, *Holding Fast the Inner Lines*, 105.
48. John F. McClymer, "The Federal Government and the Americanization Movement, 1915–24," in *Americanization, Social Control, and Philanthropy*, ed. George E. Pozzetta (New York: Garland Publishing, 1991), 234.
49. Mary Elizabeth Brown, "Henry Cabot Lodge (1850–1924): Immigration as National Policy," in *The Making of Modern Immigration: An Encyclopedia of Peoples and Ideas*, ed. Patrick J. Hayes (Santa Barbara, CA: ABC-CLIO, 2012), 500.
50. Hiroshi Motomura, *Americans in Waiting: The Lost Story of Immigration and Citizenship in the United States* (New York: Oxford University Press, 2006), 125.
51. Capozzola, *Uncle Sam Wants You*, 177; Jennifer K. Elsea, "Detention of American Citizens as Enemy Combatants," in *The Treatment of Prisoners: Legal, Moral, or Criminal?*, ed. Ralph D. McPhee (New York: Nova Publishers, 2006), 11.
52. Elliot Barkan, Hasia R. Diner, and Alan Kraut, eds., *From Arrival to Incorporation: Migrants to the U.S. in a Global Era* (New York: New York University Press, 2007),

247.

53. Barkan, Diner, and Kraut, *From Arrival to Incorporation*, 247.
54. Barkan, Diner, and Kraut, *From Arrival to Incorporation*, 247; David M. O'Brien, "Detentions and Security versus Liberty in Times of National Emergency," in *Courts and Terrorism: Nine Nations Balance Rights and Security*, ed. Mary L. Volcansek and John F. Stack Jr. (New York: Cambridge University Press, 2011), 14.
55. Barkan, Diner, and Kraut, *From Arrival to Incorporation*, 248; O'Brien, "Detentions and Security," 14.
56. Barkan, Diner, and Kraut, *From Arrival to Incorporation*, 247–48; David M. Reimers, *Unwelcome Strangers: American Identity and the Turn against Immigration* (New York: Columbia University Press, 1998), 19.
57. Edgar J. McManus and Tara Helfman, *Liberty and Union: A Constitutional History of the United States* (New York: Routledge, 2014), 325.
58. Richard Striner, *Woodrow Wilson and World War I: A Burden Too Great to Bear* (Lanham, MD: Rowman & Littlefield, 2014), 117–18.
59. Craig R. Smith, "The Red Scares," in *Silencing the Opposition: How the U.S. Government Suppressed Freedom of Speech During Major Crises*, ed. Craig R. Smith (Albany: State University of New York Press, 2011), 176.
60. Kennedy, *Over Here*, 77.
61. Striner, *Woodrow Wilson*, 119.
62. Striner, *Woodrow Wilson*, 119.
63. Nancy Gentile Ford, *Issues of War and Peace* (Westport, CT: Greenwood Press, 2002), 187.
64. Christopher M. Finan, *From the Palmer Raids to the Patriot Act: A History of the Right for Free Speech in America* (Boston, MA: Beacon Press, 2007), 2–3.
65. Susan F. Martin, *A Nation of Immigrants* (New York: Oxford University Press, 2011), 148.
66. Ross, *Propaganda for the War*, 13.
67. Capozzola, *Uncle Sam Wants You*, 180–81; Desmond King, *The Liberty of Strangers: Making the American Nation* (New York: Oxford University Press, 2005), 65.
68. Ross, *Propaganda for the War*, 2–3.
69. Vaughn, *Holding Fast the Inner Lines*, 64.
70. Capozzola, *Uncle Sam Wants You*, 177.
71. Brenton J. Malin, *Feeling Mediated: A History of Media Technology and Emotion in America* (New York: New York University Press, 2014), 34–35.

72. Malin, *Feeling Mediated*, 34; Robert A. Ferguson, *Law and Letters in American Culture* (Cambridge, MA: Harvard University Press, 1984), 231. See also Peter N. Stearns and Jan Lewis, eds., *An Emotional History of the United States* (New York: New York University Press, 1998).
73. Andrew Burstein, *Sentimental Democracy: The Evolution of America's Romantic Self-Image* (New York: Hill and Wang, 1999), 23, 140–41.
74. See, for example, Philip Gibbs, "America's New Place in the World," *Harper's Magazine* 140 (December 1919): 89–97; Winthrop D. Lane, "The National Conference of Social Work," *The Survey* 40 (June 1918): 254.
75. "Fake War Pictures Stir the East Side," *New York Times*, September 6, 1914, http://www.nytimes.com.
76. "Fake War Pictures."
77. Benedict Anderson, *Imagined Communities: Reflections on the Origin and Spread of Nationalism* (New York: Verso, 1983), 6. See also Andrew Shryock, *Nationalism and the Genealogical Imagination: Oral History and Textual Authority in Tribal Jordan* (Berkeley: University of California Press, 1997); Gayatri Chakravorty Spivak, *Nationalism and the Imagination* (New York: Seagull Books, 2015); Charles Taylor, "Nationalism and Modernity," in *The Morality of Nationalism*, ed. Robert McKim and Jeff McMahan (New York: Oxford University Press, 1997), 31–55.
78. Nina Glick Schiller, "Long Distance Nationalism," in *Encyclopedia of Diasporas: Immigrant and Refugee Cultures around the World*, ed. Melvin Ember, Carol R. Ember, and Ian Skoggard (New York: Springer Science and Business Media, 2004), 572.
79. Woodrow Wilson, "President's Topeka Speech: No Place Fuller of Fight Than Kansas, He Declares," *New York Times*, February 3, 1916, http://www.nytimes.com.
80. Wilson, "President's Topeka Speech."
81. Patrick Quinn, "The First World War: American Writing," in *The Cambridge Companion to War Writing*, ed. Kate McLoughlin (New York: Cambridge University Press, 2009), 177.
82. On the book's popular uptake, see "The Hyphen," *Booklist: A Guide to the Best New Books* 17 (1921): 219; "A Two-Decker," *New York Medical Journal*, January 29, 1921, 211.
83. Margaret Blake [Lida C. Schem], *The Hyphen* (New York: E.P. Dutton 1920), 438.
84. Blake [Schem], *The Hyphen*, 441.
85. Blake [Schem], *The Hyphen*, 442.

86. John F. McClymer, "Gender and the 'American Way of Life': Women in the Americanization Movement," *Journal of American Ethnic History* 10 (1991): 3.
87. Mirel, *Patriotic Pluralism*, 6.
88. Robert Carlson, *The Quest for Conformity: Americanization through Education* (New York: Wiley, 1975), 8.
89. Kennedy, *Over Here*, 63–66; Nancy Gentile Ford, *Americans All! Foreign-Born Soldiers in World War I* (College Station: Texas A&M University Press, 2001), 11.
90. Mary Anne Trasciatti, "Americanization Campaign," in *The Home Front Encyclopedia: United States, Britain, and Canada in World Wars I and II*, ed. James Ciment and Thaddeus Russell (Santa Barbara, CA: ABC-CLIO, 2007), 232.
91. Gwendolyn Mink, *The Wages of Motherhood: Inequality in the Welfare State, 1917–1942* (Ithaca, NY: Cornell University Press, 1996).
92. Mink, *The Wages of Motherhood*, 81.
93. Mink, *The Wages of Motherhood*, 81–82.
94. Mink, *The Wages of Motherhood*, 80.
95. Edward George Hartmann, *The Movement to Americanize the Immigrant* (New York: Columbia University Press, 1948), 124.
96. Hartmann, *The Movement to Americanize the Immigrant*, 126.
97. McClymer, "Gender and the 'American Way of Life,'" 5.
98. Carlson, *Quest for Conformity*, 107.
99. Frances A. Kellor, "Americanization by Industry," *Immigrants in America Review* 2 (1916): 15.
100. Kellor, "Americanization by Industry," 15.
101. McClymer, "Gender and the 'American Way of Life,'" 5.
102. Alex Carey, *Taking the Risk out of Democracy: Corporate Propaganda versus Freedom and Liberty*, ed. Andrew Lohrey (Champaign-Urbana: University of Illinois Press, 1997), 49.
103. McClymer, "Gender and the 'American Way of Life,'" 3.
104. Royal Dixon, *Americanization* (New York: Macmillan, 1916), 6.
105. Dixon, *Americanization*, 6.
106. Dixon, *Americanization*, 194–95.
107. Dixon, *Americanization*, 194.
108. Dixon, *Americanization*, 194.
109. Dixon, *Americanization*, 195.
110. On the concept of civil religion, see Catherine L. Albanese, *America: Religions and Religion* (Belmont, CA: Wadsworth Publishing, 1981); Marcela Cristi, *From*

Civil to Political Religion: The Intersection of Culture, Religion and Politics (Waterloo, ON: Wilfrid Laurier University Press, 2001); Carlton J. H. Hayes, Nationalism: A Religion (New York: Macmillan, 1960); Martin E. Marty, The New Shape of American Religion (New York: Harper & Row, 1959).

111. Vaughn, Holding Fast the Inner Lines, 48–49.
112. Mirel denotes the emotional devotion of immigrants to the United States as "patriotic pluralism," arguing that foreign press journalists surveyed during World War II espoused an "intense" emotional commitment to "the United States and American democracy." While his analysis rightly acknowledges the complex negotiations immigrants engaged in during this period, he overlooks concentrated attempts by earlier Americanization authorities to solicit that very emotional commitment. See Mirel, Patriotic Pluralism, 104.
113. Amy Dayton-Wood, "Teaching English for 'A Better America,'" Rhetoric Review 27 (2008): 400–407; Elizabeth Wiatr, "Between Word, Image and the Machine: Visual Education and the Films of Industrial Process," Historical Journal of Film, Radio and Television 22 (2002): 333–36.
114. Gladys Bollman and Henry Bollman, Motion Pictures for Community Needs: A Practical Manual of Information and Suggestion for Educational, Religious and Social Work (New York: Henry Holt, 1922), 151.
115. Bollman and Bollman, Motion Pictures for Community Needs, iii.
116. Dixon, Americanization, 195.
117. Émile Durkheim, The Elementary Forms of Religious Life, trans. Joseph Ward Swain (1915; Mineola, NY: Dover Publications, 2008), 262.
118. See, for example, Sara Ahmed, The Cultural Politics of Emotion (New York: Routledge, 2004); J. M. Barbalet, Emotion, Social Theory, and Social Structure: A Macrosociological Approach (New York: Cambridge University Press, 2001); Gillian Bendelow and Simon J. Williams, eds., Emotions in Social Life: Critical Themes and Contemporary Issues (New York: Routledge, 1998); Lauren Gail Berlant, ed., Compassion: The Culture and Politics of an Emotion (New York: Routledge, 2004).
119. Jeanne Fahnestock, Rhetorical Figures in Science (New York: Oxford University Press, 1999), 8–11.
120. Marcus Tullius Cicero, Cicero on Oratory and Orators with His Letters to Quintus and Brutus, trans. J. S. Watson (London: Bell and Daldy, 1871), 399.
121. John Richard Dugan, Making a New Man: Ciceronian Self-Fashioning in the Rhetorical Works (New York: Oxford University Press, 2005), 157.
122. Erik Gunderson, Staging Masculinity: The Rhetoric of Performance in the Roman

World (Ann Arbor: University of Michigan, 2000), 66.

123. Giambattista Vico, *The New Science*, trans. Thomas Goddard Bergin and Max Harold Fisch (Ithaca, NY: Cornell University Press, 1948).

124. David L. Marshall, *Vico and the Transformation of Rhetoric in Early Modern Europe* (New York: Cambridge University Press, 2010), 19.

125. Paul Ricoeur, *The Rule of Metaphor: Multi-Disciplinary Studies of the Creation of Meaning in Language* (Toronto: University of Toronto Press, 2000), 7.

126. Ernesto Laclau argues that social structures can only be fully interrogated by analyzing the tropological schemes of representation that create the values of a given order. He attends to synecdoche, metonymy, and metaphor to show how hegemony makes the contingent appear stable. Kenneth Burke treats tropes as playing a role in the discovery of truth. Hayden White insists that tropes are constitutive of the data appearing on a historical field. See Ernesto Laclau, *The Rhetorical Foundations of Society* (New York: Verso, 2014); Kenneth Burke, *A Grammar of Motives* (Berkeley: University of California Press, 1969), 403–518; Hayden White, *Metahistory: The Historical Imagination in Nineteenth Century Europe* (Baltimore, MD: Johns Hopkins University Press, 1975). See also Paul de Man, *The Rhetoric of Romanticism* (New York: Columbia University, 1984); Christian O. Lundberg, *Lacan in Public: Psychoanalysis and the Science of Rhetoric* (Tuscaloosa: University of Alabama Press, 2012); Ricoeur, *The Rule of Metaphor*.

127. In his recent work on Jacques Lacan, Christian Lundberg maintains that while rhetoricians have often treated tropes as ornamental or as conduits to persuasion, the tropological aspect of rhetoric bears an ontological status in the constitution of representation, subjectivity, and communication. See Lundberg, *Lacan in Public*, 88.

128. Here, I am suggesting that Burke and White are focused on symbols or signs of representation as opposed to those scholars who read tropes as linguistic, including Laclau and de Man, among others.

129. Gabriel R. Ricci, *Time Consciousness: The Philosophical Uses of History* (New Brunswick, NJ: Transaction Publishers, 2002), xxxvii.

130. Ricoeur, *The Rule of Metaphor*, 7.

131. Ricoeur, *The Rule of Metaphor*, 7.

132. Ricoeur, *The Rule of Metaphor*, 199.

133. Lawrence J. Prelli, "Rhetorics of Display: An Introduction," in *Rhetorics of Display*, ed. Lawrence J. Prelli (Columbia: University of South Carolina, 2006), 1.

134. McClymer, "Gender and the 'American Way of Life,'" 9; Michael R. Olneck, "Americanization and the Education of Immigrants, 1900–1925: An Analysis of Symbolic Action," *American Journal of Education* 97 (1989): 398–423.
135. Jane S. Sutton and Mari Lee Mifsud, "Introduction: A Revolution in Tropes," in *A Revolution in Tropes: Alloiostrophic Rhetoric*, ed. Jane S. Sutton and Mari Lee Mifsud (Lanham, MD: Lexington Books, 2015), xvii.
136. Shawn Michelle Smith, *American Archives: Gender, Race, and Class in Visual Culture* (Princeton, NJ: Princeton University Press, 1999).
137. Smith, *American Archives*, 6.
138. For a similar argument on another set of texts, see Emily Fourmy Cutrer, "A Pragmatic Mode of Seeing: James, Howells, and the Politics of Vision," in *American Iconology: New Approaches to Nineteenth-Century Art and Literature*, ed. David C. Miller (New Haven, CT: Yale University Press, 1993), 261.

Chapter Two. The Visual Pedagogy of Americanization

1. House Committee on Immigration and Naturalization, *Education and Americanization Hearings*, 66th Cong., 1st Sess. (Washington, DC: U.S. Government Printing Office, 1919), 5–6.
2. House Committee, *Education and Americanization*, 6.
3. House Committee, *Education and Americanization*, 84–85.
4. House Committee, *Education and Americanization*, 85.
5. See, for example, Terry Lindvall, *Sanctuary Cinema: Origins of the Christian Film Industry* (New York: New York University Press, 2007), 87–91; Katerina Loukopoulou, "Museum at Large: Aesthetic Education through Film," in *Learning with the Lights Off: Educational Film in the United States*, ed. Devin Orgeron, Marsha Orgeron, and Dan Streible (New York: Oxford University Press, 2012), 348; Devin Orgeron, Marsha Orgeron, and Dan Streible, "A History of Learning with the Lights Off," in Orgeron, Orgeron, and Streible, *Learning with the Lights Off*, 22; Jay Winter, "Imaginings of War: Posters and the Shadow of the Lost Generation," in *Picture This: World War I Posters and Visual Culture*, ed. Pearl James (Lincoln: University of Nebraska Press, 2009), 51.
6. Henry Dyson, *Prolepsis and Ennoia in the Early Stoa* (Berlin: Walter de Gruyter, 2009), xxix, 25.
7. For argumentation scholars, following from the ancient Athenians and Romans, prolepsis is an argumentative strategy of anticipating objections. See Richard Besel, "Prolepsis and the Environmental Rhetoric of Congressional Politics:

Defeating the Climate Stewardship Act of 2003," *Environmental Communication* 6 (2012): 233–49. For scholars of rhetorical figures, prolepsis is a type of anticipation crafted through the construction of speech. See James Jasinski, *Sourcebook on Rhetoric* (Thousand Oaks, CA: Sage, 2001), 554–56.

8. Lee Grieveson, *Policing Cinema: Movies and Censorship in Early-Twentieth-Century America* (Berkeley: University of California, 2004), 15–18; Lea Jacobs, "Reformers and Spectators: The Film Education Movement in the Thirties," *Camera Obscura* 8 (1990): 33–34.

9. Desmond King, *Making Americans: Immigrants, Race, and the Origins of the Diverse Democracy* (Cambridge, MA: Harvard University Press, 2002), 85–126; Arthur F. McClure, James Riley Chrisman, and Perry Mock, *Education for Work: The Historical Evolution of Vocational and Distributive Education in America* (Cranberry, NJ: Associated University Presses, 1985), 71–77.

10. Uffa Jensen, "Mrs. Gaskell's Anxiety," in *Learning How to Feel: Children's Literature and Emotional Socialization, 1870–1970*, ed. Ute Frevert et al. (New York: Oxford University Press, 2014), 25–26. For a popular period example, see George Herbert Betts, *The Mind and Its Education* (1906; New York: D. Appleton and Co., 1916), 239–53. Betts was an acclaimed educator. On Betts's career, see John F. Ohles, ed., *Biographical Dictionary of American Educators* (Westport, CT: Greenwood Press, 1978), 1:126–27.

11. William James, "What Is an Emotion?" *Mind* 9 (1884): 188–205; Carl Georg Lange, "The Mechanism of the Emotions," in *The Classical Psychologists*, ed. Benjamin Rand (1885; Boston: Houghton Mifflin, 1912), 672–84. See also J. C. Banerjee, *Encyclopaedic Dictionary of Psychological Terms* (New Delhi: MD Publications Pvt. Ltd., 1994), 152–53. In 1994, for the one hundredth anniversary edition of *Psychological Review*, the journal released a special issue focused on William James and the James-Lange theory of emotions as it evolved into contemporary behaviorism. See Walter Kintsch and John T. Cacioppo, eds., "The Centennial Issue of the Psychological Review," *Psychological Review* 101 (1994).

12. Paul Stob, *William James and the Art of Popular Statement* (East Lansing: Michigan State University Press, 2013), 75.

13. Stob, *William James*, 77.

14. Stob, *William James*, 98–108.

15. Richard Butsch, *The Citizen Audience: Crowds, Public, and Individuals* (New York: Routledge, 2008).

16. Ernesto Laclau, *On Populist Reason* (New York: Verso, 2005), 40–52.

17. Laclau, *On Populist Reason*, 43.
18. A number of empirical and psychological theorists during the late nineteenth and early twentieth centuries investigated the senses of the body as central to the process of influence and persuasion. Popular theories in this tradition situated feeling, touch, sight, and sound as gateways to both body and mind. As contemporary scholar Jonathan Crary chronicles, simple positivistic accounts of vision popularized in the 1880s were slowly complicated by theories of vision that attempted to describe the complex relationship between the stimulating object and the psychobiological responses of the human body. See Jonathan Crary, *Suspensions of Perception: Attention, Spectacle, and Modern Culture* (Cambridge, MA: MIT Press, 2001).
19. James Ozro Engleman, *Moral Education in School and Home* (Chicago: Benjamin H. Sanborn and Co., 1918), 22–23.
20. Engleman, *Moral Education*, 22.
21. Engleman, *Moral Education*, 23.
22. Engleman, *Moral Education*, 100.
23. Dyson, *Prolepsis*, 17.
24. Dyson, *Prolepsis*, xxix.
25. Dyson, *Prolepsis*, xxix.
26. H. D. Rickard, "Use of the Stereopticon," in *Proceedings Americanization Conference Held under the Auspices of the Americanization Division, Bureau of Education, Department of the Interior, Washington, May 12, 13, 14, 15, 1919* (Washington, DC: U.S. Government Printing Office, 1919), 60–67.
27. Rickard, "Use of the Stereopticon," 61.
28. Rickard, "Use of the Stereopticon," 62.
29. Rickard, "Use of the Stereopticon," 62.
30. Rickard, "Use of the Stereopticon," 61.
31. Brenton J. Malin, "Looking White and Middle-Class: Stereoscopic Imagery and Technology in the Early Twentieth-Century United States," *Quarterly Journal of Speech* 93 (2007): 403–24.
32. Jonathan Crary, *Techniques of the Observer: On Vision and Modernity in the 19th Century* (Cambridge, MA: MIT Press, 1992), 125.
33. Rickard, "Use of the Stereopticon," 67.
34. Rickard, "Use of the Stereopticon," 67.
35. Rickard, "Use of the Stereopticon," 63.
36. Rickard, "Use of the Stereopticon," 63.

37. David Lanier Lewis, *The Public Image of Henry Ford: An American Folk Hero and His Company* (Detroit: Wayne State University Press, 1976), 115–16; Lee Grieveson, "The Work of Film in the Age of Fordist Mechanization," *Cinema Journal* 51 (2012): 47.
38. Grieveson, "The Work of Film," 26–27.
39. On the YMCA's use of teachers for its films, see Ronald Walter Greene, "Y Movies: Film and the Modernization of Pastoral Power," *Communication and Critical/Cultural Studies* 2 (2005): 20–36.
40. Grieveson, "The Work of Film," 28.
41. See, for example, "'Americanization'—The Teacher's New Task," *Moderator-Topics* 40 (January 1920): 255; "'Americanization'—The Teacher's New Task," *Primary Education* 28 (January 1920): 53.
42. Grieveson, "The Work of Film," 41.
43. Ford Educational Weekly Collection, National Archives and Records Administration, RG2429, RG2430, RG2431, RG2432, RG2433, College Park, MD. In the early 1920s, many theaters banned the films after Henry Ford published a number of anti-Semitic comments in the *Dearborn Independent*. The sharp decline in distribution numbers ended the series. See Grieveson, "The Work of Film," 47; Lewis, *The Public Image of Henry Ford*, 116.
44. "A New Tool for the 'Brain Factory,'" *Popular Educator* (November 1919): 122.
45. Stephen Meyer, "Adapting the Immigrant to the Line: Americanization in the Ford Factory, 1914–1921," *Journal of Social History* 14 (1980): 67–82.
46. H. H. Wheaton, "The United States Bureau of Education and the Immigrant," *Annals of the American Academy of Political and Social Science* 67 (1916): 278.
47. H. H. Wheaton, "The America First Campaign," *Immigration Journal* 1 (June 1916): 92.
48. Alex Carey, *Taking the Risk out of Democracy: Corporate Propaganda versus Freedom and Liberty*, ed. Andrew Lohrey (Champaign-Urbana: University of Illinois Press, 1997), 49.
49. Carey, *Taking the Risk out of Democracy*, 50. Historical sources corroborate Carey's statistic, while Hartmann indicates that this number is much lower but notes a wider variety of media distributed for this purpose. As he wrote, the Bureau of Education distributed "96,948 circulars, newsletters, schedules of standards and syllabi, 29,400 new releases on programs of the movement, 57,000 enrollment blanks, 9,265 'America First' posters, 5,719 pamphlets and bulletins, and a large quantity of other material to aid the movement during 1916." See

Edward George Hartmann, *The Movement to Americanize the Immigrant* (New York: Columbia University Press, 1948), 159.

50. "Chambers of Commerce in 'America First' Campaign," *American City* 15 (December 1916): 680. See also Frederic Ernest Farrington, "The Interior Department and the Immigrant," *Catholic Educational Review* 13 (April 1917): 433; "Immigrants and Night Schools," *School and Society* 4 (1916): 592–93.
51. Wheaton, "The United States Bureau of Education," 277.
52. Wheaton, "The United States Bureau of Education," 278.
53. Wheaton, "The United States Bureau of Education," 278.
54. Wheaton, "The America First Campaign," 92.
55. Laclau, *On Populist Reason*, 52.
56. Sara Ahmed, *The Promise of Happiness* (Durham, NC: Duke University Press, 2010), 38.
57. Cyril O'Regan, *The Heterodox Hegel* (Albany: State University of New York Press, 1994), 10. See also Alice Bennett, *Afterlife and Narrative in Contemporary Fiction* (New York: Palgrave Macmillan, 2012); Mark Currie, *About Time: Narrative, Fiction, and the Philosophy of Time* (Edinburgh: Edinburgh University Press, 2006).
58. Dyson, *Prolepsis*, xxix.
59. "Getting the American Viewpoint," *New York Times*, August 21, 1921, http://www.nytimes.com.
60. The civic-oriented textbooks published by AVS included *We and Our History*, *We and Our Government*, *We and Our Work*, *We and the Constitution of the United States*, and *We and Our Health*. They also published one volume for children with minimal illustrations: *The Spirit of America*.
61. Albert Bushnell Hart, foreword to *We and Our History* (Albany, NY: American Viewpoint Society, 1923); Jeremiah Whipple Jenks and Rufus Daniel Smith, front matter in *We and Our Government* (Albany, NY: American Viewpoint Society, 1922).
62. Hart, foreword to *We and Our History*.
63. F.H.H., "Classified Book Notes: *We and Our History*," *Journal of Social Forces* 2 (May 1924): 628.
64. W. G. Kimmel, "The Visual Appeal in Education for Citizenship," *School Review* 31 (January 1923): 70.
65. Guy Thomas Buswell, "A New Type of Pictured Textbook," *Elementary School Journal* 23 (November 1922): 232; N.W.W., "Review," *High School Journal* 7 (May–October 1924): 232.

66. Kimmel, "Visual Appeal," 69–70; "Briefer Notices," *American Political Science Review* 16 (November 1922): 724.
67. Mary O. Cowper, "Utopias, Biographies and Things," *Journal of Social Forces* 1 (September 1923): 630.
68. Buswell, "A New Type," 232.
69. Kimmel, "Visual Appeal," 70.
70. David K. Glidden, "Parrots, Pyrrhonists, and Native Speakers," in *Language*, ed. Stephen Everson (New York: Cambridge University Press, 1994), 129–48.
71. Dyson, *Prolepsis*, 112–19.
72. Dyson, *Prolepsis*, 68.
73. The volume with limited illustrations was *The Spirit of America* by Angelo Patri.
74. David Morley, *Media, Modernity and Technology: The Geography of the New* (London: Routledge, 2007), 235–38.
75. Nancy Gentile Ford, *Americans All! Foreign-Born Soldiers in World War I* (College Station: Texas A&M University Press, 2001), 24. Given that Lady Liberty was heavily used to promote war bonds during World War I, by the 1920s she was readily associated with the concept of freedom and specifically seen as a symbol of freedom's promise for new arrivals. Her visage was so ingrained in this conception of the American Dream that she was employed to critique the nightmare of hyper-loyalty demanded during the Great War.
76. Kristin L. Hoganson, *Consumers' Imperium: The Global Production of American Domesticity, 1865–1920* (Chapel Hill: University of North Carolina Press, 2007), 254.
77. Brian Massumi, *Parables for the Virtual: Movement, Affect, Sensation* (Durham, NC: Duke University Press, 2002), 15.
78. Jenks and Smith, *We and Our Government*, 5.
79. René Nünlist, *The Ancient Critic at Work: Terms and Concepts of Literary Criticism in Greek Scholia* (New York: Cambridge University Press, 2009), 42–43.
80. Dyson, *Prolepsis*, 68.
81. Jenks and Smith, *We and Our Government*, 76.
82. Jenks and Smith, *We and Our Government*, 16.
83. Jenks and Smith, *We and Our Government*, 23; Hart, *History*, 273.
84. Jenks and Smith, *We and Our Government*, 21.
85. Jenks and Smith, *We and Our Government*, 23.
86. Hart, *We and Our History*, 273.
87. Jenks and Smith, *We and Our Government*, 79–86.

88. I will discuss the concept of racial hierarchy more in chapter 6 and in the conclusion, but this quotation is obviously a nod to the 1917 quota act and the exclusions it put into place.
89. Nünlist, *Ancient Critic at Work*, 38.
90. Sara Ahmed has insightfully argued that the promise of happiness is structured by longing, even or especially in the absence of happiness. See Ahmed, *Promise of Happiness*.
91. Zizi Papacharissi, *Affective Publics: Sentiment, Technology, and Politics* (New York: Oxford University Press, 2015), 16.
92. Gregory J. Seigworth and Melissa Gregg, "An Inventory of Shimmers," in *The Affect Theory Reader*, ed. Gregory J. Seigworth and Melissa Gregg (Durham, NC: Duke University Press, 2010), 4.

Chapter Three. The American Lifestyle through Housing Reform

1. "A Governor's Message," *Housing Betterment* 6 (January 1917): 13.
2. Kenneth Baar, "The National Movement to Halt the Spread of Multifamily Housing, 1890–1926," *Journal of the American Planning Association* 58 (1992): 39–48.
3. Theresa Enos, ed., *Encyclopedia of Rhetoric and Composition: Communication from Ancient Times to the Information Age* (New York: Routledge, 2013), 72.
4. Michel de Certeau, *The Practice of Everyday Life*, trans. Steven Rendall (Berkeley: University of California Press, 1984), 101.
5. de Certeau, *Practice*, 101.
6. Yoosun Park and Susan P. Kemp, "'Little Alien Colonies': Representations of Immigrants and Their Neighborhoods in Social Work Discourse, 1875–1924," *Social Service Review* 80 (2006): 705–34.
7. On Roosevelt's position on immigration and assimilation, see Leroy G. Dorsey, *We Are All Americans, Pure and Simple: Theodore Roosevelt and the Myth of Americanism* (Tuscaloosa: University of Alabama Press, 2007).
8. Theodore Roosevelt, "Americanism," in *Immigration and Americanization: Selected Readings*, ed. Philip Davis and Bertha Schwartz (Boston: Ginn and Co., 1920), 657–58. Speech originally delivered before the Knights of Columbus, Carnegie Hall, New York City, October 12, 1915.
9. Christopher J. Kauffman, *Patriotism and Fraternalism in the Knights of Columbus: A History of the Fourth Degree* (New York: Crossroad, 2001), 34; Thomas S.

Bremer, *Formed from This Soil: An Introduction to the Diverse History of Religion in America* (Malden, MA: Wiley, 2015), 357.

10. Tyler Anbinder, *Five Points: The 19th Century New York Neighborhood That Invented Tap Dance, Stole Elections, and Became the World's Most Notorious Slum* (New York: Simon & Schuster, 2001), 243–51; Andrew Ross, "'Nothing Gained by Overcrowding': The History and Politics of Urban Population Control," in *The New Blackwell Companion to the City*, ed. Gary Bridge and Sophie Watson (New York: John Wiley & Sons, 2011), 172; David Ward, *Poverty, Ethnicity and the American City, 1840–1925: Changing Conceptions of the Slum and the Ghetto* (New York: Cambridge University Press, 1989).

11. Grace Abbott, "The Immigrant as a Problem in Community Planning," *Publications of the American Sociological Society* 12 (1916): 168–69.

12. Abbott, "The Immigrant as a Problem," 169.

13. Abbott, "The Immigrant as a Problem," 169.

14. Henry Pratt Fairchild, *Immigration: A World Movement and Its American Significance* (New York: Macmillan, 1918), 242.

15. Fairchild, *Immigration*, 252.

16. Simon J. Lubin, "California and the Problems of the Immigrant: A Discussion of the Existing and Future Situation in the State," *California Outlook*, November 15, 1913, 27.

17. Lubin, "California and the Problems of the Immigrant," 27.

18. Frederic Jennings Haskin, *The Immigrant: An Asset and a Liability* (New York: Fleming H. Revell, 1913), 92.

19. Haskin, *The Immigrant*, 21, 92.

20. Beginning in the mid-nineteenth century, housing reform became a popular endeavor for social advocates, religious groups, and the philanthropic aristocracy of most major cities of the United States. As increasing numbers moved to the cities, the rise in slipshod construction and tenements resulted in what became known as slums—downtrodden and deleterious areas predominantly inhabited by the poor and the recently immigrated. In the Progressive Era, rehabilitation of poor housing accommodations focused on codes for construction, housing laws, and the manufacture of model dwellings. See Ross, "Nothing Gained by Overcrowding," 169–72; Roy Lubove, *The Progressives and the Slums: Tenement House Reform in New York City, 1890–1917* (Pittsburgh: University of Pittsburgh Press, 1962), 4–11; Jon A. Peterson, "The Impact of Sanitary Reform upon American Urban Planning, 1840–1890," *Journal of Social History* 13 (1979): 83–103;

Ward, *Poverty, Ethnicity and the American City*.

21. On the boom in company towns, see Linda Carlson, *Company Towns of the Pacific Northwest* (Seattle: University of Washington Press, 2003); Margaret Crawford, *Building the Workingman's Paradise: The Design of American Company Towns* (New York: Verso, 1995); Margaret Crawford, "Earle S. Draper and the Company Town in the American South," in *The Company Town: Architecture and Society in the Early Industrial Age*, ed. John Garner (New York: Oxford University Press, 1992), 139–72; Leland Roth, "Company Towns in the Western United States," in Garner, *The Company Town*, 173–206; Margaret M. Mulrooney, "A Legacy of Coal: The Coal Company Towns of Southwestern Pennsylvania," *Perspectives in Vernacular Architecture* 4 (1991): 130–37; Crandall Shifflett, *Coal Towns: Life, Work, and Culture in Company Towns of Southern Appalachia, 1880–1960* (Knoxville: University of Tennessee Press, 1991).

22. See, for example, "Housing Cause Advanced a Generation," *Housing Betterment* 7 (May 1918): 29–30; U.S. Department of Labor, *Report of the United States Housing Corporation* (Washington, DC: U.S. Government Printing Office, 1919), 2:19–23.

23. Crawford, *Building the Workingman's Paradise*, 159.

24. Crawford, *Building the Workingman's Paradise*, 7.

25. "Better Homes for the Immigrant Workmen: Americanization Committee's Novel House Competition Will Be a Big Factor in Its Vigorous Campaign to Assimilate Aliens," *New York Times*, May 28, 1916, http://www.nytimes.com.

26. Hartmann notes that the contest was so popular that the NAC formed a housing committee to attend to correspondence and publicity. See Edward George Hartmann, *The Movement to Americanize the Immigrant* (New York: Columbia University Press, 1948), 139.

27. "The Immigrant Housing Competition," *Immigrants in America Review* 2 (April 1916): 55.

28. See, for example, "Better Homes for the Immigrant Workmen," *Architect and Engineer* 44 (March 1916): 108; "Housing Competition," *Journal of the Engineers Society of Pennsylvania* 8 (April 1916): 89; "The Immigrant Housing Competition," 55–57.

29. "Better Homes for the Immigrant Workmen."

30. "Better Homes for the Immigrant Workmen."

31. Frances A. Kellor, "The Application of Americanization to Housing," *Architectural Review* 5 (January 1917): 1.

32. Kellor, "The Application of Americanization to Housing," 1.

33. Kellor, "The Application of Americanization to Housing," 1.
34. National Americanization Committee (NAC), cited in "Better Homes for the Immigrant Workmen."
35. "The Immigrant Housing Competition," 55.
36. "The Immigrant Housing Competition," 57.
37. Cited in Kenneth E. Miller, *From Progressive to New Dealer: Frederic C. Howe and American Liberalism* (University Park: Penn State University Press, 2010), 215.
38. Sara Ahmed, *The Promise of Happiness* (Durham, NC: Duke University Press, 2010), 37.
39. Ahmed, *Promise of Happiness*, 37.
40. "The Immigrant Housing Competition," 57.
41. Hayden White, *Metahistory: The Historical Imagination in Nineteenth-Century Europe* (Baltimore, MD: Johns Hopkins University Press, 1975), 34.
42. White, *Metahistory*, 36.
43. Crawford, *Building the Workingman's Paradise*, 45–48.
44. While the Pullman community was initially touted as the very best accommodations workers could imagine, Pullman's own authoritarian rule resulted in the town's demise. Other communities succeeded in attracting high-quality workers, yet the costs of materials during the war halted construction. The NAC and COC contest explicitly sought to overcome the problems of high construction costs and radicalized workers by building homes that were both cost-efficient and aesthetically pleasing enough to satisfy residents.
45. Kellor, "The Application of Americanization to Housing," 2.
46. E. T. Hartmann, "Housing Essentials," *Architectural Review* 5 (January 1917): 24.
47. Hartmann, "Housing Essentials," 23.
48. Stanley Buder, *Visionaries and Planners: The Garden City Movement and the Modern Community* (New York: Oxford University Press, 1990).
49. Standish Meacham, *Regaining Paradise: Englishness and the Early Garden City Movement* (New Haven, CT: Yale University Press, 1999), 37.
50. Crawford, *Building the Workingman's Paradise*, 70; Lubove, *The Progressives and the Slums*, 221–24; Ben Minteer, *The Landscape of Reform: Civic Pragmatism and Environmental Thought in America* (Cambridge, MA: MIT Press, 2006), 54–56.
51. Kellor, "The Application of Americanization to Housing," 1.
52. Kellor, "The Application of Americanization to Housing," 2.
53. Crawford, *Building the Workingman's Paradise*, 101.
54. Crawford, *Building the Workingman's Paradise*, 112.

55. "The Prize Designs in the National Americanization Committee Immigrant Housing Competition: Accompanied by the Competitor's Full Specifications and Descriptions," *Architectural Review* 5 (January 1917): 8.
56. Hartmann, "Housing Essentials," 23.
57. Kellor, "The Application of Americanization to Housing," 1.
58. Kellor, "The Application of Americanization to Housing," 1.
59. Crawford, *Building the Workingman's Paradise*.
60. See Frances Kellor's reasoning in "The Application of Americanization to Housing" on this point.
61. Joseph Mayper, "Americanizing Barren Island," in *Americanization: Principles of Americanism, Essentials of Americanization, Technic of Race Assimilation, Annotated Bibliography*, ed. Winthrop Talbot (New York: H.W. Wilson Co., 1917), 283–84. Reprint of an essay in *Immigrants in America Review* from July 1916.
62. Mayper, "Americanizing Barren Island," 286.
63. Mayper, "Americanizing Barren Island," 286.
64. Mayper, "Americanizing Barren Island," 286.
65. Mayper, "Americanizing Barren Island," 283.
66. Mayper, "Americanizing Barren Island," 290.
67. Henry Ezekiel Jackson, *A Community Center: What It Is and How to Organize It* (New York: Macmillan Co., 1918), 14.
68. Jackson, *A Community Center*, 15.
69. Jackson, *A Community Center*, 14.
70. John Daniels, *America via the Neighborhood* (New York: Harper & Brothers, 1920), 18–20.
71. Daniels, *America via the Neighborhood*, 212.
72. Daniels refers to a certain population as Bohemian. Given the preferences of the period, he is likely referring to a collection of Slavic peoples.
73. Daniels, *America via the Neighborhood*, 319.
74. Isaac Baer Berkson, *Theories of Americanization* (New York: Columbia University Press, 1920), 1.
75. Berkson, *Theories of Americanization*, 223.
76. Berkson, *Theories of Americanization*, 70.
77. Berkson, *Theories of Americanization*, 12–13.
78. Berkson, *Theories of Americanization*, 13.
79. Berkson, *Theories of Americanization*, 149.
80. Berkson, *Theories of Americanization*, 125.

81. Thomas Docherty, *Aesthetic Democracy* (Stanford, CA: Stanford University Press, 2006), 135.
82. Ahmed, *Promise of Happiness*, 142–44.

Chapter Four. Displaying Americanization in Public Celebration

1. Woodrow Wilson, "Address to Naturalized Citizens at Convention Hall, Philadelphia," The Presidency Project, May 10, 1915, http://www.presidency.ucsb.edu/ws/index.php?pid=65388.
2. On the concept of the foreigner as bearing the promise of democratic practice, see Bonnie Honig, *Democracy and the Foreigner* (Princeton, NJ: Princeton University Press, 2001).
3. Wilson, "Address to Naturalized Citizens at Convention Hall." On the audience for this speech, see Elizabeth W. Baker, *Great Speeches* (Norwood, MA: Norwood Press, 1927), 5.
4. Wilson, "Address to Naturalized Citizens at Convention Hall."
5. "Spread of Americanization Day Plans," *The Survey*, June 19, 1915, 261.
6. Convention Hall does not have pillars. Thus, I am inferring that the pillars described by *The Survey* must have been installed for the event. "Spread of Americanization Day Plans," 261.
7. "Spread of Americanization Day Plans," 261.
8. "Spread of Americanization Day Plans," 261.
9. "Spread of Americanization Day Plans," 261.
10. Edward George Hartmann, *The Movement to Americanize the Immigrant* (New York: Columbia University Press, 1948), 116–19.
11. Hartmann, *The Movement to Americanize the Immigrant*, 116.
12. Daniel Fischlin, *In Small Proportions: A Poetics of the English Ayre, 1596–1622* (Detroit: Wayne State University Press, 1998), 174.
13. David Hackett Fischer, *Albion's Seed: Four British Folkways in America* (New York: Oxford University Press, 1989), 5–7.
14. Peter Novick, *That Noble Dream: The "Objectivity Question" and the American Historical Profession* (New York: Cambridge University Press, 1988), 87–88.
15. Rutledge Dennis, "W.E.B. Du Bois's Concept of Double-Consciousness," in *Race and Ethnicity: Comparative and Theoretical Approaches*, ed. John Stone and Rutledge Dennis (Malden, MA: Blackwell, 2003), 13–14.
16. Novick, *That Noble Dream*, 88.

17. Russell Andrew Kazal, *Becoming Old Stock: The Paradox of German American Identity* (Princeton, NJ: Princeton University Press, 2004), 120–28.
18. Nancy Tomes, *The Gospel of Germs: Men, Women, and the Microbe in American Life* (Cambridge, MA: Harvard University Press, 1999).
19. Kathleen M. Brown, *Foul Bodies: Cleanliness in Early America* (New Haven, CT: Yale University Press, 2009), 366–67.
20. Woodrow Wilson, "Loyalty, Address at Citizenship Convention, Washington, 13 July 1916," in *Selected Addresses and Public Papers of Woodrow Wilson*, ed. Albert Bushnell Hart (New York: Boni and Liveright, 1918), 140.
21. Wilson, "Loyalty," 142.
22. Woodrow Wilson, "Address to the Daughters of the American Revolution, Washington, October 11, 1915," in *President Wilson's Great Speeches and Other History Making Documents* (Chicago: Stanton and Van Vliet, 1918), 72.
23. Wilson, "Address to the Daughters," 76.
24. Wilson, "Address to the Daughters," 75.
25. Wilson, "Address to the Daughters," 73–74.
26. Wilson, "Address to the Daughters," 77.
27. Wilson, "Address to the Daughters," 78.
28. Richard K. Campbell, *Annual Report of the Commissioner of Naturalization to the Secretary of Labor* (Washington, DC: U.S. Government Printing Office, 1917), 78.
29. Campbell, *Annual Report*, 78.
30. Vanessa B. Beasley, *You, the People: American National Identity in Presidential Rhetoric* (College Station: Texas A&M University Press, 2004), 80.
31. Ernest Boyd, "The Elusive American and the Ex-European," *Scribner's Magazine* 72 (July 1922): 27.
32. Boyd, "The Elusive American," 28.
33. Boyd, "The Elusive American," 27.
34. Walter Lippmann, *Public Opinion* (1922; New York: Free Press, 1997), 57.
35. Brian Cummings, "Metalepsis: The Boundaries of Metaphor," in *Renaissance Figures of Speech*, ed. Sylvia Adamson, Gavin Alexander, and Katrin Ettenhuber (New York: Cambridge University Press, 2007), 222.
36. Wilson, "Address to Naturalized Citizens at Convention Hall"; John Higham, *Strangers in the Land: Patterns of American Nativism, 1860–1925* (Piscataway, NJ: Rutgers University Press, 2002), 243; June Granatir Alexander, *Ethnic Pride, American Patriotism: Slovaks and Other New Immigrants in the Interwar Era* (Philadelphia: Temple University Press, 2004), 18–19.

37. Higham, *Strangers*, 243.
38. See, for example, "President Marches up Avenue at Head of 60,000 Paraders," *Evening Star*, June 14, 1916, 1. Other newspapers prominently featured the photograph of President Wilson as the parade marshal in D.C.
39. Alexander, *Ethnic Pride, American Patriotism*, 19.
40. John E. Bodnar, *Remaking America: Public Memory, Commemoration, and Patriotism in the Twentieth Century* (Princeton, NJ: Princeton University Press, 1992), 96. America First was a war slogan for isolationists as well as a political campaign fashioned Wilson's administration to forward nationalist sentiment and Americanization efforts.
41. Alexander, *Ethnic Pride, American Patriotism*, 19–20.
42. Woodrow Wilson, "Insults and Aggressions of Germany," in Hart, *Selected Addresses*, 217. This speech was delivered on Flag Day (June 14, 1917) in Washington, DC. Notably, one of the primary authors for the American Viewpoint Society edited this volume.
43. "Italian Boys to March July 4th," *Syracuse Herald*, June 18, 1916, 32; John J. Miller, *The Unmaking of Americans: How Multiculturalism Has Undermined America's Assimilation Ethic* (New York: Free Press, 1998), 67; Alex Carey, *Taking the Risk out of Democracy: Corporate Propaganda versus Freedom and Liberty*, ed. Andrew Lohrey (Champaign-Urbana: University of Illinois Press, 1997), 49.
44. See, for example, "Americanization Movement of Hour," *Waterloo Times-Tribune*, June 15, 1915, 4; "Civic Education of Immigrants," *Eau Claire Leader*, June 23, 1915, 6; "To Greet New Citizens," *Emporia Gazette*, June 22, 1915, 4.
45. "Citizenship Receptions," *School and Society*, June 19, 1915, 880–81.
46. See, for example, "Americanization Day Proves Big Success," *Dallas Morning News*, July 6, 1915, 7; "New Citizens Sing 'America,'" *Dallas Morning News*, July 5, 1915, 1; "Italian Boys to March July 4th," 32.
47. "President Marches up Avenue," 1.
48. "Italian Boys to March July 4th," 32.
49. Robert Justin Goldstein, *Political Repression in Modern America from 1870 to 1976* (Champaign-Urbana: University of Illinois Press, 2001), 100.
50. Roy Rosenzweig, *Eight Hours for What We Will: Workers and Leisure in an Industrial City, 1870–1920* (New York: Cambridge University Press, 1985), 158–59.
51. Robert James Branham and Stephen J. Hartnett, *Sweet Freedom's Song: "My Country 'Tis of Thee" and Democracy in America* (New York: Oxford University Press, 2002), 63–71, 120–21.

52. Karen J. Blair, *The Torchbearers: Women and Their Amateur Arts Associations in America, 1890–1930* (Bloomington: Indiana University Press, 1994), 50–68.
53. E. Christina Chang, "The Singing Program of World War I: The Crusade for a Singing Army," *Journal of Historical Research in Music Education* 23 (2001): 19–45.
54. Weaver Pangburn, "The War and Community Movement," *American Journal of Sociology* 26 (1920): 84.
55. Pangburn, "The War and Community Movement," 92.
56. Anne Shaw Faulkner, *Americanization Songs: Liberty Chorus Song Book for Home, School and Community Singing* (Chicago: McKinley Music Co., 1920), 1–2.
57. "Music Always in Advance Guard of National Movements," *Dallas Morning News*, October 14, 1917, 16.
58. "Community Chorus Will Start Today," *New York Times*, March 23, 1919, 23.
59. Back matter in *Music Supervisor's Journal* 6 (1919).
60. Back matter in *Music Supervisor's Journal* 6 (1919).
61. Charles Rosebault, "Golden Rule for Aliens," *New York Times*, July 25, 1920, 71.
62. "Community Chorus Will Start Today," 23.
63. "Settlement Turns out Its Thousand," *New York Times*, March 3, 1918, 59.
64. Alfred Emanuel Smith, "Choral Music, Americanization, and Taste," *The Outlook*, April 23, 1919, 682.
65. Smith, "Choral Music," 682.
66. Robert J. Branham, "'Of Thee I Sing': Contesting 'America,'" *American Quarterly* 48 (1996): 629–30.
67. Branham, "Of Thee I Sing," 629.
68. Faulkner, *Americanization Songs*, 2.
69. Faulkner, *Americanization Songs*, 2.
70. Branham and Hartnett, *Sweet Freedom's Song*, 63.
71. John Hollander, *The Figure of Echo: A Mode of Allusion in Milton and After* (Berkeley: University of California Press, 1981), 114.
72. Fischlin, *In Small Proportions*, 173; Cummings, "Metalepsis," 219; John Pier, afterword to *Metalepsis in Popular Culture*, ed. Karin Kukkonen and Sonja Klimek (Berlin: Walter de Gruyter, 2011), 268.
73. Cummings, "Metalepsis," 222.
74. Gérard Genette, *Narrative Discourse: An Essay in Method*, trans. Jane E. Lewin (Ithaca, NY: Cornell University Press, 1983), 235–36. See also Debra Malina, *Breaking the Frame: Metalepsis and the Construction of the Subject* (Columbus: Ohio State University Press, 2002), 1–2.

75. "Spanish Congregation in New York," *New York Times*, January 13, 1918, SM6.
76. William A. Weber, "Archibald T. Davison: Faith in Good Music," *Harvard Crimson*, February 17, 1961, http://www.thecrimson.com/article/1961/2/17/archibald-t-davison-faith-in-good/.
77. Archibald T. Davison, "Good Music for Community Singing," *The Playground* 16 (January 1923): 455.
78. Davison, "Good Music," 455, 457.
79. Judith Butler and Gayatri Chakravorty Spivak, *Who Sings the Nation-State? Language, Politics, Belonging* (Oxford, UK: Seagull Books, 2007), 59–61.
80. Butler and Spivak, *Who Sings the Nation-State?*, 73.
81. Frank Crane, "Music and Democracy," *Recreation* 16 (January 1923): 458.
82. Crane, "Music and Democracy," 458.
83. Crane, "Music and Democracy," 458.
84. Robert Hariman and John Louis Lucaites, *No Caption Needed: Iconic Photographs, Public Culture, and Liberal Democracy* (Chicago: University of Chicago Press, 2007), 17.
85. Cummings, "Metalepsis," 223.
86. Thomas Woods Stevens, "Community Gatherings and Recreation," in *Proceedings Americanization Conference: Held under the Auspices of the Americanization Division, Bureau of Education, Department of the Interior* (Washington, DC: U.S. Government Printing Office, 1919), 309–19.
87. Stevens, "Community Gatherings and Recreation," 313.
88. Stevens, "Community Gatherings and Recreation," 314.
89. Stevens, "Community Gatherings and Recreation," 309.

CHAPTER FIVE. RECOGNIZING AMERICANS THROUGH SCOUTING

1. Helen Josephine Ferris, *Girls' Clubs, Their Organization and Management* (New York: E. P. Dutton, 1918), 50.
2. Ferris, *Girls' Clubs*, 51.
3. Many period authorities on recreation and clubs supported a philosophy similar to Ferris on girls' clubs. See, for example, Royal Dixon, *Americanization* (New York: Macmillan, 1916), 96–99; Luther Halsey Gulick, *A Philosophy of Play* (New York: Scribner, 1920); Mary Eliza Moxcey, *Physical Health and Recreation for Girls* (New York: Methodist Book Concern, 1920).
4. Gavin Alexander, "Prosopopoeia: The Speaking Figure," in *Renaissance Figures of Speech*, ed. Sylvia Adamson, Gavin Alexander, and Katrin Ettenhuber (New York:

Cambridge University Press, 2007), 101.

5. Paul de Man, "Autobiography as De-Facement," *MLN* 94 (1979): 926; Paul de Man, "Shelley Disfigured," in *Deconstruction and Criticism*, ed. Harold Bloom (New York: Continuum Press, 1979), 68. See also Megan Foley, "Voicing Terri Schiavo: Prosopopeic Citizenship in the Democratic Aporia between Sovereignty and Biopower," *Communication and Critical/Cultural Studies* 7 (2010): 381–400; E. Johanna Hartelius, "Face-ing Immigration: Prosopopeia and the 'Muslim-Arab-Middle Eastern' Other," *Rhetoric Society Quarterly* 43 (2013): 311–34; Ned Lukacher, *Primal Scenes: Literature, Philosophy, Psychoanalysis* (Ithaca, NY: Cornell University Press, 1986), 84–93; J. Hillis Miller, *Tropes, Parables, and Performatives: Essays on Twentieth-Century Literature.* (Durham, NC: Duke University Press, 1991), 245–59.
6. John E. Bodnar, *The Transplanted: A History of Immigrants in Urban America* (Bloomington: Indiana University Press, 1985), 190–92.
7. John Rogers Commons, *Races and Immigrants in America* (1907; New York: Macmillan, 1920), 170.
8. U.S. Immigration Commission, *Reports of the Immigration Commission: Immigration and Crime*, 61st Cong., 3rd Sess. (Washington, DC: U.S. Government Printing Office, 1911), 36, 268.
9. U.S. Immigration Commission, *Reports of the Immigration Commission*, 266.
10. Sophonisba Preston Breckinridge and Edith Abbott, *The Delinquent Child and the Home* (1912; New York: Arno, 1970), 14.
11. Breckinridge and Abbott, *Delinquent Child*, 55.
12. Rachel Devlin, "Female Juvenile Delinquency and the Problem of Sexual Authority in America, 1945–1965," in *Delinquents and Debutantes: Twentieth-Century American Girls' Cultures*, ed. Sherrie A. Inness (New York: New York University Press, 1998), 87.
13. Mabel Carter Rhoades, *The Case Study of Delinquent Boys in the Juvenile Court of Chicago* (Chicago: University of Chicago Press, 1907).
14. Commons, *Races and Immigrants in America*, 170–71.
15. Commons, *Races and Immigrants in America*, 171.
16. Ruth M. Alexander, *The Girl Problem: Female Sexual Delinquency in New York, 1900–1930* (Ithaca, NY: Cornell University Press, 1995); Mary E. Odem, *Delinquent Daughters: Protecting and Policing Adolescent Female Sexuality in the United States, 1885–1920* (Chapel Hill: University of North Carolina Press, 1995).
17. June Purcell-Guild, "A Study of One-Hundred and Thirty-One Delinquent Girls

Held at the Juvenile Detention Home in Chicago, 1917," *Journal of the American Institute of Criminal Law and Criminology* 10 (1919): 474.
18. Joseph Moreau, "Rise of the (Catholic) American Nation: United States History and Parochial Schools, 1878–1925," *American Studies* 38 (1997): 67–90.
19. Breckinridge and Abbott, *Delinquent Child*, 55–56.
20. Jane Addams, *The Spirit of Youth and the City Streets* (New York: Macmillan, 1909), 5.
21. Breckinridge and Abbott, *Delinquent Child*, 76–77.
22. Breckinridge and Abbott, *Delinquent Child*, 76–77.
23. Robert Archey Woods and Albert J. Kennedy, *Young Working Girls: A Summary of Evidence from Two Thousand Social Workers* (Boston: Houghton Mifflin, 1913), 34–36.
24. Martha P. Falconer, "Causes of Delinquency among Girls," *Annals of the American Academy of Political and Social Science* 36 (1910): 79.
25. H. W. Lytle and John Dillon, *From Dance Hall to White Slavery* (Chicago: Charles C. Thompson, 1912), 48. Reformers during this period launched a major campaign against the dance hall, nickel theatre, and amusement park as establishments that allowed for white slavery. See David J. Pivar, *Purity and Hygiene: Women, Prostitution, and the "American Plan," 1900–1930* (Westport, CT: Greenwood, 2002).
26. Lytle and Dillon, *From Dance Hall to White Slavery*, 48.
27. Lytle and Dillon, *From Dance Hall to White Slavery*, 50.
28. Lytle and Dillon, *From Dance Hall to White Slavery*, 48.
29. Harriet McDoual Daniels and the Association of Neighborhood Workers, *The Girl and Her Chance* (New York: Fleming H. Revell, 1914), 9, 25.
30. Daniels, *The Girl and Her Chance*, 25.
31. Reform authorities often berated immigrant mothers for unsanitary housekeeping methods as the root cause of spreading disease. See Suellen Hoy, *Chasing Dirt: The American Pursuit of Cleanliness* (New York: Oxford University Press, 1995), 113–16; Nancy Tomes, *The Gospel of Germs: Men, Women, and the Microbe in American Life* (Cambridge, MA: Harvard University Press, 1998).
32. Olivia Howard Dunbar, "Teaching the Immigrant Woman," in *Americanization: Principles of Americanism, Essentials of Americanization, Technic of Race-Assimilation, Annotated Bibliography*, ed. Winthrop Talbot (New York: H. W. Wilson, 1920), 256.
33. Dunbar, "Teaching the Immigrant Woman," 256.

34. Kathie Friedman-Kasaba, *Memories of Migration: Gender, Ethnicity, and Work in the Lives of Jewish and Italian Women in New York, 1870–1924* (Albany: State University of New York, 1996), 111.
35. North American Civic League for Immigrants, "Domestic Education among Immigrants," in Talbot, *Americanization*, 257.
36. North American Civic League for Immigrants, "Domestic Education," 257–58.
37. Woods and Kennedy, *Young Working Girls*, 136.
38. Ferris, *Girls' Clubs*, 277.
39. Ferris, *Girls' Clubs*, 277.
40. Luther Halsey Gulick, "Recreation and Youth," *Proceedings of the Academy of Political Science* 2 (1912): 119–20.
41. The growth of the early Camp Fire Girls astounded its founders with over 4,700 local groups by December 1913. The Girl Scouts rivaled the Camp Fire Girls, if not in full numbers, in rapid popularity. It was not, however, until the advent of cookie sales that the Girl Scouts would outnumber the Camp Fire Girls. See Helen Buckler, Mary F. Fiedler, and Martha F. Allen, *Wo-He-Lo: The Story of Camp Fire Girls, 1910–1960* (New York: Holt, 1961), 83; Juliette Low, "Girl Scouts as an Educational Force," *Bulletin* (U.S. Bureau of Education) 33 (1919): 3; Laureen Tedesco, "Making a Girl into a Scout: Americanizing Scouting for Girls," in Inness, *Delinquents and Debutantes*, 25.
42. Frances C. Jeffrey, "The New Fourth of July," *Wohelo*, May 1915, 2. For more evidence, see Laureen Tedesco, "Progressive Era Girl Scouts and the Immigrant: *Scouting for Girls* (1920) as a Handbook for American Girlhood," *Children's Literature Association Quarterly* 31 (2006): 363; Lillian S. Williams, *A Bridge to the Future: The History of Diversity in Girl Scouting* (New York: Girl Scouts of the USA, 1996), 11.
43. Low, "Girl Scouts," 8.
44. Mrs. Frank H. Bliss, "Scout for 'America First,'" *The Rally*, January 1918, 3.
45. Rowe Wright, "The Makers of Americans," *Wohelo*, February 1919, 212.
46. Tedesco, "Progressive Era Girl Scouts," 348–49. Americanization work virtually disappears from the magazines of both groups after the early 1920s. Tedesco notes that the Girl Scouts diminished their Americanization activities in the early 1920s, while the guidebooks revised in 1927 and 1933 on the 1920 model retain some of the Americanization tone. While internal documentation from the Camp Fire Girls was destroyed in a fire, virtually the last original Camp Fire Girls handbook to list Americanization honors was published in 1924.

47. Several authors briefly mention the Americanization work of Girl Scouts and to a minimal extent the Camp Fire Girls. See Rima D. Apple and Joanne Passet, "Learning to Be a Woman: Lessons from Girl Scouting and Home Economics, 1920–1970," in *Defining Print Culture for Youth: The Cultural Work of Children's Literature*, ed. Anne Lundin and Wayne Wiegand (Westport, CT: Libraries Unlimited, 2003), 140; Sherrie A. Inness, "Girl Scouts, Camp Fire Girls, and Woodcraft Girls: The Ideology of Girls' Scouting Novels, 1910–1935," in *Continuities in Popular Culture: The Present in the Past and the Past in the Present and Future*, ed. Ray B. Browne and Ronald J. Ambrosetti (Bowling Green, OH: Bowling Green State University Popular Press, 1993), 235–36; Julia Kirk Blackwelder, *Now Hiring: The Feminization of Work in the United States, 1900–1995* (College Station: Texas A&M University Press, 1997), 85–89, 128–31; Mary Jane McCallum, "'The Fundamental Things': Camp Fire Girls and Authenticity, 1910–20," *Canadian Journal of History* 40 (2005): 45–66; David I. Macleod, *Building Character in the American Boy: The Boy Scouts, YMCA, and Their Forerunners, 1870–1920* (Madison: University of Wisconsin Press, 1983), 50–51; Clifford Putney, *Muscular Christianity: Manhood and Sports in Protestant America, 1880–1920* (Cambridge, MA: Harvard University Press, 2001), 158–60; Tedesco, "Making a Girl into a Scout," 19–39.
48. Tedesco, "Progressive Era Girl Scouts," 350.
49. Tedesco, "Progressive Era Girl Scouts," 347.
50. Leslie Paris, "The Adventures of Peanut and Bo: Summer Camps and Early-Twentieth-Century American Girlhood," *Journal of Women's History* 12 (2001): 49; Rebekah E. Revzin, "American Girlhood in the Early Twentieth Century: The Ideology of Girl Scout Literature, 1913–1930," *Library Quarterly* 68 (1998): 261–75. There is one exception to this scholarship with Elisabeth Israels Perry, who details the happenings of an African American troop in Tennessee. See Elisabeth Israels Perry, "From Achievement to Happiness: Girl Scouting in Middle Tennessee, 1910s–1960s," *Journal of Women's History* 5 (1993): 75–94; Elisabeth Israels Perry, "'The Very Best Influence': Josephine Holloway and Girl Scouting in Nashville's African-American Community," *Tennessee Historical Quarterly* 52 (1993): 73–85.
51. de Man, "Autobiography as De-Facement"; de Man, "Shelley Disfigured."
52. On the groups' inability to consolidate, see Report of the Director to the Executive Committee of Girl Scouts, 12 June 1919, Girl Scouts of the United States of America National Historic Preservation Center (hereafter GSNHPC), New York City, 26; Report of the Director to the Executive Committee of Girl

Scouts, 11 September 1919, GSNHPC, New York City, 36; Luther Halsey Gulick to General Baden-Powell, 17 January 1913, GSNHPC, New York City; Stephanie Wallach, "Luther Halsey Gulick and the Salvation of the American Adolescent" (PhD diss., Columbia University, 1989), 352–79.

53. Wright, "Makers of Americans," 211.
54. Rowe Wright, "Scouting for Girls Is Making Americans," *The Rally*, January 1918, 8. This article might point to an instance in which immigrants could take up Girl Scouting without abandoning their ethnicity. However, the focus on American cooking and American freedoms seems to belie the possibility.
55. Wright, "Scouting for Girls," 8.
56. Caroline E. Lewis, "Camping with Girl Scouts," *The Rally*, July 1918, 2.
57. Kenneth Burke, *A Rhetoric of Motives* (Berkeley: University of California Press, 1969), 21.
58. Wright, "Makers of Americans," 212.
59. Bonnie Honig, *Democracy and the Foreigner* (Princeton, NJ: Princeton University Press, 2001), 3.
60. *The Book of the Camp Fire Girls* (New York: George H. Doran, 1913), 20.
61. *The Book of the Camp Fire Girls* (New York: Press of Thos. B. Brooks, 1922), 13–14. For another analysis of this, see Philip Deloria, *Playing Indian* (New Haven, CT: Yale University Press, 1998), 111–21.
62. *Book of the Camp Fire Girls* (1922), 13.
63. I have chosen to use the terms American Indian and indigenous peoples over Native American, first peoples, First Nations, etc. While the word Indian is obviously problematic in that it was originally used to place peoples as those inhabiting India, the phrase American Indian is more appropriate to the analytical work I am performing in this chapter. I do so in as limited a fashion as possible, and try to quote primary sources when possible to highlight the authors' own prejudices. I omitted Native American because period sources such as Madison Grant use the term to mean Nordic peoples. Given no term is a perfect fit and there is ample contestation of these titles, I will sometimes use the phrase indigenous peoples. My choices are informed by the following sources: Kathryn Walbert, "American Indian vs. Native American: A Note on Terminology," Learn NC, http://www.learnnc.org/lp/editions/nc-american-indians/5526; David E. Wilkins and Heidi Kiiwetinepinesiik Stark, *American Indian Politics and the American Political System* (Lanham, MD: Rowman & Littlefield, 2011), xvii; Michael Yellow Bird, "Indian, American Indian, and Native Americans:

Counterfeit Identities," *Winds of Change: A Magazine for American Indian Education and Opportunity* 14 (1999): 1.

64. S. Elizabeth Bird, ed., *Dressing in Feathers: The Construction of the Indian in American Popular Culture* (Boulder, CO: Westview, 1996); Brian W. Dippie, *The Vanishing American: White Attitudes and U.S. Indian Policy* (Lawrence: University Press of Kansas, 1982), 16–20; Gretchen Bataille and Charles L. P. Silet, eds., *The Pretend Indians: Images of Native Americans in the Movies* (Ames: Iowa State University Press, 1980); Robert F. Berkhofer Jr., *The White Man's Indian: Images of the American Indian from Columbus to the Present* (New York: Vintage Books, 1978), 29; James A. Clifton, ed., *Invented Indian: Cultural Fictions and Government Policies* (New Brunswick, NJ: Transaction Publishers, 1990); Jay Mechling, "'Playing Indian' and the Search for Authenticity in Modern White America," *Prospects* 5 (1980): 17–33; Richard Morris and Mary E. Stuckey, "Destroying the Past to Save the Present: Pastoral Voice and Native Identity," in *Cultural Diversity and the U.S. Media*, ed. Yahya R. Kamalipour and Theresa Carilli (Albany: State University of New York Press, 1998), 137–48; Raymond William Stedman, *Shadows of the Indian: Stereotypes in American Culture* (Norman: University of Oklahoma Press, 1982); Bruce Ziff and Pratima V. Rao, eds., *Borrowed Power: Essays in Cultural Appropriation* (New Brunswick, NJ: Rutgers University Press, 1997).
65. *Book of the Camp Fire Girls* (1913), 21.
66. *Book of the Camp Fire Girls* (1922), 13.
67. *Book of the Camp Fire Girls* (1913), 20.
68. Luther Gulick, "Camp Fire Is an Army Not a Hospital," *Wohelo*, March 1915, 14.
69. W. J. Hoxie, *How Girls Can Help Their Country: The 1913 Handbook for Girl Scouts* (Bedford, MA: Applewood Books, 2001), 6.
70. Hoxie, *How Girls Can Help Their Country*, 6.
71. Hoxie, *How Girls Can Help Their Country*, 6.
72. Hoxie, *How Girls Can Help Their Country*, 6.
73. Girl Scouts of the United States of America (hereafter GSUSA), *Scouting for Girls: Official Handbook of the Girl Scouts* (New York: Girl Scouts, 1920), 20.
74. GSUSA, *Scouting for Girls*, 21.
75. GSUSA, *Scouting for Girls*, 20.
76. GSUSA, *Scouting for Girls*, 20.
77. GSUSA, *Scouting for Girls*, 21.
78. GSUSA, *Scouting for Girls*, 22.

79. GSUSA, *Scouting for Girls*, 22.
80. GSUSA, *Scouting for Girls*, 22.
81. GSUSA, *Scouting for Girls*, 22.
82. GSUSA, *Scouting for Girls*, 23.
83. Alexander, "Prosopopoeia," 102.
84. For an article on the tremendous growth of the Girl Guides in the UK, see Richard A. Voeltz, "The Antidote to 'Khaki Fever'? The Expansion of the British Girl Guides during the First World War," *Journal of Contemporary History* 27 (1992): 627–38.
85. Blackwelder, *Now Hiring*, 85.
86. Macleod, *Building Character in the American Boy*, 184.
87. Macleod, *Building Character in the American Boy*, 184.
88. Inness, "Girl Scouts, Camp Fire Girls, and Woodcraft Girls," 231.
89. Blackwelder, *Now Hiring*, 85–86.
90. Tedesco, "Making a Girl into a Scout," 30.
91. Tedesco, "Making a Girl into a Scout," 20.
92. Tedesco, "Making a Girl into a Scout," 25.
93. Erin McMurray, "Camp Fire Girls," in *Girlhood in America: An Encyclopedia*, ed. Miriam Forman-Brunell (Santa Barbara, CA: ABC-CLIO, 2001), 1:87.
94. McMurray, "Camp Fire Girls," 87.
95. Kathryn R. Kent, *Making Girls into Women: American Women's Writing and the Rise of Lesbian Identity* (Durham, NC: Duke University Press, 2003), 110.
96. Kent, *Making Girls into Women*, 110. On how the contemporary Boy Scouts similarly addressed gender role concerns, see Jay Mechling, "Boy Scouts and the Manly Art of Cooking," *Food and Foodways* 13 (2005): 67–89; Jay Mechling, *On My Honor: Boy Scouts and the Making of American Youth* (Chicago: University of Chicago Press, 2004).
97. Macleod, *Building Character in the American Boy*, 184.
98. Kent, *Making Girls into Women*, 110.
99. Macleod, *Building Character in the American Boy*, 184.
100. *Book of the Camp Fire Girls* (1913), 63.
101. Juliette Gordon Low, *How Girls Can Help Their Country* (Savannah, GA: Press of M.S. & D.A. Byck, 1917), 131–41.
102. Low, *How Girls Can Help Their Country*, 25.
103. Hoxie, *How Girls Can Help Their Country*, 130–35; Low, *How Girls Can Help Their Country*, 35–47; GSUSA, *Scouting for Girls*, 504–24.

104. Low, *How Girls Can Help Their Country*, 112; GSUSA, *Scouting for Girls*, 519.
105. "A Democratic Camp," *The Rally*, October 1917, 9.
106. "A Democratic Camp," 9.
107. *Book of the Camp Fire Girls* (1922), 41–42.
108. Tammy Proctor, *Scouting for Girls: A Century of Girl Guides and Girl Scouts* (Santa Barbara, CA: ABC-CLIO, 2009), 29.
109. Importantly, the Girl Scouts did not integrate the troops for decades, with black girls segregated into their own regiments.
110. Lawrence J. Prelli, introduction to *Rhetorics of Display*, ed. Lawrence J. Prelli (Columbia: University of South Carolina Press, 2006), 2.
111. Juliette Low, *Leaders' Manual for Girl Scouts* (New York: Girl Scouts, 1915), 25.
112. *The Book of the Camp Fire Girls with War Program and Illustrations* (New York: National Headquarters, 1917), vi–vii; *The Book of the Camp Fire Girls* (New York: Camp Fire Girls, 1921), 10; Wallach, "Luther Halsey Gulick," 281.
113. *Book of the Camp Fire Girls* (1917), xi.
114. McMurray, "Camp Fire Girls," 87.
115. McMurray, "Camp Fire Girls," 87.
116. McMurray, "Camp Fire Girls," 87.
117. Sally Dwyer-McNulty, *Common Threads: A Cultural History of Clothing in American Catholicism* (Chapel Hill: University of North Carolina Press, 2014), 104.
118. Susan A. Miller, *Growing Girls: The Natural Origins of Girls' Organizations in America* (New Brunswick, NJ: Rutgers University Press, 2007), 36.
119. *Book of the Camp Fire Girls* (1913), 24. The term "squaw" is deeply racist and misogynistic, used as slang for a woman's vagina and a whole host of other problematic meanings. See Mark Monmonier, *From Squaw Tit to Whorehouse Meadow: How Maps Name, Claim, and Inflame* (Chicago: University of Chicago Press, 2006), 2–5.
120. *Book of the Camp Fire Girls* (1921), 13.
121. S. Elizabeth Bird, "Savage Desires: The Gendered Construction of American Indian in Popular Media," in *Selling the Indian: Commercializing and Appropriating American Indian Cultures*, ed. Carter Jones Meyer and Diana Royer (Tucson: University of Arizona Press, 2001), 79.
122. Deloria, *Playing Indian*, 113–14.
123. Deloria, *Playing Indian*, 114.
124. "Scouting for All Girls—Not a Few," *The Rally*, May 1918, 4.

125. "Scouting for All Girls," 1.
126. Jeffrey, "New Fourth of July," 1–2.
127. See, for example, Charlotte Canning, *The Most American Thing in the World: Circuit Chautauqua as Performance* (Iowa City: University of Iowa Press, 2005), 42; Frances A. Kellor, "Americanization: A Conservation Policy for Industry," *Annals of the American Academy of Political Science* 65 (May 1916): 240–44.
128. Charles Simpson Meek, *English To-day: Grade Seven* (New York: Scribner's, 1920), 80.
129. Karen Strassler, *Refracted Visions: Popular Photography and National Modernity in Java* (Durham, NC: Duke University Press, 2010), 26.
130. Inness, "Girl Scouts, Camp Fire Girls, and Woodcraft Girls," 234.
131. See, for example, Meryl Irwin, "On Becoming 'Citizen': The Rhetorical Work of 'Immigrancy' in the American National Fantasy" (PhD diss., University of Iowa, 2012), Desmond King, *The Liberty of Strangers: Making the American Nation* (New York: Oxford University Press, 2005); Desmond King, *Making Americans: Immigration, Race, and the Origins of the Diverse Democracy* (Cambridge, MA: Harvard University Press, 2002); Jeffrey Mirel, *Patriotic Pluralism: Americanization Education and European Immigrants* (Cambridge, MA: Harvard University Press, 2010), 154–55; Sherrow O. Pinder, *The Politics of Race and Ethnicity in the United States: Americanization, De-Americanization, and Racialized Ethnic Groups* (New York: Palgrave Macmillan, 2010).
132. Paul de Man, *The Resistance to Theory* (Minneapolis: University of Minnesota Press, 1986), 49.
133. de Man, *Resistance to Theory*, 50.

Chapter Six. The Paradox of Americanization

1. Abram I. Elkus and Felix Adler, *Americanization: Report of the Committee on Education of Governor Smith's Reconstruction Commission* (Albany, NY: J.B. Lyon Co., 1919), 4.
2. Elkus and Adler, *Americanization*, 4.
3. John F. McClymer, "Gender and the 'American Way of Life': Women in the Americanization Movement," *Journal of American Ethnic History* 10 (1991): 9; Michael R. Olneck, "Americanization and the Education of Immigrants, 1900–1925: An Analysis of Symbolic Action," *American Journal of Education* 97 (1989): 398–423.
4. See, for example, Robert Carlson, *The Quest for Conformity: Americanization*

through Education (New York: Wiley, 1975), 458; McClymer, "Gender and the 'American Way of Life,'" 7; Stephen Meyer, "Adapting the Immigrant to the Line: Americanization in the Ford Factory, 1914–1921," *Journal of Social History* 14 (1980): 78; Olneck, "Americanization and the Education of Immigrants," 398; Jeffrey E. Mirel, *Patriotic Pluralism: Americanization Education and European Immigrants* (Cambridge, MA: Harvard University Press, 2010), 11.

5. See, for example, Don E. Carleton, *Red Scare: Right-Wing Hysteria, Fifties Fanaticism, and Their Legacy in Texas* (Austin: University of Texas Press, 2014), 9–10; Petra DeWitt, *Degrees of Allegiance: Harassment and Loyalty in Missouri's German-American Community during World War I* (Athens: Ohio University Press, 2012), 52; Jay Feldman, *Manufacturing Hysteria: A History of Scapegoating, Surveillance, and Secrecy in Modern America* (New York: Anchor Books, 2011), xi–xviii, 17–64; Robert K. Murray, *Red Scare: A Study in National Hysteria, 1919–1920* (Minneapolis: University of Minnesota Press, 1955); Tammy M. Proctor, "'Patriotic Enemies': Germans in the Americas, 1914–1920," in *Germans as Minorities during the First World War: A Global Comparative Perspective*, ed. Panikos Panayi (Burlington, VT: Ashgate, 2014), 213–34.

6. Petra DeWitt, "World War I and German Americans," in *Germany and the Americas: Culture, Politics, and History*, ed. Thomas Adam (Santa Barbara, CA: ABC-CLIO, 2005), 1166; DeWitt, *Degrees of Allegiance*, 58–59.

7. Harriet C. Frazier, *Lynchings in Kansas, 1850s to 1932* (Jefferson, NC: McFarland and Co., 2015), 155. See also James C. Juhnke, "Mob Violence and Kansas Mennonites in 1918," *Kansas Historical Quarterly* 3 (1977): 334–50.

8. DeWitt, "World War I," 1166.

9. Frederick C. Luebke, *Bonds of Loyalty: German-Americans and World War I* (DeKalb: Northern Illinois University Press, 1974), 279–81; Mark Ellis, "German Americans in World War I," in *Enemy Images in American History*, ed. Ragnhild Fiebig-von Hase and Ursula Lehmkuhl (Providence, RI: Berghahn Books, 1997), 201.

10. Geoffrey R. Stone, *Perilous Times: Free Speech in Wartime from the Sedition Act of 1798 to the War on Terrorism* (New York: W.W. Norton & Co., 2004), 188.

11. "Prager Lynchers Quickly Acquitted," *New York Times*, June 2, 1918, http://www.nytimes.com.

12. Thomas A. Hollihan, "Propagandizing in the Interest of the War: A Rhetorical Study of the Committee on Public Information," *Southern Speech Communication Journal* 49 (1984): 241–57; James J. Kimble, "Whither

Propaganda? Agonism and 'The Engineering of Consent,'" *Quarterly Journal of Speech* 91 (2005): 201–18; J. Michael Sproule, *Propaganda and Democracy: The American Experience of Media and Mass Persuasion* (New York: Cambridge University Press, 1997); Stephen Vaughn, *Holding Fast the Inner Lines: Democracy, Nationalism, and the Committee on Public Information* (Chapel Hill: University of North Carolina Press, 1980).

13. Wayne A. Wiegand, *An Active Instrument for Propaganda: The American Public Library during World War I* (Westport, CT: Greenwood Press, 1989), 120.

14. Americanization Registration Cards for Immigrant Societies, March–April 1918, Records of the Committee on Public Information, RG63, Box 1, National Archives Records Administration, College Park, MD.

15. Of the dozens cataloged, responses largely emerged from Wisconsin, California, Texas, and Pennsylvania.

16. Letter from Henry G. Stott, Americanization Registration Cards for Immigrant Societies, March–April 1918, Records of the Committee on Public Information, RG63, Box 1, National Archives Records Administration, College Park, MD.

17. Stott, Americanization Registration Cards, Records of the Committee on Public Information.

18. Stott, Americanization Registration Cards, Records of the Committee on Public Information.

19. Registration Card from Elizabeth B. Suchman, Americanization Registration Cards for Immigrant Societies, March–April 1918, Records of the Committee on Public Information, RG63, Box 1, National Archives Records Administration, College Park, MD.

20. Letter from George Gona, Americanization Registration Cards for Immigrant Societies, March–April 1918, Records of the Committee on Public Information, RG63, Box 1, National Archives Records Administration, College Park, MD.

21. Gona, Americanization Registration Cards, Records of the Committee on Public Information.

22. Registration Card from Nick Nistor, Americanization Registration Cards for Immigrant Societies, March–April 1918, Records of the Committee on Public Information, RG63, Box 1, National Archives Records Administration, College Park, MD.

23. Registration Card from E. J. Avey, Americanization Registration Cards for Immigrant Societies, March–April 1918, Records of the Committee on Public Information, RG63, Box 1, National Archives Records Administration, College

Park, MD.
24. Gona, Americanization Registration Cards, Records of the Committee on Public Information.
25. Gona, Americanization Registration Cards, Records of the Committee on Public Information.
26. David M. Kennedy, *Over Here: The First World War and American Society* (New York: Oxford University Press, 2004), 65; Ross A. Kennedy, *A Companion to Woodrow Wilson* (Malden, MA: Wiley-Blackwell, 2013), 316.
27. Letter from Manuel Alaniz, Americanization Registration Cards for Immigrant Societies, March–April 1918, Records of the Committee on Public Information, RG63, Box 1, National Archives Records Administration, College Park, MD.
28. Registration Card from George Polinka, Americanization Registration Cards for Immigrant Societies, March–April 1918, Records of the Committee on Public Information, RG63, Box 1, National Archives Records Administration, College Park, MD.
29. Dorothee Schneider, *Crossing Borders: Migration and Citizenship in the Twentieth-Century United States* (Cambridge, MA: Harvard University Press, 2011), 162–63.
30. Mae M. Ngai, *Impossible Subjects: Illegal Aliens and the Making of Modern America* (Princeton, NJ: Princeton University Press, 2004), 3.
31. See, for example, Desmond King, *Making Americans: Immigration, Race, and the Origins of the Diverse Democracy* (Cambridge, MA: Harvard University Press, 2002); Nancy Ordover, *American Eugenics: Race, Queer Anatomy, and the Science of Nationalism* (Minneapolis: University of Minnesota Press, 2003).
32. Raymond Tatalovich, *Nativism Reborn? The Official English Language Movement and the American States* (Lexington: University of Kentucky Press, 1995), 72; Gary Gerstle, *American Crucible: Race and Nation in the Twentieth Century* (Princeton, NJ: Princeton University Press, 2001), 117; Jonathan Spiro, *Defending the Master Race: Conservation, Eugenics, and the Legacy of Madison Grant* (Burlington: University of Vermont Press, 2009), 223.
33. Kenneth Burke, *A Rhetoric of Motives* (Berkeley: University of California Press, 1969).
34. Kenneth Burke, "Psychology and Form," *The Dial* 79 (July 1925): 35.
35. Paul de Man, *The Rhetoric of Romanticism* (New York: Columbia University Press, 1984), 114–15.
36. See, for example, King, *Making Americans*; Ordover, *American Eugenics*.
37. Madison Grant, *The Passing of the Great Race: Or, the Racial Basis of European*

History (1916; New York: Charles Scribner's Sons, 1918).

38. Spiro, *Defending the Master Race*, 202–10.
39. Jeanne D. Petit, *The Men and Women We Want: Gender, Race, and the Progressive Era Literacy Test Debate* (Rochester, NY: University of Rochester Press, 2010), 129–30.
40. Speech by Ellison DuRant Smith, April 9, 1924, *Congressional Record*, 68th Cong., 1st Sess. (Washington, DC: U.S. Government Printing Office, 1924), 65:5961.
41. Speech by Rep. Nathan Perlman, *Congressional Record*, 68th Cong., 1st Sess. (Washington, DC: U.S. Government Printing Office, 1924), 65:5651. Also cited in Chin Jou, "Contesting Nativism: The New York Congressional Delegation's Case against the Immigration Act of 1924," *Federal History* 3 (January 2011): 74.
42. Jou, "Contesting Nativism," 74. See Speech by Emanuel Celler, April 8, 1924, *Congressional Record*, 68th Cong., 1st Sess. (Washington, DC: U.S. Government Printing Office, 1924), 65:5913.
43. Petit, *The Men and Women We Want*, 132. See James A. Gallivan, April 8, 1924, *Congressional Record*, 68th Cong., 1st Sess. (Washington, DC: U.S. Government Printing Office, 1924), 65:5849.
44. Indeed, opponents of the bill were often lambasted for their own racial stock; as Petit notes, "The racial identity of Congressmen of southern and eastern European descent—especially Jewish Congressmen—became a cudgel that could be used against them." See Petit, *The Men and Women We Want*, 131.
45. Spiro, *Defending the Master Race*, 233.
46. Ngai, *Impossible Subjects*, 7, 24.
47. Matthew Frye Jacobson, *Whiteness of a Different Color: European Immigrants and the Alchemy of Race* (Cambridge, MA: Harvard University Press, 1999), 88.
48. DuRant Smith, *Congressional Record*, 65:5961.
49. Speech by Grant Hudson, April 5, 1924, *Congressional Record*, 68th Cong., 1st Sess. (Washington, DC: U.S. Government Printing Office, 1924), 65:5641.
50. Hudson, *Congressional Record*, 65:5641.
51. See, for example, Speech by Robert H. Clancy, April 8, 1924, *Congressional Record*, 68th Cong., 1st Sess. (Washington, DC: U.S. Government Printing Office, 1924), 65:5929–32; Petit, *The Men and Women We Want*, 132.
52. Speech by Adolph Sabath, April 4, 1924, *Congressional Record*, 68th Cong., 1st Sess. (Washington, DC: U.S. Government Printing Office, 1924), 65:5578.
53. Speech by Jeremiah O'Connell, April 8, 1924, *Congressional Record*, 68th Cong., 1st Sess. (Washington, DC: U.S. Government Printing Office, 1924), 65:5836.

54. Speech by John D. McSwain, April 5, 1924, *Congressional Record*, 68th Cong., 1st Sess. (Washington, DC: U.S. Government Printing Office, 1924), 65:5683.
55. Statement by Scott Leavitt, April 12, 1924, *Congressional Record*, 68th Cong., 1st Sess. (Washington, DC: U.S. Government Printing Office, 1924), 65:6265.
56. Speech by Stanley Kunz, April 5, 1924, *Congressional Record*, 68th Cong., 1st Sess. (Washington, DC: U.S. Government Printing Office, 1924), 65:5659.
57. Kunz, *Congressional Record*, 65:5659.
58. Statement by Elton Watkins, April 5, 1924, *Congressional Record*, 68th Cong., 1st Sess. (Washington, DC: U.S. Government Printing Office, 1924), 65:5659.
59. Speech by James F. Byrnes, April 5, 1924, *Congressional Record*, 68th Cong., 1st Sess. (Washington, DC: U.S. Government Printing Office, 1924), 65:5652.
60. Byrnes, *Congressional Record*, 65:5653.
61. Speech by Ira G. Hersey, April 8, 1924, *Congressional Record*, 68th Cong., 1st Sess. (Washington, DC: U.S. Government Printing Office, 1924), 65:5868.
62. Speech by Benjamin Rosenbloom, April 5, 1924, *Congressional Record*, 68th Cong., 1st Sess. (Washington, DC: U.S. Government Printing Office, 1924), 65:5851.
63. Speech by John M. Robsion, April 5, 1924, *Congressional Record*, 68th Cong., 1st Sess. (Washington, DC: U.S. Government Printing Office, 1924), 65:5665.
64. Robsion, *Congressional Record*, 65:5665.
65. Robsion, *Congressional Record*, 65:5665.
66. Rosenbloom, *Congressional Record*, 65:5851.
67. Speech by Samuel D. McReynolds, April 8, 1924, *Congressional Record*, 68th Cong., 1st Sess. (Washington, DC: U.S. Government Printing Office, 1924), 65:5853.
68. Statement by Robert E. L. Allen, April 5, 1924, *Congressional Record*, 68th Cong., 1st Sess. (Washington, DC: U.S. Government Printing Office, 1924), 65:5693.
69. Speech by John F. Miller, April 8, 1924, *Congressional Record*, 68th Cong., 1st Sess. (Washington, DC: U.S. Government Printing Office, 1924), 65:5855.
70. Frances A. Kellor, "What Is Americanization?" *Yale Review* 8 (January 1919): 289.
71. Mirel, *Patriotic Pluralism*, 90.
72. See, for example, Robert A. Carlson, "Americanization as an Early Twentieth-Century Adult Education Movement," *History of Education Quarterly* 10 (1970): 440–64; Gary Gerstle, "Liberty, Coercion, and the Making of Americans," *Journal of American History* 84 (1997): 524–58; Seth Korelitz, "'A Magnificent Piece of Work': The Americanization Work of the National Council of Jewish Women,"

American Jewish History 83 (1995): 201; Mirel, *Patriotic Pluralism*, 90–91.

73. See, for example, Edward George Hartmann, *The Movement to Americanize the Immigrant* (New York: Columbia University Press, 1948); Paul McBride, "Peter Roberts and the YMCA Americanization Program, 1907–World War I," *Pennsylvania History* 44 (1977): 145–62; Olneck, "Americanization and the Education of Immigrants," 398–423.

74. As Peter de Bolla notes of Harold Bloom's philosophy, "A trope will become a larger unit than a single word; a trope will become a historical principle of generation of discourse." See Peter de Bolla, *Harold Bloom: Towards Historical Rhetorics* (New York: Routledge, 1988), 143.

75. Robert Hariman and John Louis Lucaites, *No Caption Needed: Iconic Photographs, Public Culture, and Liberal Democracy* (Chicago: University of Chicago Press, 2007), 107.

Conclusion

1. Woodrow Wilson, "Address of President Wilson at Flag Day Exercises of the Treasury Department, June 14, 1915" (Washington, DC: U.S. Government Printing Office, 1915), 3.
2. Wilson, "Address of President Wilson," 3.
3. Wilson, "Address of President Wilson," 5.
4. "Flag Day June 14, 1924. Ceremonies on the Ellipse at 10:30." Flag Day Program. Printed Ephemera Collection, Portfolio 208, Folder 37a. Retrieved from American Memory Project, Library of Congress, http://memory.loc.gov.
5. "Progress of Catholic Education: Interesting Notes from Many Fields," *National Catholic Welfare Conference Bulletin* 6 (July 1924): 31.
6. Cecilia Elizabeth O'Leary, *To Die For: The Paradox of American Patriotism* (Princeton, NJ: Princeton University Press, 1999), 4.
7. O'Leary, *To Die For*, 4–5.
8. Jennifer R. Mercieca, *Founding Fictions* (Tuscaloosa: University of Alabama Press, 2010), 14.
9. Desmond King, *Making Americans: Immigration, Race, and the Origins of the Diverse Democracy* (Cambridge, MA: Harvard University Press, 2002).
10. Desmond King, *The Liberty of Strangers: Making the American Nation* (New York: Oxford University Press, 2005), 176.
11. King, *Liberty of Strangers*, 31.
12. See, for example, Emory Stephen Bogardus, *Essentials of Americanization* (Los

Angeles: University of Southern California Press, 1920); Franklin K. Lane, Department of the Interior, *America, Americanism, Americanization* (Washington, DC: U.S. Government Printing Office, 1919).

13. See Bogardus, *Essentials of Americanization*; Lane, Department of the Interior, *America, Americanism, Americanization*.
14. Jeffrey E. Mirel, *Patriotic Pluralism: Americanization Education and European Immigrants* (Cambridge, MA: Harvard University Press, 2010), 154–55; King, *Making Americans*, 159–64.
15. W.E.B. Du Bois, "Opinion," *The Crisis: A Record of the Darker Races* 24 (August 1922): 152.
16. Du Bois, "Opinion," 154.
17. Du Bois, "Opinion," 154.
18. Du Bois, "Opinion," 154.
19. Michael A. Kaplan, *Friendship Fictions: The Rhetoric of Citizenship in the Liberal Imaginary* (Tuscaloosa: University of Alabama Press, 2010), 206.
20. James R. Barrett and David Roediger, "Inbetween Peoples: Race, Nationality and the 'New Immigrant' Working Class," *Journal of American Ethnic History* 16 (1997): 3–44; Gary Gerstle, *American Crucible: Race and Nation in the Twentieth Century* (Princeton, NJ: Princeton University Press, 2001); Katrina Irving, *Immigrant Mothers: Narratives of Race and Maternity, 1890–1925* (Champaign-Urbana: University of Illinois Press, 2000); Jeanne D. Petit, *The Men and Women We Want: Gender, Race, and the Progressive Era Literacy Test Debate* (Rochester, NY: University of Rochester Press, 2010); David R. Roediger, *Working toward Whiteness: How America's Immigrants Became White* (New York: Basic Books, 2005). Whiteness studies have generated considerable responses from numerous scholarly perspectives. See Andrew Hartman, "The Rise and Fall of Whiteness Studies," *Race and Class* 46 (2004): 22–38; Katherine Ellinghaus, Jane Carey, and Leigh Boucher, eds., *Re-Orienting Whiteness: A New Agenda for the Field* (New York: Palgrave Macmillan, 2009); Joe L. Kincheloe, Shirley R. Steinberg, Nelson M. Rodriguez, Ronald E. Chennault, eds., *White Reign: Deploying Whiteness in America* (New York: Palgrave Macmillan, 2000).
21. Aristotle, *Rhetoric* (Oxford: Grant and Matthewson, 1816), 143.
22. Kenneth Burke, *A Grammar of Motives* (Berkeley: University of California Press, 1969), 403–518; Giambattista Vico, *The New Science*, trans. Thomas Goddard Bergin and Max Harold Fisch (Ithaca, NY: Cornell University Press, 1948).
23. Paul Ricoeur, *The Rule of Metaphor: Multi-Disciplinary Studies of the Creation of*

Meaning in Language (Toronto: University of Toronto Press, 2000), 199.
24. Ricoeur, *Rule of Metaphor*, 199.
25. Ricoeur, *Rule of Metaphor*, 199.
26. W.J.T. Mitchell, *Picture Theory: Essays on Verbal and Visual Representation* (Chicago: University of Chicago Press, 1995), 284.
27. Peter G. Platt, *Shakespeare and the Culture of Paradox* (Burlington, VT: Ashgate, 2009), 47.
28. Bonnie Honig, *Emergency Politics: Paradox, Law, Democracy* (Princeton, NJ: Princeton University Press, 2009), 13–19.
29. See, for example, Sarah LeTrent, "Mr. President, Who Are You Wearing?," *CNN.com*, October 15, 2012, http://www.cnn.com; John Avlon, "6 Worthy Policy Ideas from Obama's 2012 State of the Union Speech," *DailyBeast.com*, January 25, 2012, http://www.thedailybeast.com; Ellie Krupnick, "Romney's Flag Pin Is Bigger Than Obama's at Debate . . . And What's with That Strange Blob?," *HuffingtonPost.com*, October 4, 2012, http://www.huffingtonpost.com.
30. Stanley Renshon, "The Political Mind: Obama Denounces Flag-Pin Patriotism," *Politico.com*, October 23, 2007, http://www.politico.com/story/2007/10/the-political-mind-obama-denounces-flag-pin-patriotism-006502.
31. Charles Kesler, "The Corner: Flagging an Issue," *National Review*, October 23, 2012, http://www.nationalreview.com/corner/331355/flagging-issue-charles-kesler.
32. Kesler, "The Corner."
33. Kesler, "The Corner."
34. Gilbert Cruz, "A Brief History of the Flag Lapel Pin," *Time*, July 3, 2008, http://content.time.com/time/nation/article/0,8599,1820023,00.html.
35. Renshon, "The Political Mind."
36. Renshon, "The Political Mind."
37. See, for example, Thierry Devos and Debbie S. Ma, "How 'American' Is Barack Obama? The Role of National Identity in a Historic Bid for the White House," *Journal of Applied Social Psychology* 43 (2013): 214–26; Nilanjana Dasgupta and Kumar Yogeeswaran, "Obama-Nation? Implicit Beliefs about American Nationality and the Possibility of Redefining Who Counts as 'Truly' American," in *The Obamas and a (Post) Racial America*, ed. Gregory Parks and Matthew Hughey (New York: Oxford University Press, 2011), 72–90; Carmen R. Lugo-Lugo and Mary K. Bloodsworth-Lugo, "Black as Brown: The 2008 Obama Primary Campaign and the U.S. Browning of Terror," *Journal of African American Studies* 13 (2009): 110–20; Gregory S. Parks and Jeffrey J. Rachlinksi, "Barack Obama's

Candidacy and the Collateral Consequences of the 'Politics of Fear,'" in *Barack Obama and African American Empowerment: The Rise of Black America's New Leadership*, ed. Manning Marable and Kristen Clarke (New York: Palgrave Macmillan, 2009), 232–39; Jonathan P. Rossing, "Comic Provocations in Racial Culture: Barack Obama and the 'Politics of Fear,'" *Communication Studies* 62 (2011): 422–38.

38. Lauren Gail Berlant, *The Queen of America Goes to Washington City: Essays on Sex and Citizenship* (Durham, NC: Duke University Press, 1997), 189.
39. Berlant, *Queen of America*, 189.
40. See, for example, Sara Ahmed, *The Cultural Politics of Emotions* (New York: Routledge, 2004); Martha C. Nussbaum, *Political Emotions: Why Love Matters for Justice* (Cambridge, MA: Harvard University Press, 2013); David Lemmings and Ann Brooks, eds., *Emotions and Social Change: Historical and Sociological Perspectives* (New York: Routledge, 2014).
41. Antoine J. Banks, *Anger and Racial Politics: The Emotional Foundation of Racial Attitudes in America* (New York: Cambridge University Press, 2014).
42. Jeremy Engels, *The Politics of Resentment: A Genealogy* (University Park: Penn State University Press, 2015).
43. This phrase is often attributed to Mark Twain, though there is no compelling evidence that it is his. As such, I referred to this statement as a popular aphorism.
44. Jacques Rancière, *Disagreement: Politics and Philosophy* (Minneapolis: University of Minnesota Press, 2004), 96–101.
45. On the possibilities enabled by democratic paradoxes, see Mary E. Stuckey, *Defining Americans: The Presidency and National Identity* (Lawrence: University Press of Kansas, 2004), 335–54.

Bibliography

ARCHIVAL COLLECTIONS

Americanization Registration Cards for Immigrant Societies. Records of the Committee on Public Information. National Archives Records Administration, College Park, MD.

Camp Fire Girls Publications. New York Public Library, New York, NY.

Ford Educational Weekly Collection. National Archives and Records Administration, College Park, MD.

Girl Scout Archives. Girl Scouts of the United States of America National Historic Preservation Center, New York, NY.

Printed Ephemera Collection. American Memory Project, Library of Congress. Https://memory.loc.gov/ammem.

PRIMARY SOURCES

Abbott, Grace. "The Immigrant as a Problem in Community Planning." *Publications of the American Sociological Society* 12 (1916): 166–73.

Addams, Jane. *The Spirit of Youth and the City Streets.* New York: Macmillan, 1909.

"Americanization Movement of Hour." *The Waterloo Times-Tribune* (IA), June 15, 1915.

"'Americanization'—The Teacher's New Task." *Moderator-Topics* 40 (January 1920).

"'Americanization'—the Teacher's New Task." *Primary Education* 28 (January 1920).

Berkson, Isaac Baer. *Theories of Americanization.* New York: Columbia University Press, 1920.

"Better Homes for the Immigrant Workmen." *Architect and Engineer* (March 1916).

"Better Homes for the Immigrant Workmen: Americanization Committee's Novel House Competition Will Be a Big Factor in Its Vigorous Campaign to Assimilate Aliens." *New York Times,* May 28, 1916.

Betts, George Herbert. *The Mind and Its Education.* 1906. New York: D. Appleton and Company, 1916.

Blake, Margaret [Lida C. Schem]. *The Hyphen.* New York: E. P. Dutton, 1920.

Bliss, Mrs. Frank H. "Scout for 'America First.'" *The Rally,* January 1918.

Breckinridge, Sophonisba Preston, and Edith Abbott. *The Delinquent Child and the Home.* 1912. New York: Arno, 1970.

Bogardus, Emory Stephen. *Essentials of Americanization.* 1919. Los Angeles: University of Southern California Press, 1920.

Bollman, Gladys, and Henry Bollman. *Motion Pictures for Community Needs: A Practical Manual of Information and Suggestion for Educational, Religious and Social Work.* New York: Henry Holt, 1922.

The Book of the Camp Fire Girls. New York: George H. Doran, 1913.

The Book of the Camp Fire Girls. New York: Camp Fire Girls, 1921.

The Book of the Camp Fire Girls. New York: Press of Thos. B. Brooks, 1922.

The Book of the Camp Fire Girls with War Program and Illustrations. New York: National Headquarters, 1917.

Boyd, Ernest. "The Elusive American and the Ex-European." *Scribner's Magazine* 72 (July 1922).

"Briefer Notices." *American Political Science Review* 16 (November 1922).

Buswell, Guy Thomas. "A New Type of Pictured Textbook." *Elementary School Journal* 23 (November 1922).

Campbell, Richard K. *Annual Report of the Commissioner of Naturalization to the Secretary of Labor.* Washington, DC: U.S. Government Printing Office, 1917.

"Chambers of Commerce in 'America First' Campaign." *American City* 15 (December 1916).

"Citizenship Receptions." *School and Society* (June 1915).

"Civic Education of Immigrants." *The Eau Claire Leader* (WI), June 23, 1915.

Commons, John Rogers. *Races and Immigrants in America*. 1907. New York: Macmillan, 1920.

"Community Chorus Will Start Today." *New York Times*, March 23, 1919.

Cowper, Mary O. "Utopias, Biographies and Things." *Journal of Social Forces* 1 (September 1923): 621–33.

Crane, Frank. "Music and Democracy." *Recreation* 16 (January 1923).

Daniels, Harriet McDoual, and the Association of Neighborhood Workers. *The Girl and Her Chance*. New York: Fleming H. Revell, 1914.

Daniels, John. *America via the Neighborhood*. New York: Harper & Brothers, 1920.

Davison, Archibald T. "Good Music for Community Singing." *The Playground* 16 (January 1923).

"A Democratic Camp." *The Rally*, October 1917.

Dixon, Royal. *Americanization*. New York: Macmillan, 1916.

Du Bois, W.E.B. "Opinion." *The Crisis: A Record of the Darker Races* 24 (August 1922).

Dunbar, Olivia Howard. "Teaching the Immigrant Woman." In *Americanization: Principles of Americanism, Essentials of Americanization, Technic of Race-Assimilation, Annotated Bibliography*, edited by Winthrop Talbot, 252–55. New York: H. W. Wilson, 1920.

Durkheim, Émile. *The Elementary Forms of Religious Life*. Translated by Joseph Ward Swain. 1915. Mineola, NY: Dover Publications, 2008.

Elkus, Abram I., and Felix Adler. *Americanization: Report of the Committee on Education of Governor Smith's Reconstruction Commission*. Albany, NY: J.B. Lyon Company, 1919.

Engleman, James Ozro. *Moral Education in School and Home*. Chicago: Benjamin H. Sanborn and Company, 1918.

Fairchild, Henry Pratt. *Immigration: A World Movement and Its American Significance*. New York: Macmillan, 1918.

"Fake War Pictures Stir the East Side." *New York Times*, September 6, 1914.

Falconer, Martha P. "Causes of Delinquency among Girls." *Annals of the American Academy of Political and Social Science* 36 (1910): 77–79.

Farrington, Frederic Ernest. "Immigrants and Night Schools." *School and Society* 4 (1916): 592–93.

———. "The Interior Department and the Immigrant." *Catholic Educational Review* 13 (April 1917): 432–35.

Faulkner, Anne Shaw. *Americanization Songs: Liberty Chorus Song Book for Home,*

School and Community Singing. Chicago: McKinley Music Company, 1920.

Ferris, Helen Josephine. *Girls' Clubs, Their Organization and Management*. New York: E. P. Dutton, 1918.

F.H.H. "Classified Book Notes: *We and Our History*." *Journal of Social Forces* 2 (May 1924): 628.

"Getting the American Viewpoint." *New York Times*, August 21, 1921.

Gibbs, Philip. "America's New Place in the World." *Harper's Magazine* 140 (December 1919).

Girl Scouts of the United States of America. *Scouting for Girls: Official Handbook of the Girl Scouts*. New York: Girl Scouts, 1920.

"A Governor's Message." *Housing Betterment* 6 (January 1917).

Grant, Madison. *The Passing of the Great Race: Or, the Racial Basis of European History*. 1916. New York: Charles Scribner's Sons, 1918.

Gulick, Luther. "Camp Fire Is an Army Not a Hospital." *Wohelo*, March 1915.

———. *A Philosophy of Play*. New York: Scribner's, 1920.

———. "Recreation and Youth." *Proceedings of the Academy of Political Science* 2 (1912): 118–22.

Hart, Albert Bushnell. *We and Our History*. Albany, NY: American Viewpoint Society, 1923.

Hartmann, E. T. "Housing Essentials." *Architectural Review* 5 (January 1917): 22–24.

Haskin, Frederic Jennings. *The Immigrant: An Asset and a Liability*. New York: Fleming H. Revell, 1913.

House Committee on Immigration and Naturalization. *Education and Americanization Hearings*. 66th Cong., 1st Sess. Washington, DC: U.S. Government Printing Office, 1919.

"Housing Cause Advanced a Generation." *Housing Betterment* 7 (May 1918).

"Housing Competition." *Journal of the Engineers Society of Pennsylvania* (April 1916).

Hoxie, W. J. *How Girls Can Help Their Country: The 1913 Handbook for Girl Scouts*. 1913. Bedford, MA: Applewood Books, 2001.

"The Hyphen." *Booklist: A Guide to the Best New Books*, March 1921.

"The Immigrant Housing Competition." *Immigrants in America Review* 2 (April 1916).

Immigration Commission. *Brief Statement of the Conclusions and Recommendations of the Immigration Commission, with Views of the Minority*. Washington, DC: U.S. Government Printing Office, 1910.

"Italian Boys to March July 4th." *The Syracuse Herald*, June 18, 1916.

Jackson, Henry Ezekiel. *A Community Center: What It Is and How to Organize It*. New

York: Macmillan Company, 1918.

James, William. "What Is an Emotion?" *Mind* 9 (1884): 188–205.

Jeffrey, Frances C. "The New Fourth of July." *Wohelo*, May 1915.

Jenks, Jeremiah Whipple, and Rufus Daniel Smith. *We and Our Government*. Albany, NY: American Viewpoint Society, 1922.

Kellor, Frances A. "Americanization: A Conservation Policy for Industry." *Annals of the American Academy of Political Science* 65 (May 1916): 240–44.

———. "Americanization by Industry." *Immigrants in America Review* 2 (1916): 15–26.

———. "The Application of Americanization to Housing." *Architectural Review* 5 (January 1917): 1–2.

———. "What Is Americanization?" *Yale Review* 8 (January 1919): 282–99.

Kimmel, W. G. "The Visual Appeal in Education for Citizenship." *School Review* 31 (January 1923): 69–70.

Lane, Franklin K., and the Department of the Interior. *America, Americanism, Americanization*. Washington, DC: U.S. Government Printing Office, 1919.

Lane, Winthrop D. "The National Conference of Social Work." *The Survey* 40 (June 1918): 251–57.

Lange, Carl Georg. "The Mechanism of the Emotions." In *The Classical Psychologists*, edited by Benjamin Rand, 672–84. 1885. Boston: Houghton Mifflin, 1912.

Lewis, Caroline E. "Camping with Girl Scouts." *The Rally*, July 1918.

Lippmann, Walter. *Public Opinion*. 1922. New York: Free Press, 1997.

Low, Juliette. "Girl Scouts as an Educational Force." *Bulletin* (U.S. Bureau of Education) 33 (1919): 1–8.

———. *How Girls Can Help Their Country*. Savannah, GA: Press of M.S. & D.A. Byck, 1917.

———. *Leaders' Manual for Girl Scouts*. New York: Girl Scouts, 1915.

Lubin, Simon J. "California and the Problems of the Immigrant: A Discussion of the Existing and Future Situation in the State." *California Outlook*, November 15, 1913.

Lytle, H. W., and John Dillon. *From Dance Hall to White Slavery*. Chicago: Charles C. Thompson, 1912.

Mayper, Joseph. "Americanizing Barren Island." In *Americanization: Principles of Americanism, Essentials of Americanization, Technic of Race Assimilation, Annotated Bibliography*, edited by Winthrop Talbot, 281–90. New York: H. W. Wilson Company, 1917.

Meek, Charles Simpson. *English To-day: Grade Seven*. New York: Scribner's, 1920.

Moxcey, Mary Eliza. *Physical Health and Recreation for Girls*. New York: Methodist Book Concern, 1920.

"Music Always in Advance Guard of National Movements." *Dallas Morning News*, October 14, 1917.

"New Citizens Sing 'America.'" *Dallas Morning News*, July 5, 1915.

"A New Tool for the 'Brain Factory.'" *Popular Educator* (November 1919): 122.

North American Civic League for Immigrants. "Domestic Education among Immigrants." In *Americanization: Principles of Americanism, Essentials of Americanization, Technic of Race-Assimilation, Annotated Bibliography*, edited by Winthrop Talbot, 256–58. New York: H. W. Wilson, 1920.

N.W.W. "Review." *High School Journal* 7 (May–October 1924).

Pangburn, Weaver. "The War and Community Movement." *American Journal of Sociology* 26 (1920): 82–95.

"Prager Lynchers Quickly Acquitted." *New York Times*, June 2, 1918.

"President Marches up Avenue at Head of 60,000 Paraders." *Evening Star* (DC), June 14, 1916.

"President's Topeka Speech: No Place Fuller of Fight Than Kansas, He Declares." *New York Times*, February 3, 1916.

"The Prize Designs in the National Americanization Committee Immigrant Housing Competition: Accompanied by the Competitor's Full Specifications and Descriptions." *Architectural Review* 5 (January 1917).

"Progress of Catholic Education: Interesting Notes from Many Fields." *National Catholic Welfare Conference Bulletin* 6 (July 1924).

Purcell-Guild, June. "A Study of One-Hundred and Thirty-One Delinquent Girls Held at the Juvenile Detention Home in Chicago, 1917." *Journal of the American Institute of Criminal Law and Criminology* 10 (1919): 441–76.

Rhoades, Mabel Carter. *The Case Study of Delinquent Boys in the Juvenile Court of Chicago*. Chicago: University of Chicago Press, 1907.

Rickard, H. D. "Use of the Stereopticon." In *Proceedings Americanization Conference Held under the Auspices of the Americanization Division, Bureau of Education, Department of the Interior, Washington, May 12, 13, 14, 15, 1919*, 60–67. Washington, DC: U.S. Government Printing Office, 1919.

Roosevelt, Theodore. "Americanism." In *Immigration and Americanization: Selected Readings*, edited by Philip Davis and Bertha Schwartz, 657–58. Boston: Ginn and Company, 1920.

Rosebault, Charles. "Golden Rule for Aliens." *New York Times*, July 25, 1920.

"Settlement Turns out Its Thousand." *New York Times*, March 3, 1918.

"Scouting for All Girls—Not a Few." *The Rally*, May 1918.

Smith, Alfred Emanuel. "Choral Music, Americanization, and Taste." *The Outlook*. April 23, 1919.

"Spanish Congregation in New York." *New York Times*, January 13, 1918.

"Spread of Americanization Day Plans." *The Survey*, June 19, 1915.

Stevens, Thomas Woods. "Community Gatherings and Recreation." In *Proceedings Americanization Conference: Held under the Auspices of the Americanization Division, Bureau of Education, Department of the Interior*, 309–19. Washington, DC: U.S. Government Printing Office, 1919.

"To Greet New Citizens." *The Emporia Gazette* (KS), June 22, 1915.

"A Two-Decker." *New York Medical Journal*, January 29, 1921.

U.S. Congress. *Congressional Record*. 68th Cong., 1st Sess. Vol. 65. Washington, DC: U.S. Government Printing Office, 1924.

U.S. Department of Labor. *Report of the United States Housing Corporation*. Vol. 2. Washington, DC: U.S. Government Printing Office, 1919.

U.S. Immigration Commission. *Reports of the Immigration Commission*. 61st Cong., 2nd Sess. Vols. 1 and 2. Washington, DC: U.S. Government Printing Office, 1911.

———. *Reports of the Immigration Commission, Dictionary of Races or Peoples*. 61st Cong., 2nd Sess. Vol. 5. Washington, DC: U.S. Government Printing Office, 1911.

———. *Reports of the Immigration Commission: Immigration and Crime*. 61st Cong., 3rd Sess. Washington, DC: U.S. Government Printing Office, 1911.

Wheaton, H. H. "The America First Campaign." *Immigration Journal* (June 1916).

———. "The United States Bureau of Education and the Immigrant." *Annals of the American Academy of Political and Social Science* 67 (1916): 273–83.

Wilson, Woodrow. "Address to the Daughters of the American Revolution, Washington, October 11, 1915." In *President Wilson's Great Speeches and Other History Making Documents*, 72–78. Chicago: Stanton and Van Vliet, 1918.

———. "Address to Naturalized Citizens at Convention Hall, Philadelphia." The Presidency Project, May 10, 1915. Http://www.presidency.ucsb.edu.

———. "Address of President Wilson at Flag Day Exercises of the Treasury Department, June 14, 1915." Washington, DC: U.S. Government Printing Office, 1915.

———. "Insults and Aggressions of Germany." In *Selected Addresses and Public Papers of Woodrow Wilson*, edited by Albert Bushnell Hart, 210–17. New York: Boni and Liveright, 1918.

———. "Loyalty, Address at Citizenship Convention, Washington 13 July 1916." In *Selected Addresses and Public Papers of Woodrow Wilson*, edited by Albert Bushnell Hart, 139–43. New York: Boni and Liveright, 1918.

———. "Proclamation 1335—Flag Day." The Presidency Project, May 30, 1916. Http://www.presidency.ucsb.edu.

Woods, Robert Archey, and Albert J. Kennedy. *Young Working Girls: A Summary of Evidence from Two Thousand Social Workers*. Boston: Houghton Mifflin, 1913.

Wright, Rowe. "The Makers of Americans." *Wohelo*, February 1919.

———. "Scouting for Girls Is Making Americans." *The Rally*, January 1918.

SECONDARY SOURCES

Ahmed, Sara. *The Cultural Politics of Emotion*. New York: Routledge, 2004.

———. *The Promise of Happiness*. Durham, NC: Duke University Press, 2010.

Albanese, Catherine L. *America: Religions and Religion*. Belmont, CA: Wadsworth Publishing, 1981.

Alexander, Gavin. "Prosopopoeia: The Speaking Figure." In *Renaissance Figures of Speech*, edited by Sylvia Adamson, Gavin Alexander, and Katrin Ettenhuber, 97–114. New York: Cambridge University Press, 2007.

Alexander, June Granatir. *Ethnic Pride, American Patriotism: Slovaks and Other New Immigrants in the Interwar Era*. Philadelphia: Temple University Press, 2004.

Alexander, Ruth M. *The Girl Problem: Female Sexual Delinquency in New York, 1900–1930*. Ithaca, NY: Cornell University Press, 1995.

Anbinder, Tyler. *Five Points: The 19th Century New York Neighborhood That Invented Tap Dance, Stole Elections, and Became the World's Most Notorious Slum*. New York: Simon & Schuster, 2001.

Anderson, Benedict. *Imagined Communities: Reflections on the Origin and Spread of Nationalism*. New York: Verso, 1983.

Apple, Rima D., and Joanne Passet. "Learning to Be a Woman: Lessons from Girl Scouting and Home Economics, 1920–1970." In *Defining Print Culture for Youth: The Cultural Work of Children's Literature*, edited by Anne Lundin and Wayne Wiegand, 139–54. Westport, CT: Libraries Unlimited, 2003.

Aristotle. *Rhetoric*. Oxford: Grant and Matthewson, 1816.

Arneson, Eric, ed. *Encyclopedia of U.S. Labor and Working Class History*. Vol. 1. New York: Routledge, 2007.

Asato, Noriko. "Mandating Americanization: Japanese Language Schools and the Federal Survey of Education in Hawai'i, 1916–1920." *History of Education*

Quarterly 43 (2003): 10–38.
Avlon, John. "6 Worthy Policy Ideas from Obama's 2012 State of the Union Speech." *DailyBeast.com*, January 25, 2012.
Baar, Kenneth. "The National Movement to Halt the Spread of Multifamily Housing, 1890–1926." *Journal of the American Planning Association* 58 (1992): 39–48.
Baker, Elizabeth W. *Great Speeches*. Norwood, MA: Norwood Press, 1927.
Banerjee, J. C. *Encyclopaedic Dictionary of Psychological Terms*. New Delhi: MD Publications Pvt. Ltd., 1994.
Banks, Antoine J. *Anger and Racial Politics: The Emotional Foundation of Racial Attitudes in America*. New York: Cambridge University Press, 2014.
Barbalet, J. M. *Emotion, Social Theory, and Social Structure: A Macrosociological Approach*. New York: Cambridge University Press, 2001.
Barkan, Elliot, Hasia R. Diner, and Alan Kraut, eds. *From Arrival to Incorporation: Migrants to the U.S. in a Global Era*. New York: New York University Press, 2007.
Barrett, James R. "Americanization from the Bottom Up: Immigration and the Remaking of the Working Class in the United States, 1880–1930." *Journal of American History* 79 (1992): 996–1020.
Barrett, James R., and David Roediger. "Inbetween Peoples: Race, Nationality and the 'New Immigrant' Working Class." *Journal of American Ethnic History* 16 (1997): 3–44.
Bataille, Gretchen, and Charles L. P. Silet, eds. *The Pretend Indians: Images of Native Americans in the Movies*. Ames: Iowa State University Press, 1980.
Beasley, Vanessa B. *You, the People: American National Identity in Presidential Rhetoric*. College Station: Texas A&M University Press, 2004.
Bendelow, Gillian, and Simon J. Williams, eds. *Emotions in Social Life: Critical Themes and Contemporary Issues*. New York: Routledge, 1998.
Bennett, Alice. *Afterlife and Narrative in Contemporary Fiction*. New York: Palgrave Macmillan, 2012.
Berkhofer, Robert F., Jr. *The White Man's Indian: Images of the American Indian from Columbus to the Present*. New York: Vintage Books, 1978.
Berlant, Lauren Gail, ed. *Compassion: The Culture and Politics of an Emotion*. New York: Routledge, 2004.
———. *The Queen of America Goes to Washington City: Essays on Sex and Citizenship*. Durham, NC: Duke University Press, 1997.
Besel, Richard. "Prolepsis and the Environmental Rhetoric of Congressional Politics: Defeating the Climate Stewardship Act of 2003." *Environmental Communication*

6 (2012): 233–49.

Bird, S. Elizabeth, ed. *Dressing in Feathers: The Construction of the Indian in American Popular Culture*. Boulder, CO: Westview, 1996.

———. "Savage Desires: The Gendered Construction of the American Indian in Popular Media." In *Selling the Indian: Commercializing and Appropriating American Indian Cultures*, edited by Carter Jones Meyer and Diana Royer, 62–98. Tucson: University of Arizona Press, 2001.

Blackwelder, Julia Kirk. *Now Hiring: The Feminization of Work in the United States, 1900–1995*. College Station: Texas A&M University Press, 1997.

Blair, Karen J. *The Torchbearers: Women and Their Amateur Arts Associations in America, 1890–1930*. Bloomington: Indiana University Press, 1994.

Bodnar, John E. *Remaking America: Public Memory, Commemoration, and Patriotism in the Twentieth Century*. Princeton, NJ: Princeton University Press, 1992.

———. *The Transplanted: A History of Immigrants in Urban America*. Bloomington: Indiana University Press, 1985.

Branham, Robert J. "'Of Thee I Sing': Contesting 'America.'" *American Quarterly* 48 (1996): 623–52.

Branham, Robert James, and Stephen J. Hartnett. *Sweet Freedom's Song: "My Country 'Tis of Thee" and Democracy in America*. New York: Oxford University Press, 2002.

Bremer, Thomas S. *Formed from This Soil: An Introduction to the Diverse History of Religion in America*. Malden, MA: Wiley, 2015.

Brophy, Anne. "'The Committee . . . Has Stood out against Coercion': The Reinvention of Detroit Americanization, 1915–1931." *Michigan Historical Review* 29 (2003): 1–39.

Brown, Kathleen M. *Foul Bodies: Cleanliness in Early America*. New Haven, CT: Yale University Press, 2009.

Brown, Mary Elizabeth. "Henry Cabot Lodge (1850–1924): Immigration Restriction as National Policy." In *The Making of Modern Immigration: An Encyclopedia of Peoples and Ideas*, edited by Patrick J. Hayes, 491–504. Santa Barbara, CA: ABC-CLIO, 2012.

Buckler, Helen, Mary F. Fiedler, and Martha F. Allen. *Wo-He-Lo: The Story of Camp Fire Girls, 1910–1960*. New York: Holt, 1961.

Buder, Stanley. *Visionaries and Planners: The Garden City Movement and the Modern Community*. New York: Oxford University Press, 1990.

Bukowczyk, John J. "The Transformation of Working-Class Ethnicity: Corporate Control, Americanization, and the Polish Immigrant Middle Class in Bayonne,

New Jersey, 1915–1925." *Labor History* 25 (1984): 53–82.

Burke, Kenneth. *A Grammar of Motives*. Berkeley: University of California Press, 1969.

———. "Psychology and Form." *The Dial* 79 (July 1925): 34–46.

———. *A Rhetoric of Motives*. Berkeley: University of California Press, 1969.

Burstein, Andrew. *Sentimental Democracy: The Evolution of America's Romantic Self-Image*. New York: Hill and Wang, 1999.

Butler, Judith, and Gayatri Chakravorty Spivak. *Who Sings the Nation-State? Language, Politics, Belonging*. Oxford, UK: Seagull Books, 2007.

Butsch, Richard. *The Citizen Audience: Crowds, Public, and Individuals*. New York: Routledge, 2008.

Canning, Charlotte. *The Most American Thing in the World: Circuit Chautauqua as Performance*. Iowa City: University of Iowa Press, 2005.

Capozzola, Christopher. *Uncle Sam Wants You: World War I and the Making of the Modern American Citizen*. New York: Oxford University Press, 2010.

Carey, Alex. *Taking the Risk out of Democracy: Corporate Propaganda versus Freedom and Liberty*. Edited by Andrew Lohrey. Champaign-Urbana: University of Illinois Press, 1997.

Carleton, Don E. *Red Scare: Right-Wing Hysteria, Fifties Fanaticism, and Their Legacy in Texas*. Austin: University of Texas Press, 2014.

Carlson, Linda. *Company Towns of the Pacific Northwest*. Seattle: University of Washington Press, 2003.

Carlson, Robert. "Americanization as an Early Twentieth-Century Adult Education Movement." *History of Education Quarterly* 10 (1970): 440–64.

———. *The Quest for Conformity: Americanization through Education*. New York: Wiley, 1975.

Cashman, Sean Dennis. *America Ascendant: From Theodore Roosevelt to FDR in the Century of American Power, 1901–1945*. New York: New York University Press, 1998.

Chang, E. Christina. "The Singing Program of World War I: The Crusade for a Singing Army." *Journal of Historical Research in Music Education* 23 (2001): 19–45.

Cicero, Marcus Tullius. *Cicero on Oratory and Orators with His Letters to Quintus and Brutus*. Translated by J. S. Watson. London: Bell and Daldy, 1871.

Clifton, James A., ed. *The Invented Indian: Cultural Fictions and Government Policies*. New Brunswick, NJ: Transaction Publishers, 1990.

Crary, Jonathan. *Suspensions of Perception: Attention, Spectacle, and Modern Culture*. Cambridge, MA: MIT Press, 2001.

———. *Techniques of the Observer: On Vision and Modernity in the 19th Century.* Cambridge, MA: MIT Press, 1992.

Crawford, Margaret. *Building the Workingman's Paradise: The Design of American Company Towns.* New York: Verso, 1995.

———. "Earle S. Draper and the Company Town in the American South." In *The Company Town: Architecture and Society in the Early Industrial Age*, edited by John Garner, 139–72. New York: Oxford University Press, 1992.

Cristi, Marcela. *From Civil to Political Religion: The Intersection of Culture, Religion and Politics.* Waterloo, ON: Wilfrid Laurier University Press, 2001.

Cruz, Gilbert. "A Brief History of the Flag Lapel Pin." *Time*, July 3, 2008. Http://content.time.com/time/nation.

Cummings, Brian. "Metalepsis: The Boundaries of Metaphor." In *Renaissance Figures of Speech*, edited by Sylvia Adamson, Gavin Alexander, and Katrin Ettenhuber, 217–36. New York: Cambridge University Press, 2007.

Currie, Mark. *About Time: Narrative, Fiction, and the Philosophy of Time.* Edinburgh: Edinburgh University Press, 2006.

Cutrer, Emily Fourmy. "A Pragmatic Mode of Seeing: James, Howells, and the Politics of Vision." In *American Iconology: New Approaches to Nineteenth-Century Art and Literature*, edited by David C. Miller, 259–75. New Haven, CT: Yale University Press, 1993.

Dasgupta, Nilanjana, and Kumar Yogeeswaran. "Obama-Nation? Implicit Beliefs about American Nationality and the Possibility of Redefining Who Counts as 'Truly' American." In *The Obamas and a (Post) Racial America*, edited by Gregory Parks and Matthew Hughey, 72–90. New York: Oxford University Press, 2011.

Dayton-Wood, Amy. "Teaching English for 'A Better America.'" *Rhetoric Review* 27 (2008): 397–414.

de Bolla, Peter. *Harold Bloom: Towards Historical Rhetorics.* New York: Routledge, 1988.

de Certeau, Michel. *The Practice of Everyday Life.* Translated by Steven Rendall. Berkeley: University of California, 1984.

Deloria, Philip. *Playing Indian.* New Haven, CT: Yale University Press, 1998.

de Man, Paul. "Autobiography as De-Facement." *MLN* 94 (1979): 919–30.

———. *The Resistance to Theory.* Minneapolis: University of Minnesota Press, 1986.

———. *The Rhetoric of Romanticism.* New York: Columbia University Press, 1984.

———. "Shelley Disfigured." In *Deconstruction and Criticism*, edited by Harold Bloom, 32–61. New York: Continuum, 1979.

Demo, Anne Teresa, and Bradford Vivian, eds. *Rhetoric, Remembrance, and Visual Form:*

Sighting Memory. New York: Routledge, 2012.

Dennis, Rutledge. "W.E.B. Du Bois's Concept of Double-Consciousness." In *Race and Ethnicity: Comparative and Theoretical Approaches*, edited by John Stone and Rutledge Dennis, 13–27. Malden, MA: Blackwell, 2003.

Devlin, Rachel. "Female Juvenile Delinquency and the Problem of Sexual Authority in America, 1945–1965." In *Delinquents and Debutantes: Twentieth-Century American Girls' Cultures*, edited by Sherrie A. Inness, 83–107. New York: New York University Press, 1998.

Devos, Thierry, and Debbie S. Ma. "How 'American' Is Barack Obama? The Role of National Identity in a Historic Bid for the White House." *Journal of Applied Social Psychology* 43 (2013): 214–26.

DeWitt, Petra. *Degrees of Allegiance: Harassment and Loyalty in Missouri's German-American Community during World War I*. Athens: Ohio University Press, 2012.

———. "World War I and German Americans." In *Germany and the Americas: Culture, Politics, and History*, edited by Thomas Adam, 1163–66. Santa Barbara, CA: ABC-CLIO, 2005.

Dinnerstein, Leonard, and David M. Reimers. *Ethnic Americans: A History of Immigration and Assimilation*. New York: Dodd, Mead & Company, 1975.

Dippie, Brian W. *The Vanishing American: White Attitudes and U.S. Indian Policy.* Lawrence: University Press of Kansas, 1982.

Docherty, Thomas. *Aesthetic Democracy*. Stanford, CA: Stanford University Press, 2006.

Dorsey, Leroy. *We Are All Americans, Pure and Simple: Theodore Roosevelt and the Myth of Americanism*. Tuscaloosa: University of Alabama Press, 2007.

Dugan, John Richard. *Making a New Man: Ciceronian Self-Fashioning in the Rhetorical Works*. New York: Oxford University Press, 2005.

Dwyer-McNulty, Sally. *Common Threads: A Cultural History of Clothing in American Catholicism*. Chapel Hill: University of North Carolina Press, 2014.

Dyson, Henry. *Prolepsis and Ennoia in the Early Stoa*. Berlin: Walter de Gruyter, 2009.

Edwards, Janis L., and Carol K. Winkler. "Representative Form and the Visual Ideograph: The Iwo Jima Image in Editorial Cartoons." *Quarterly Journal of Speech* 83 (1997): 289–310.

Ellinghaus, Katherine, Jane Carey, and Leigh Boucher, eds. *Re-Orienting Whiteness: A New Agenda for the Field*. New York: Palgrave Macmillan, 2009.

Ellis, Mark. "German Americans in World War I." In *Enemy Images in American History*, edited by Ragnhild Fiebig-von Hase and Ursula Lehmkuhl, 183–208. Providence, RI: Berghahn Books, 1997.

Ellis, Richard J. *To the Flag: The Unlikely History of the Pledge of Allegiance.* Lawrence: University Press of Kansas, 2005.

Elsea, Jennifer K. "Detention of American Citizens as Enemy Combatants." In *The Treatment of Prisoners: Legal, Moral, or Criminal?*, edited by Ralph D. McPhee, 1–52. New York: Nova Publishers, 2006.

Engels, Jeremy. *The Politics of Resentment: A Genealogy.* University Park: Penn State University Press, 2015.

Enos, Theresa, ed. *Encyclopedia of Rhetoric and Composition: Communication from Ancient Times to the Information Age.* New York: Routledge, 2013.

Fahnestock, Jeanne. *Rhetorical Figures in Science.* New York: Oxford University Press, 1999.

———. *Rhetorical Style: The Uses of Language in Persuasion.* New York: Oxford University Press, 2011.

Feldman, Jay. *Manufacturing Hysteria: A History of Scapegoating, Surveillance, and Secrecy in Modern America.* New York: Anchor Books, 2011.

Ferguson, Robert A. *Law and Letters in American Culture.* Cambridge, MA: Harvard University Press, 1984.

Finan, Christopher M. *From the Palmer Raids to the Patriot Act: A History of the Right for Free Speech in America.* Boston, MA: Beacon Press, 2007.

Finnegan, Cara. "The Naturalistic Enthymeme and Visual Argument: Photographic Representation in the 'Skull Controversy.'" *Argumentation & Advocacy* 37 (2001): 133–49.

Fischer, David Hackett. *Albion's Seed: Four British Folkways in America.* New York: Oxford University Press, 1989.

Fischlin, Daniel. *In Small Proportions: A Poetics of the English Ayre, 1596–1622.* Detroit: Wayne State University Press, 1998.

Foley, Megan. "Voicing Terri Schiavo: Prosopopeic Citizenship in the Democratic Aporia between Sovereignty and Biopower." *Communication and Critical/Cultural Studies* 7 (2010): 381–400.

Ford, Nancy Gentile. *Americans All! Foreign-Born Soldiers in World War I.* College Station: Texas A&M University Press, 2001.

———. *The Great War and America: Civil-Military Relations during World War I.* Westport, CT: Praeger, 2008.

———. *Issues of War and Peace.* Westport, CT: Greenwood Press, 2002.

Frazier, Harriet C. *Lynchings in Kansas, 1850s to 1932.* Jefferson, NC: McFarland and Company, 2015.

Friedman-Kasaba, Kathie. *Memories of Migration: Gender, Ethnicity, and Work in the Lives of Jewish and Italian Women in New York, 1870–1924*. Albany: State University of New York, 1996.

Garcia, Mario T. "Americanization and the Mexican Immigrant, 1880–1930." *Journal of Ethnic Studies* 6 (1978): 19–34.

Genette, Gérard. *Narrative Discourse: An Essay in Method*. Translated by Jane E. Lewin. Ithaca, NY: Cornell University Press, 1983.

Gerstle, Gary. *American Crucible: Race and Nation in the Twentieth Century*. Princeton, NJ: Princeton University Press, 2001.

———. "Liberty, Coercion, and the Making of Americans." *Journal of American History* 84 (1997): 524–58.

Glassberg, David. *American Historical Pageantry: The Uses of Tradition in the Early Twentieth Century*. Chapel Hill: University of North Carolina Press, 1990.

Glidden, David K. "Parrots, Pyrrhonists, and Native Speakers." In *Language*, edited by Stephen Everson, 129–48. New York: Cambridge University Press, 1994.

Goldstein, Robert Justin. *Political Repression in Modern America from 1870 to 1976*. Champaign-Urbana: University of Illinois Press, 2001.

Greene, Ronald Walter. "Rhetorical Pedagogy as Postal System: Circulating Subjects through Michael Warner's 'Publics and Counterpublics.'" *Quarterly Journal of Speech* 88 (2002): 434–43.

———. "Y Movies: Film and the Modernization of Pastoral Power." *Communication and Critical/Cultural Studies* 2 (2005): 20–36.

Grieveson, Lee. *Policing Cinema: Movies and Censorship in Early-Twentieth-Century America*. Berkeley: University of California, 2004.

———. "The Work of Film in the Age of Fordist Mechanization." *Cinema Journal* 51 (2012): 25–51.

Gunderson, Erik. *Staging Masculinity: The Rhetoric of Performance in the Roman World*. Ann Arbor: University of Michigan, 2000.

Gullett, Gayle. "Women Progressives and the Politics of Americanization in California, 1915–1920." *Pacific Historical Review* 64 (1995): 71–94.

Gutek, Gerald L. *An Historical Introduction to American Education*. Long Grove, IL: Waveland Press, 2013.

Gyory, Andrew. *Closing the Gate: Race, Politics, and the Chinese Exclusion Act*. Chapel Hill: University of North Carolina Press, 1998.

Hariman, Robert, and John Louis Lucaites. *No Caption Needed: Iconic Photographs, Public Culture, and Liberal Democracy*. Chicago: University of Chicago Press,

2007.

———. "Visual Tropes and Late-Modern Emotion in U.S. Public Culture." *Poroi* 5 (2008): 47–93.

Hartelius, E. Johanna. "Face-ing Immigration: Prosopopeia and the 'Muslim-Arab-Middle Eastern' Other." *Rhetoric Society Quarterly* 43 (2013): 311–34.

Hartman, Andrew. "The Rise and Fall of Whiteness Studies." *Race and Class* 46 (2004): 22–38.

Hartmann, Edward George. *The Movement to Americanize the Immigrant*. New York: Columbia University Press, 1948.

Hayes, Carlton J. H. *Nationalism: A Religion*. New York: Macmillan, 1960.

Higham, John. *Strangers in the Land: Patterns of American Nativism, 1860–1925*. New Brunswick, NJ: Rutgers University Press, 2002.

Hogan, J. Michael. "Introduction: Rhetoric and Reform in the Progressive Era." In *Rhetoric and Reform in the Progressive Era*, edited by J. Michael Hogan, vii–xvii. East Lansing: Michigan State University Press, 2003.

Hoganson, Kristin L. *Consumers' Imperium: The Global Production of American Domesticity, 1865–1920*. Chapel Hill: University of North Carolina Press, 2007.

Hollander, John. *The Figure of Echo: A Mode of Allusion in Milton and After*. Berkeley: University of California Press, 1981.

Hollihan, Thomas A. "Propagandizing in the Interest of the War: A Rhetorical Study of the Committee on Public Information." *Southern Speech Communication Journal* 49 (1984): 241–57.

Honig, Bonnie. *Democracy and the Foreigner*. Princeton, NJ: Princeton University Press, 2001.

———. *Emergency Politics: Paradox, Law, Democracy*. Princeton, NJ: Princeton University Press, 2009.

Hoy, Suellen. *Chasing Dirt: The American Pursuit of Cleanliness*. New York: Oxford University Press, 1995.

Inness, Sherrie A. "Girl Scouts, Camp Fire Girls, and Woodcraft Girls: The Ideology of Girls' Scouting Novels, 1910–1935." In *Continuities in Popular Culture: The Present in the Past and the Past in the Present and Future*, edited by Ray B. Browne and Ronald J. Ambrosetti, 229–40. Bowling Green, OH: Bowling Green State University Popular Press, 1993.

Irving, Katrina. *Immigrant Mothers: Narratives of Race and Maternity, 1890–1925*. Champaign-Urbana: University of Illinois Press, 2000.

Irwin, Meryl. "On Becoming 'Citizen': The Rhetorical Work of 'Immigrancy' in the

American National Fantasy." PhD diss., University of Iowa, 2012.

Jacobs, Lea. "Reformers and Spectators: The Film Education Movement in the Thirties." *Camera Obscura* 8 (1990): 28–49.

Jacobson, Matthew Frye. *Whiteness of a Different Color: European Immigrants and the Alchemy of Race*. Cambridge, MA: Harvard University Press, 1999.

Jasinski, James. *Sourcebook on Rhetoric*. Thousand Oaks, CA: Sage, 2001.

Jensen, Uffa. "Mrs. Gaskell's Anxiety." In *Learning How to Feel: Children's Literature and Emotional Socialization, 1870–1970*, edited by Ute Frevert et al., 21–39. New York: Oxford University Press, 2014.

Johannesen, Richard L., Rennard Strickland, and Ralph T. Eubanks. "Richard M. Weaver on the Nature of Rhetoric: An Interpretation." In *The Vision of Richard Weaver*, edited by Joseph Scotchie, 93–110. New Brunswick, NJ: Transaction Publishers, 1995.

Jou, Chin. "Contesting Nativism: The New York Congressional Delegation's Case against the Immigration Act of 1924." *Federal History* 3 (January 2011): 66–79.

Juhnke, James C. "Mob Violence and Kansas Mennonites in 1918." *Kansas Historical Quarterly* 3 (1977): 334–50.

Kaplan, Michael A. *Friendship Fictions: The Rhetoric of Citizenship in the Liberal Imaginary*. Tuscaloosa: University of Alabama Press, 2010.

Karabel, Jerome. *The Chosen: The Hidden History of Admission and Exclusion at Harvard, Yale, and Princeton*. New York: Houghton Mifflin Harcourt, 2005.

Kauffman, Christopher J. *Patriotism and Fraternalism in the Knights of Columbus: A History of the Fourth Degree*. New York: Crossroad, 2001.

Kazal, Russell Andrew. *Becoming Old Stock: The Paradox of German American Identity*. Princeton, NJ: Princeton University Press, 2004.

Kennedy, David M. *Over Here: The First World War and American Society*. New York: Oxford University Press, 2004.

Kennedy, Ross A. *A Companion to Woodrow Wilson*. Malden, MA: Wiley-Blackwell, 2013.

Kent, Kathryn R. *Making Girls into Women: American Women's Writing and the Rise of Lesbian Identity*. Durham, NC: Duke University Press, 2003.

Kesler, Charles. "The Corner: Flagging an Issue." *National Review*, October 23, 2012. Http://www.nationalreview.com/corner/331355/flagging-issue-charles-kesler.

Kimble, James J. "Whither Propaganda? Agonism and 'The Engineering of Consent.'" *Quarterly Journal of Speech* 91 (2005): 201–18.

Kincheloe, Joe L., Shirley R. Steinberg, Nelson M. Rodriguez, and Ronald E.

Chennault, eds. *White Reign: Deploying Whiteness in America*. New York: Palgrave Macmillan, 2000.

King, Desmond. *The Liberty of Strangers: Making the American Nation*. New York: Oxford University Press, 2005.

———. *Making Americans: Immigration, Race, and the Origins of the Diverse Democracy*. Cambridge, MA: Harvard University Press, 2002.

Kintsch, Walter, and John T. Cacioppo, eds. "The Centennial Issue of the Psychological Review." *Psychological Review* 101 (1994).

Korelitz, Seth. "'A Magnificent Piece of Work': The Americanization Work of the National Council of Jewish Women." *American Jewish History* 83 (1995): 177–203.

Krupnick, Ellie. "Romney's Flag Pin Is Bigger Than Obama's at Debate . . . And What's with That Strange Blob?" *HuffingtonPost.com*, October 4, 2012.

Laclau, Ernesto. *On Populist Reason*. New York: Verso, 2005.

———. *The Rhetorical Foundations of Society*. New York: Verso, 2014.

Leepson, Marc. *Flag: An American Biography*. New York: St. Martin's, 2007.

Lemmings, David, and Ann Brooks, eds. *Emotions and Social Change: Historical and Sociological Perspectives*. New York: Routledge, 2014.

LeTrent, Sarah. "Mr. President, Who Are You Wearing?" *CNN.com*, October 15, 2012. Http://www.cnn.com/2012/10/15/living/presidential-fashion/.

Lewis, David Lanier. *The Public Image of Henry Ford: An American Folk Hero and His Company*. Detroit: Wayne State University Press, 1976.

Lindvall, Terry. *Sanctuary Cinema: Origins of the Christian Film Industry*. New York: New York University Press, 2007.

Loukopoulou, Katerina. "Museum at Large: Aesthetic Education through Film." In *Learning with the Lights Off: Educational Film in the United States*, edited by Devin Orgeron, Marsha Orgeron, and Dan Streible, 356–76. New York: Oxford University Press, 2012.

Lubove, Roy. *The Progressives and the Slums: Tenement House Reform in New York City, 1890–1917*. Pittsburgh, PA: University of Pittsburgh Press, 1962.

Luebke, Frederick C. *Bonds of Loyalty: German-Americans and World War I*. DeKalb: Northern Illinois University Press, 1974.

Lugo-Lugo, Carmen R., and Mary K. Bloodsworth-Lugo. "Black as Brown: The 2008 Obama Primary Campaign and the U.S. Browning of Terror." *Journal of African American Studies* 13 (2009): 110–20.

Lukacher, Ned. *Primal Scenes: Literature, Philosophy, Psychoanalysis*. Ithaca, NY: Cornell University Press, 1986.

Lundberg, Christian O. *Lacan in Public: Psychoanalysis and the Science of Rhetoric*. Tuscaloosa: University of Alabama Press, 2012.

Macleod, David I. *Building Character in the American Boy: The Boy Scouts, YMCA, and Their Forerunners, 1870–1920*. Madison: University of Wisconsin Press, 1983.

Malin, Brenton J. *Feeling Mediated: A History of Media Technology and Emotion in America*. New York: New York University Press, 2014.

———. "Looking White and Middle-Class: Stereoscopic Imagery and Technology in the Early Twentieth-Century United States." *Quarterly Journal of Speech* 93 (2007): 403–24.

Malina, Debra. *Breaking the Frame: Metalepsis and the Construction of the Subject*. Columbus: Ohio State University Press, 2002.

Marshall, David L. *Vico and the Transformation of Rhetoric in Early Modern Europe*. New York: Cambridge University Press, 2010.

Martin, Susan F. *A Nation of Immigrants*. New York: Oxford University Press, 2011.

Martinez, Ramiro, Jr. "Coming to America: The Impact of New Immigration on Crime." In *Immigration and Crime: Race, Ethnicity, and Violence*, edited by Ramiro Martinez Jr. and Abel Valenzuela, 1–19. New York: New York University Press, 2006.

Marty, Martin E. *The New Shape of American Religion*. New York: Harper & Row, 1959.

Massumi, Brian. *Parables for the Virtual: Movement, Affect, Sensation*. Durham, NC: Duke University Press, 2002.

McBride, Paul. "Peter Roberts and the YMCA Americanization Program, 1907–World War I." *Pennsylvania History* 44 (1977): 145–62.

McCallum, Mary Jane. "'The Fundamental Things': Camp Fire Girls and Authenticity, 1910–20." *Canadian Journal of History* 40 (2005): 45–66.

McClure, Arthur F., James Riley Chrisman, and Perry Mock. *Education for Work: The Historical Evolution of Vocational and Distributive Education in America*. Cranberry, NJ: Associated University Presses, 1985.

McClymer, John F. "The Federal Government and the Americanization Movement, 1915–24." In *Americanization, Social Control, and Philanthropy*, edited by George E. Pozzetta, 233–52. New York: Garland Publishing, 1991.

———. "Gender and the 'American Way of Life': Women in the Americanization Movement." *Journal of American Ethnic History* 10 (1991): 3–20.

McManus, Edgar J., and Tara Helfman. *Liberty and Union: A Constitutional History of the United States*. New York: Routledge, 2014.

McMurray, Erin. "Camp Fire Girls." In *Girlhood in America: An Encyclopedia*, edited by

Miriam Forman-Brunell, 1:85–90. Santa Barbara, CA: ABC-CLIO, 2001.

McPherson, Christina Ziegler. "Dillingham Commission." In *Anti-Immigration in the United States, A-R*, edited by Kathleen Arnold, 158–60. Santa Barbara, CA: ABC-CLIO, 2011.

Meacham, Standish. *Regaining Paradise: Englishness and the Early Garden City Movement*. New Haven, CT: Yale University Press, 1999.

Mechling, Jay. "Boy Scouts and the Manly Art of Cooking." *Food and Foodways* 13 (2005): 67–89.

———. *On My Honor: Boy Scouts and the Making of American Youth*. Chicago: University of Chicago Press, 2004.

———. "'Playing Indian' and the Search for Authenticity in Modern White America." *Prospects* 5 (1980): 17–33.

Medhurst, Martin J., and Michael A. DeSousa. "Political Cartoons as Rhetorical Form: A Taxonomy of Graphic Discourse." *Communication Monographs* 48 (1981): 197–236.

Mercieca, Jennifer R. *Founding Fictions*. Tuscaloosa: University of Alabama Press, 2010.

Meyer, Stephen. "Adapting the Immigrant to the Line: Americanization in the Ford Factory, 1914–1921." *Journal of Social History* 14 (1980): 67–82.

Miller, J. Hillis. *Tropes, Parables, and Performatives: Essays on Twentieth-Century Literature*. Durham, NC: Duke University Press, 1991.

Miller, John J. *The Unmaking of Americans: How Multiculturalism Has Undermined America's Assimilation Ethic*. New York: Free Press, 1998.

Miller, Kenneth E. *From Progressive to New Dealer: Frederic C. Howe and American Liberalism*. University Park: Penn State University Press, 2010.

Miller, Susan A. *Growing Girls: The Natural Origins of Girls' Organizations in America*. New Brunswick, NJ: Rutgers University Press, 2007.

Mink, Gwendolyn. *The Wages of Motherhood: Inequality in the Welfare State, 1917–1942*. Ithaca, NY: Cornell University Press, 1996.

Minteer, Ben. *The Landscape of Reform: Civic Pragmatism and Environmental Thought in America*. Cambridge, MA: MIT Press, 2006.

Mirel, Jeffrey E. *Patriotic Pluralism: Americanization Education and European Immigrants*. Cambridge, MA: Harvard University Press, 2010.

Mitchell, W.J.T. *Picture Theory: Essays on Verbal and Visual Representation*. Chicago: University of Chicago Press, 1995.

Monmonier, Mark. *From Squaw Tit to Whorehouse Meadow: How Maps Name, Claim, and Inflame*. Chicago: University of Chicago Press, 2006.

Moreau, Joseph. "Rise of the (Catholic) American Nation: United States History and Parochial Schools, 1878–1925." *American Studies* 38 (1997): 67–90.

Morley, David. *Media, Modernity and Technology: The Geography of the New.* London: Routledge, 2007.

Morris, Richard, and Mary E. Stuckey. "Destroying the Past to Save the Present: Pastoral Voice and Native Identity." In *Cultural Diversity and the U.S. Media*, edited by Yahya R. Kamalipour and Theresa Carilli, 137–48. Albany: State University of New York Press, 1998.

Motomura, Hiroshi. *Americans in Waiting: The Lost Story of Immigration and Citizenship in the United States.* New York: Oxford University Press, 2006.

Mulrooney, Margaret M. "A Legacy of Coal: The Coal Company Towns of Southwestern Pennsylvania." *Perspectives in Vernacular Architecture* 4 (1991): 130–37.

Murray, Robert K. *Red Scare: A Study in National Hysteria, 1919–1920.* Minneapolis: University of Minnesota Press, 1955.

Nelson, John S. *Tropes of Politics: Science, Theory, Rhetoric, Action.* Madison: University of Wisconsin Press, 1998.

Nemanic, Mary Lou. *One Day for Democracy: Independence Day and the Americanization of Iron Range Immigrants.* Athens: Ohio University Press, 2007.

Ngai, Mae M. *Impossible Subjects: Illegal Aliens and the Making of Modern America.* Princeton, NJ: Princeton University Press, 2004.

Novick, Peter. *That Noble Dream: The "Objectivity Question" and the American Historical Profession.* New York: Cambridge University Press, 1988.

Nünlist, René. *The Ancient Critic at Work: Terms and Concepts of Literary Criticism in Greek Scholia.* New York: Cambridge University Press, 2009.

Nussbaum, Martha C. *Political Emotions: Why Love Matters for Justice.* Cambridge, MA: Harvard University Press, 2013.

O'Brien, David M. "Detentions and Security versus Liberty in Times of National Emergency." In *Courts and Terrorism: Nine Nations Balance Rights and Security*, edited by Mary L. Volcansek and John F. Stack Jr., 9–32. New York: Cambridge University Press, 2011.

Odem, Mary E. *Delinquent Daughters: Protecting and Policing Adolescent Female Sexuality in the United States, 1885–1920.* Chapel Hill: University of North Carolina Press, 1995.

Ohles, John F., ed. *Biographical Dictionary of American Educators.* Vol. 1. Westport, CT: Greenwood Press, 1978.

O'Leary, Cecilia Elizabeth. *To Die For: The Paradox of American Patriotism.* Princeton,

NJ: Princeton University Press, 1999.

Olneck, Michael R. "Americanization and the Education of Immigrants, 1900–1925: An Analysis of Symbolic Action." *American Journal of Education* 97 (1989): 398–423.

Ordover, Nancy. *American Eugenics: Race, Queer Anatomy, and the Science of Nationalism*. Minneapolis: University of Minnesota Press, 2003.

O'Regan, Cyril. *The Heterodox Hegel*. Albany: State University of New York Press, 1994.

Orgeron, Devin, Marsha Orgeron, and Dan Streible. "A History of Learning with the Lights Off." In *Learning with the Lights Off: Educational Film in the United States*, edited by Devin Orgeron, Marsha Orgeron, and Dan Streible, 15–66. New York: Oxford University Press, 2012.

Palczewski, Catherine. "The Male Madonna and the Feminine Uncle Sam: Visual Argument, Icons, and Ideographs in 1909 Anti–Woman Suffrage Postcards." *Quarterly Journal of Speech* 91 (2005): 365–94.

Papacharissi, Zizi. *Affective Publics: Sentiment, Technology, and Politics*. New York: Oxford University Press, 2015.

Papillion, Terry. "Isocrates' Techne and Rhetorical Pedagogy." *Rhetoric Society Quarterly* 25 (1995): 149–63.

Paris, Leslie. "The Adventures of Peanut and Bo: Summer Camps and Early-Twentieth-Century American Girlhood." *Journal of Women's History* 12 (2001): 47–76.

Park, Yoosun, and Susan P. Kemp. "'Little Alien Colonies': Representations of Immigrants and Their Neighborhoods in Social Work Discourse, 1875–1924." *Social Service Review* 80 (2006): 705–34.

Parks, Gregory S., and Jeffrey J. Rachlinksi. "Barack Obama's Candidacy and the Collateral Consequences of the 'Politics of Fear.'" In *Barack Obama and African American Empowerment: The Rise of Black America's New Leadership*, edited by Manning Marable and Kristen Clarke, 225–40. New York: Palgrave Macmillan, 2009.

Perry, Elisabeth Israels. "From Achievement to Happiness: Girl Scouting in Middle Tennessee, 1910s–1960s." *Journal of Women's History* 5 (1993): 75–94.

———. "'The Very Best Influence': Josephine Holloway and Girl Scouting in Nashville's African-American Community." *Tennessee Historical Quarterly* 52 (1993): 73–85.

Peters, John Durham, and Peter Simonson, eds. *Mass Communication and American Social Thought: Key Texts, 1919–1968*. Lanham, MD: Rowman & Littlefield, 2004.

Peterson, Jon A. "The Impact of Sanitary Reform upon American Urban Planning, 1840–1890." *Journal of Social History* 13 (1979): 83–103.

Petit, Jeanne D. *The Men and Women We Want: Gender, Race, and the Progressive Era*

Literacy Test Debate. Rochester, NY: University of Rochester Press, 2010.

Pier, John. Afterword to *Metalepsis in Popular Culture*, edited by Karin Kukkonen and Sonja Klimek, 268–76. Berlin: Walter de Gruyter, 2011.

Platt, Peter G. *Shakespeare and the Culture of Paradox*. Burlington, VT: Ashgate, 2009.

Pinder, Sherrow O. *The Politics of Race and Ethnicity in the United States: Americanization, De-Americanization, and Racialized Ethnic Groups*. New York: Palgrave Macmillan, 2010.

Pivar, David J. *Purity and Hygiene: Women, Prostitution, and the "American Plan," 1900–1930*. Westport, CT: Greenwood, 2002.

Pope, S. W. *Patriotic Games: Sporting Traditions in the American Imagination, 1876–1926*. New York: Oxford University Press, 1997.

Prelli, Lawrence J. "Rhetorics of Display: An Introduction." In *Rhetorics of Display*, edited by Lawrence J. Prelli, 1–40. Columbia: University of South Carolina Press, 2006.

Proctor, Tammy M. "'Patriotic Enemies': Germans in the Americas, 1914–1920." In *Germans as Minorities during the First World War: A Global Comparative Perspective*, edited by Panikos Panayi, 213–34. Burlington, VT: Ashgate, 2014.

———. *Scouting for Girls: A Century of Girl Guides and Girl Scouts*. Santa Barbara, CA: ABC-CLIO, 2009.

Putney, Clifford. *Muscular Christianity: Manhood and Sports in Protestant America, 1880–1920*. Cambridge, MA: Harvard University Press, 2001.

Quinn, Patrick. "The First World War: American Writing." In *The Cambridge Companion to War Writing*, edited by Kate McLoughlin, 175–84. New York: Cambridge University Press, 2009.

Rancière, Jacques. *Disagreement: Politics and Philosophy*. Minneapolis: University of Minnesota Press, 2004.

Ray, Angela. *The Lyceum and Public Culture in the Nineteenth-Century United States*. East Lansing: Michigan State University Press, 2005.

Reimers, David M. *Unwelcome Strangers: American Identity and the Turn against Immigration*. New York: Columbia University Press, 1998.

Renshon, Stanley. "The Political Mind: Obama Denounces Flag-Pin Patriotism." *Politico.com*, October 23, 2007. Http://www.politico.com.

Revzin, Rebekah E. "American Girlhood in the Early Twentieth Century: The Ideology of Girl Scout Literature, 1913–1930." *Library Quarterly* 68 (1998): 261–75.

Ricci, Gabriel R. *Time Consciousness: The Philosophical Uses of History*. New Brunswick, NJ: Transaction Publishers, 2002.

Ricoeur, Paul. *The Rule of Metaphor: Multi-Disciplinary Studies of the Creation of Meaning in Language.* Toronto: University of Toronto Press, 2000.

Roediger, David R. *Working toward Whiteness: How America's Immigrants Became White.* Cambridge, MA: Perseus Books, 2005.

Rosenzweig, Roy. *Eight Hours for What We Will: Workers and Leisure in an Industrial City, 1870–1920.* New York: Cambridge University Press, 1985.

Ross, Andrew. "'Nothing Gained by Overcrowding': The History and Politics of Urban Population Control." In *The New Blackwell Companion to the City*, edited by Gary Bridge and Sophie Watson, 169–78. New York: John Wiley & Sons, 2011.

Ross, Stewart Halsey. *Propaganda for the War: How the United States Was Conditioned to Fight the Great War of 1914–1918.* Jefferson, NC: McFarland & Company, 1996.

Rossing, Jonathan P. "Comic Provocations in Racial Culture: Barack Obama and the 'Politics of Fear.'" *Communication Studies* 62 (2011): 422–38.

Roth, Leland. "Company Towns in the Western United States." In *The Company Town: Architecture and Society in the Early Industrial Age*, edited by John Garner, 173–206. New York: Oxford University Press, 1992.

Rury, John L. *Education and Social Change: Contours in the History of American Schooling.* New York: Routledge, 2013.

Schiller, Nina Glick. "Long Distance Nationalism." In *Encyclopedia of Diasporas: Immigrant and Refugee Cultures around the World*, edited by Melvin Ember, Carol R. Ember, and Ian Skoggard, 570–80. New York: Springer Science and Business Media, 2004.

Schneider, Dorothee. *Crossing Borders: Migration and Citizenship in the Twentieth-Century United States.* Cambridge, MA: Harvard University Press, 2011.

Seigworth, Gregory J., and Melissa Gregg. "An Inventory of Shimmers." In *The Affect Theory Reader*, edited by Gregory J. Seigworth and Melissa Gregg, 1–28. Durham, NC: Duke University Press, 2010.

Selig, Diana. *Americans All: The Cultural Gifts Movement.* Cambridge, MA: Harvard University Press, 2008.

Shifflett, Crandall. *Coal Towns: Life, Work, and Culture in Company Towns of Southern Appalachia, 1880–1960.* Knoxville: University of Tennessee Press, 1991.

Shryock, Andrew. *Nationalism and the Genealogical Imagination: Oral History and Textual Authority in Tribal Jordan.* Berkeley: University of California Press, 1997.

Silver, M. M. *Louis Marshall and the Rise of Jewish Ethnicity in America.* Syracuse, NY: Syracuse University Press, 2013.

Smilor, Raymond W. "Creating a National Festival: The Campaign for a Safe and Sane

Fourth, 1903–1916." *Journal of American Culture* 2 (1980): 611–22.

Smith, Craig R. "The Red Scares." In *Silencing the Opposition: How the U.S. Government Suppressed Freedom of Speech during Major Crises*, edited by Craig R. Smith, 175–204. Albany: State University of New York Press, 2011.

Smith, Shawn Michelle. *American Archives: Gender, Race, and Class in Visual Culture.* Princeton, NJ: Princeton University Press, 1999.

Spiro, Jonathan. *Defending the Master Race: Conservation, Eugenics, and the Legacy of Madison Grant.* Hanover, NH: University of Vermont Press, 2009.

Spivak, Gayatri Chakravorty. *Nationalism and the Imagination.* New York: Seagull Books, 2015.

Sproule, J. Michael. *Propaganda and Democracy: The American Experience of Media and Mass Persuasion.* New York: Cambridge University Press, 1997.

Stearns, Peter N., and Jan Lewis, eds. *An Emotional History of the United States.* New York: New York University Press, 1998.

Stedman, Raymond William. *Shadows of the Indian: Stereotypes in American Culture.* Norman: University of Oklahoma Press, 1982.

Stob, Paul. *William James and the Art of Popular Statement.* East Lansing: Michigan State University Press, 2013.

Stone, Geoffrey R. *Perilous Times: Free Speech in Wartime from the Sedition Act of 1798 to the War on Terrorism.* New York: W.W. Norton & Company, 2004.

Strassler, Karen. *Refracted Visions: Popular Photography and National Modernity in Java.* Durham, NC: Duke University Press, 2010.

Striner, Richard. *Woodrow Wilson and World War I: A Burden Too Great to Bear.* Lanham, MD: Rowman & Littlefield, 2014.

Stuckey, Mary E. *Defining Americans: The Presidency and National Identity.* Lawrence: University Press of Kansas, 2004.

Sutton, Jane S., and Mari Lee Mifsud. "Introduction: A Revolution in Tropes." In *A Revolution in Tropes: Alloiostrophic Rhetoric*, edited by Jane S. Sutton and Mari Lee Mifsud, xi–xxvii. Lanham, MD: Lexington Books, 2015.

Tatalovich, Raymond. *Nativism Reborn? The Official English Language Movement and the American States.* Lexington: University of Kentucky Press, 1995.

Taylor, Charles. "Nationalism and Modernity." In *The Morality of Nationalism*, edited by Robert McKim and Jeff McMahan, 31–55. New York: Oxford University Press, 1997.

Tedesco, Laureen. "Making a Girl into a Scout: Americanizing Scouting for Girls." In *Delinquents and Debutantes: Twentieth-Century American Girls' Cultures*, edited by Sherrie A. Inness, 19–39. New York: New York University Press, 1998.

———. "Progressive Era Girl Scouts and the Immigrant: Scouting for Girls (1920) as a Handbook for American Girlhood." *Children's Literature Association Quarterly* 31 (2006): 346–68.

Tichenor, Daniel J. *Dividing Lines: The Politics of Immigration Control in America.* Princeton, NJ: Princeton University Press, 2002.

Tomes, Nancy. *The Gospel of Germs: Men, Women, and the Microbe in American Life.* Cambridge, MA: Harvard University Press, 1999.

Trasciatti, Mary Anne. "Americanization Campaign." In *The Home Front Encyclopedia: United States, Britain, and Canada in World Wars I and II*, edited by James Ciment and Thaddeus Russell, 230–32. Santa Barbara, CA: ABC-CLIO, 2007.

Vaughn, Stephen. *Holding Fast the Inner Lines: Democracy, Nationalism, and the Committee on Public Information.* Chapel Hill: University of North Carolina Press, 1980.

Vico, Giambattista. *The New Science.* Translated by Thomas Goddard Bergin and Max Harold Fisch. Ithaca, NY: Cornell University Press, 1948.

Vivian, Bradford. "Neoliberal Epideictic: Rhetorical Form and Commemorative Politics on September 11, 2002." *Quarterly Journal of Speech* 92 (2006): 1–26.

———. *Public Forgetting: The Rhetoric and Politics of Beginning Again.* University Park: Penn State University Press, 2010.

Voeltz, Richard A. "The Antidote to 'Khaki Fever'? The Expansion of the British Girl Guides during the First World War." *Journal of Contemporary History* 27 (1992): 627–38.

Vought, Hans P. *The Bully Pulpit and the Melting Pot: American Presidents and the Immigrant, 1897–1933.* Macon, GA: Mercer University Press, 2004.

Walbert, Kathryn. "American Indian vs. Native American: A Note on Terminology." Learn NC, 2009. Http://www.learnnc.org/lp/editions/nc-american-indians.

Wallach, Stephanie. "Luther Halsey Gulick and the Salvation of the American Adolescent." PhD diss., Columbia University, 1989.

Ward, David. *Poverty, Ethnicity and the American City, 1840–1925: Changing Conceptions of the Slum and the Ghetto.* New York: Cambridge University Press, 1989.

Weber, William A. "Archibald T. Davison: Faith in Good Music." *Harvard Crimson*, February 17, 1961. Http://www.thecrimson.com.

White, Hayden. *Metahistory: The Historical Imagination in Nineteenth Century Europe.* Baltimore, MD: Johns Hopkins University Press, 1975.

Wiatr, Elizabeth. "Between Word, Image and the Machine: Visual Education and the

Films of Industrial Process." *Historical Journal of Film, Radio and Television* 22 (2002): 333–51.

Wiegand, Wayne A. *An Active Instrument for Propaganda: The American Public Library during World War I.* Westport, CT: Greenwood Press, 1989.

Wilkins, David E., and Heidi Kiiwetinepinesiik Stark. *American Indian Politics and the American Political System.* Lanham, MD: Rowman & Littlefield, 2011.

Williams, Lillian S. *A Bridge to the Future: The History of Diversity in Girl Scouting.* New York: Girl Scouts of the USA, 1996.

Winter, Jay. "Imaginings of War: Posters and the Shadow of the Lost Generation." In *Picture This: World War I Posters and Visual Culture*, edited by Pearl James, 37–58. Lincoln: University of Nebraska Press, 2009.

Yellow Bird, Michael. "Indian, American Indian, and Native Americans: Counterfeit Identities." *Winds of Change: A Magazine for American Indian Education and Opportunity* 14 (1999): 1.

Ziff, Bruce, and Pratima V. Rao, eds. *Borrowed Power: Essays in Cultural Appropriation.* New Brunswick, NJ: Rutgers University Press, 1997.

Index

Page numbers in italics refer to figures.

A

Abbott, Edith, 126, 127
Abbott, Grace, 6, 16, 69–70
Addams, Jane, 127
Adler, Felix, 153–54
Aesthetic Democracy (Docherty), 87
affective stimulation, 32–35. *See also* visual aids
Ahmed, Sara, 46, 75, 88
Alaniz, Manuel, 161
Alexander, Gavin, 138–39
Alien Enemies Act, 10
Allen, Robert, 172
"America" (song), 112–13
America First poster, 42–48, 54, 213 (n. 49)
Americanization (Dixon), 18–19
Americanization Day festivities, 16, 93, 101–2, 104–8
Americanization movements: ambiguity's impact on, 154–55, 173–75, 181–83, 188–89; assimilation arguments of, 6–8; goals and programs of, xiv–xv, 15–21, 153–54, 179–80, 201 (n.46); and immigration patterns, 1–3; influence of wartime anxieties on, 8–15, 17; legacy of, 189–93; and nativist ideology, 3–6; public display emphasis of, 178–79; and

structural change avoidance, 183–84, 192–93; success markers of, 21–22; value of tropological analysis on, 22–27, 173–75, 185–88, 194–95. See also American patriotism, proof's problem

Americanization Songs (Faulkner), 110

American patriotism, proof's problem, 154–55; in immigration-restriction legislation, 162–73; and national identity standards, 181–82; with registration card initiative, 156–62; significance of mob violence on, 155–56; for structural change, 180–81; value of tropological analysis on, 155, 173–75

American Viewpoint Society (AVS). See AVS textbooks

America via the Neighborhood (Daniels), 82–83

Anderson, Benedict, 13

anger as political weapon, 191–93

Architectural Review, 76–77

Asian Exclusion Act, 171

Astor, Helen, 73

Atterbury, Grosvenor, 78

Avey, E. J., 160

AVS textbooks: chapter on Constitution, 53; civic participation promises in, 58–60; design of, 48–49; flag symbolism in, images, 59–60; future theme in, 54–58; hydroelectric and waterfall images in, 51, 53; praise for, 49–51; sequencing of images in, 51–55

B

Baden-Powell, Robert, 140

Banks, Antoine J., 191

Barren Island, New York, 80–81

Barthes, Roland, 187

Bear Mountain camp, Girl Scouts, 141

Beasley, Vanessa B., 99

Berkson, Isaac Baer, 83–84

Berlant, Lauren, 191

Bertha Fensterwald Social Centre, 159

Bird, S. Elizabeth, 144

Blake, Margaret (Lida C. Schem), 14

Boas, Franz, 6

Bollman, Gladys, 20

Bollman, Henry, 20

Booth, Hanson, 51, 52, 53, 54, 56, 57

Boyd, Ernest, 99–100

boys, delinquency explanations, 126. See also child delinquency; girls clubs

Branham, Robert, 112–13

Breckinridge, Sophonisba Preston, 126, 127

Brent, Mary, 136

Brumbaugh, Martin, 65–66

Building the Workingman's Paradise (Crawford), 78

Bureau of Education: America First poster and, 42–48, 54, 213 (n. 49); Americanization conference talk, 120–21; NAC relationship with, 17

Burke, Kenneth, xxiii, 163, 209 (n. 126)

Burleson, Albert, 10

Burns, Allen T., 82

Burstein, Andrew, 12

Butler, Judith, 116–17
Byrnes, James, 170–71

C

Campbell, Richard K., 98–99
Camp Fire Girls: citizenship instruction of, 140; founder's expectations of, 130; Indian symbolism usage of, 134–36, 138, 144–46; membership growth of, 139, 228 (n. 41); public pageantry purposes of, 146–47; uniforms of, 144; war preparedness activities of, 139–40. *See also* girls clubs
Capozzola, Christopher, 8
Carey, Alex, 43
Carlson, Robert, 9, 15–16
Carnegie Corporation, 82–83
Celler, Emanuel, 165
Chamber of Commerce, housing design contest, 72
Chicago Tribune, 17
child delinquency, 125–30
Chinese Exclusion Act, 3
choral singing, 107, 108–17, 178, 194
Cicero, 23
citizenship, liberal-democratic, 119–20
civil liberties, wartime restrictions, 10–11
Claxton, P. P., 106
Committee on Public Information (CPI), xiv, 11, 17, 19, 156–61
Commons, John Rogers, 125
community singing, 107, 108–17, 178, 194

company towns, 72–75
congressional hearings, 6, 29–30. *See also* legislation
Coolidge, Calvin, 172, 178
Cooprider, Walter, 155
cottage styles, housing design contest, 78–79
Cowper, Mary O., 50
Crane, Frank, 117–18
Crary, Jonathan, 37, 211 (n. 18)
Crawford, Margaret, 78
Creel, George, 157
Crisis, The (Du Bois), 184–85
Crist, Raymond, 29
Cruz, Gilbert, 189–90
Cummings, Brian, 101–2

D

Dallas Morning News, 110
dance halls, 128–29, 227 (n. 25)
Daniels, Harriet McDoual, 129
Daniels, John, 83
Daughters of the American Revolution (DAR). *See under* Wilson, Woodrow
Davison, Archibald T., 115–16
de Bolla, Peter, 240 (n. 75)
de Certeau, Michel, 67, 86
Defending the Master Race (Spiro), 163
Deloria, Philip, 146
de Man, Paul, 132, 150, 163
design contest, housing, 73–80, 218 (n. 26)
Dictionary of Races or Peoples (Jenks and Folkmar), 4

Dillingham, William P., 4
Dillingham Commission report, 3–5, 126
Dillon, John, 128
Dinnerstein, Leonard, 1
Dixon, Royal, 18–19, 20, 37
Docherty, Thomas, 87
domestic skills instruction, 129–30, 141, *142*, *143*
Dorsey, Leroy, 7
Du Bois, W.E.B., 184–85
Dugan, John Richard, 23
Dunbar, Olivia Howard, 129–30
DuRant Smith, Ellison, 164, 166–67
Durkheim, Émile, 21
Dyson, Henry, 34–35, 50, 55

E

efficiency/productivity motivations: America First poster and, 43, 46–47; Ford's film series and, 39–40; housing reform and, 74–75, 80; NAC mission and, 17
elephant example, prolepsis, 34–35
Elkus, Abram, 153–54
Emergency Quota Act, 162, 164, 165
"Emigrants and Immigrants" (Booth), 54
emotional nationalism. *See* American patriotism, proof's problem
employment arguments, immigrant girls, 127–28
Engels, Jeremy, 191
Engleman, James Ozro, 33–34
Espionage and Sedition Acts, 10
ethnic colony arguments, 67–71, 72, 73, 75
eugenics, 5, 7–8, 162, 163–64. *See also* Johnson-Reed Act; racial hierarchy

F

Fairchild, Henry Pratt, 70
Falconer, Martha P., 128
Faulkner, Anne Shaw, 110, 113
Ferris, Helen, 123, 130
films, 30, 39–42
First Evangelical Reform Church, Milwaukee, 158–59
Fischlin, Daniel, 94
Flag Day celebrations, xxx–xxxi, *102*, *103*, 105–8, 177–78. *See also* patriotic celebrations
flag displays, public schools, xxi
flag pins, modern significance, 189–90
Folkmar, Daniel, 4
Ford, Nancy Gentile, 9, 11
Ford Educational Weekly Series, 39–42, 213 (n.43)
Ford English School, xv
foreign-language newspapers, 10, 160–61
From Dance Hall to White Slavery (Lytle and Dillon), 128

G

Gallivan, James A., 165
garden city movement, 77–78
German Americans, 9, 10–12, 155–56
germ metaphor, 95–96, 106, 171
Gerstle, Gary, 7
girls clubs, 123–25, 132, 138–39, 147–51; with citizenship instruction, 139–41 decline of Americanization

work in, 228 (n. 46); and delinquency problem, 125–30; with domestic skills instruction, 141; gender anxiety and, 140, 144; in heroine narratives, 134–38; in preparedness activities, 139; in public demonstrations, 142–47; recruitment expectations of, 130–34; with uniforms design and uniforms of, 143–46

Girl Scouts: citizenship instruction of, 140–41; heroine narratives of, 136–38; membership growth of, 139, 228 (n. 41); merit badge categories of, 140–41; public pageantry purposes of, 146–47; uniforms of, 144; war preparedness activities of, 139–40

Glassberg, David, xx, xxi–xxii
Glidden, David K., 50
Gona, George, 159–60
Grant, Madison, 5, 163–64
Greene, Ronald Walter, xviii–xix
Grieveson, Lee, 40
Gulick, Luther, 130, 144
Gunderson, Erik, 23
Gyory, Andrew, 3

H

happiness promise: in AVS textbooks, 59–61; community participation and, 80–85; housing design and, 75–76, 79; music's potential and, 117–18. *See also* anger as political weapon

Hariman, Robert, xviii, xxiii, 119, 174
Hart, Albert Bushnell, 49, 51–53
Hartmann, E. T., xv, 16–17, 77, 79, 213 (n. 49), 218 (n. 26)
Haskins, Frederic Jennings, 71
Hersey, Ira, 171
Higham, John, 2–3
Hoganson, Kristin, 54–55
Honig, Bonnie, 134
Housing Betterment (journal), 65
housing reform, 65–67, 85–89; community participation lessons and, 80–85; design contest purposes of, 73–80; ethnic colony arguments and, 67–71; Progressive Era, 217 (n. 20)
Hoxie, R. F., 136
Hudson, Grant, 167
Hyphen, The (Blake), 14

I

imagaic prolepsis. *See* visual aids
Immigrants' Protective League, 6
Immigration Act of 1924. *See* Johnson-Reed Act
Immigration Restriction League, 6
immigration statistics, 1
imperialist nostalgia, Hoganson's argument, 54–55
Independence Day festivities, xix–xx, 103, 146
Indianapolis Americanization Parade, 104
Indian Hill, Massachusetts, 78
industrial workers: America First poster and, 43, 44, 46–47; Ford's film series and, 39–40; housing design goals and, 72–80

infection comparison, nationalism, 95–101, 104, 106
Inness, Sherrie, 149
internment of German Americans, 10

J

Jackson, Henry Ezekiel, 81–82
Jacobson, Matthew Frye, 165–66
James, William, 33
Jenks, Jeremiah Whipple, 4, 49, 53, 55, 56, 59
Johnson, Albert, 164
Johnson (textbook author), 58
Johnson-Reed Act: as Americanization rejection, 162–63, 172–73; assimilation arguments and, 167, 168–69, 170–71; codification significance in, 162, 165–66; indigestible foreigners arguments and, 170–72; invisible disloyalty arguments and, 167–70; opponent portrayals in, 238 (n. 44); race-based justifications for, 163–67; value of tropological analysis in, 162–63, 173–74
Journal of Social Forces, 49, 50
juvenile delinquency, 125–30

K

Kaplan, Michael, 185
Karabel, Jerome, 5
Kellor, Frances: Americanization Day and, 102, 104; on Americanization's failure, 173; on gardening promotion, 78; and housing reform, 73–76, 79; influence of, 6–7, 16–17

Kennedy, Albert J., 128, 130
Kennedy, David M., 9
Kent, Kathryn R., 140
Kesler, Charles, 189
Kimmel, W. G., 49, 50
King, Desmond, 5, 183
Kunz, Stanley, 170

L

Laclau, Ernesto, 209 (n. 126)
Lady Liberty imagery, 215 (n. 75)
Lange, Carl, 33
language-based tropes and images, 186–88
lantern slides, 36–39
Leavitt, Scott, 169–70
Leepson, Marc, xxi
legislation: Asian immigrants and, 3, 9 10, 171; "Star-Spangled Banner" recognition by, xxi; and wartime fears, 9–11. *See also* Johnson-Reed Act
Lewis, Caroline E., 134
Lewis and Clark Expedition, 137–38
Lindvall, Terry, xvi
Lippmann, Walter, 100
literacy tests, 4, 5, 9
living conditions problem, 69–70, 73–74. *See also* housing reform
Lodge, Henry Cabot, 4
Low, Juliette, 131
loyalty concerns, wartime anxieties, 8–15
"Loyalty" speech. *See under* Wilson, Woodrow
Lubin, Simon J., 70–71

Lucaites, John Louis, xviii, xxiii, 119, 174
Lundberg, Christian, 24, 209 (n. 127)
lyceum movement, purposes, xix
Lyon, Janet, xxiii
Lytle, H. W., 128

M

Malin, Brenton J., 12
Marshall, David, 24
Martin, Susan F., 11
mass communication, persuasion assumptions, 11–15
Massumi, Brian, 55
Mayper, Joseph, 80
McClymer, John F., 15, 17
McMurray, Erin, 144
McReynolds, Samuel D., 172
McSwain, John D., 169
Mercieca, Jennifer, 182
metalepsis concept, 94, 101–2. *See also* patriotic celebrations
metaphor and tropological analysis, 25
Meyer, Stephen, xv
Miller, John F., 172
Mink, Gwendolyn, 16
Minute Girls, Camp Fire Girls, 139, 144
Mirel, Jeffrey E., xxiv, xxvi, 1, 6, 7
Mitchell, W.J.T., 187
mob violence, wartime, 155–56
motion pictures, 30, 39–42
Movement to Americanize the Immigrant, The (Hartmann), xv
Murphy & Dana, housing design contest, 78–79

music, patriotic, xx–xxi, 107, 108–17, 178, 194
mustache anecdote, 100

N

National Americanization Committee (NAC): America First poster and, 42–43; formation of, 16–17; housing design contest and, 72–80, 218 (n. 26); patriotic celebrations and, 102
National Conference on Immigration and Americanization, 16
National Housing Association, 65–66
National Review, 189
nativist ideology, policy orientation, 3–6, 163–64. *See also* eugenics; Johnson-Reed Act; racial hierarchy
naturalization ceremony, display purposes, 91–93
Nemanic, Mary Lou, xx
New Science, The (Vico), 24
New York, 153–54
New York City, 107
New York Times, 12–13, 48, 111, 114
Ngai, Mae, 162, 165
Nistor, Nick, 160
North American Civic League (NACL), 129–30

O

Obama, Barack, 189, 190
O'Connell, Jeremiah, 168–69
O'Leary, Cecilia E., xxi, xxii, 181
Outlook, The, 112

P

Palmer, A. Mitchell, 11

Pangburn, Weaver, 110
Papacharissi, Zizi, 60
parades. *See* patriotic celebrations
parochial schools, as assimilation obstacle, 127
Passing of the Great Race, The (Grant), 5, 163–64
patriotic celebrations, 93–95, 101–2, 104, 106–7; allegiance markers at, 104–5, 107–8; choir singing at, 113–17; flag symbolism in, 105–6; and infection metaphor, 95–101, 104, 106; naturalization ceremony's purposes of, 91–93; outcome ambiguities of, 117–21. *See also* American patriotism, proof's problem
patriotic pluralism, Mirel's argument, 208 (n. 112)
patriotism. *See* Americanization movements; American patriotism, proof's problem
Perlman, Nathan, 165
Peters, John Durham, 2
Petit, Jeanne D., 165, 238 (n. 44)
Philadelphia, Americanization Day festivities, 93
photographs, paradoxical nature, 187–88. *See also* AVS textbooks
Playground, The (Davison), 115–16
Playground Association of America, xx
Pledge of Allegiance, xxi, 106
Polinka, George, 161
Popular Educator (journal), 41
Prager, Robert, 156
Prelli, Lawrence, 25

Preparedness Parades. *See* Flag Day celebrations
Proctor, Tammy, 142
productivity motivation. *See* efficiency/productivity motivations
Progressive Party, 6–7
prolepsis concept, 31–32, 34–35. *See also* visual aids
Promise of Happiness, The (Ahmed), 75
prosopopoeia concept, 124, 135. *See also* girls clubs
Purcell-Guild, June, 127

Q

Quintilian, 23, 101–2, 114

R

Races and Immigrants (Commons), 125
Races of Europe, The (Ripley), 4
racial hierarchy: in AVS textbooks, 59; in eugenics ideology, 5, 7–8, 162, 163–64; and germ metaphor, 96; girls clubs and, 149–50, 233 (n. 109); in nativist ideology, 3–6; and structural change avoidance, 183–84. *See also* Johnson-Reed Act
racial indigestion argument, 170–72
Rally, The (magazine), 131, 133, 134, 141
Ray, Angela, xix
Reconstruction Commission, 153–54
registration cards, Americanization, 156–62
Reimers, David, 1
Renshon, Stanley, 190

Revolutionary War, 105
Rhetoric of Motives, A (Burke), 163
Rhoades, Mabel Carter, 126
Rickard, H. D., 36–38
Ricoeur, Paul, 24, 25, 187
Ripley, William Z., 4
Robsion, John, 171
Romney, Mitt, 189
Roosevelt, Theodore, 3–4, 6–7, 68–69
Rosebault, Charles, 111
Rosenbloom, Benjamin, 171–72
Ross, Stewart, 11–12
Roumanian Beneficent Society, 160
rural imagery: in American First poster, 43, 44; in AVS textbooks, 51, 53, 54; for visual education, 30, 39
Russell Sage Foundation, xx

S

Sabath, Adolph, 168
Sacajawea, 137–38
Schem, Lida C. (Margaret Blake), 14
School Review, 49
Scribner's Magazine, 99
Selig, Diana, 6
Silver, Matthew, 7
Simonson, Peter, 2
Slovak Lutheran Holy Cross Church, 159–60
Smith, Al, 153
Smith, Rufus Daniel, 49, 53, 55, 56, 59
Smith, Shawn Michelle, 26
Snopes.com, flag controversies, 189
songs, patriotic, xx–xxi, 107, 108–17, 178, 194
Spirit of Youth and the City Streets,

The (Addams), 127
Spiro, Jonathan, 163
Spivak, Gayatri Chakravorty, 116–17
Sproule, J. Michael, 9
squaw, meanings, 233 (n. 119)
"Star-Spangled Banner, The," xx–xxi
stereopticon slides, 36–39
Stevens, Thomas Woods, 120–21
Stewart, Donald, 55
Stob, Paul, 33
Stoicism, 31, 34–35, 48, 55
Stott, Henry G., 158–59
Strassler, Karen, 149
Straus, Oscar, 6–7
structural argument, ethnic colony problem, 70
Stuckey, Mary E., xvii
Suchman, Elizabeth B., 159
synecdoche concept, 66–67. *See also* housing reform
Syracuse schools, stereopticon slides, 36–38

T

Talks to Teachers (James), 33
Tedesco, Laureen, 131, 139, 228 (n. 46)
textbook images, 48–61
theater pageantry, 120–21
Tichenor, Daniel, 4
Time (magazine), 189–90
tropes, Bloom's philosophy, 240 (n. 75)
tropological analysis, benefits, 22–26, 173–74, 185–88, 209 (n. 126). *See also* American patriotism, proof's problem; patriotic celebrations

U

Uncle Sam imagery, 44

V

Vaughn, Stephen, 9, 19
Verchères, Marie-Madeleine Jarret de, 136–37
Vico, Giambattista, 24
Victrola advertisement, 111
visual aids, 29–35, 47–48, 61–63; with America First poster, 42–48; with Ford's film series, 39–42; with stereopticon slides, 36–39; with textbook illustrations, 48–61
visual logic, from tropological analysis, xxiii–xxiv, 24–27, 194–95, 209 (n. 126). *See also* American patriotism, proof's problem; patriotic celebrations
Vivian, Bradford, xxiii
von Estritz, Guido (in *The Hyphen*), 14–15
Vought, Hans P., 6–7

W

Walsh, Frank, 75
wartime imagery, worries about, 12–15
Watkins, Elton, 170
We and Our Government (Jenks and Smith), 49, 53, 55, 56, 59
We and Our History (Hart), 49, 51–53, 54, 59
We and Our Work (Johnson), 58
Weeks, John W., 178
Wheaton, H. H., 42–44
White, Hayden, 75, 209 (n. 126)
Who Sings the Nation State? (Butler and Spivak), 116
Williams, Raymond, xxiii
Wilson, Margaret, 110–11
Wilson, Woodrow: in Americanization campaign, 17; DAR speech, 97–98; Flag Day speech, 105, 177–78; literacy test veto of, 9; "Loyalty" speech, 96–97; naturalization ceremony speech, 91–92; in patriotic celebrations, 102, 103; pro-war sentiment campaign of, 9, 11; "Star-Spangled Banner" authorization by, xxi; on war and immigrants, 13–14
Wohelo (magazine), 131, 133, 134, 146
Woods, Robert Archey, 128, 130
World War I, 8–15, 105
Wright, Rowe, 133

Y

Young Men's Christian Association (YMCA), xvi, 40

Z

Zradska, Stefania, 128